Cézanne

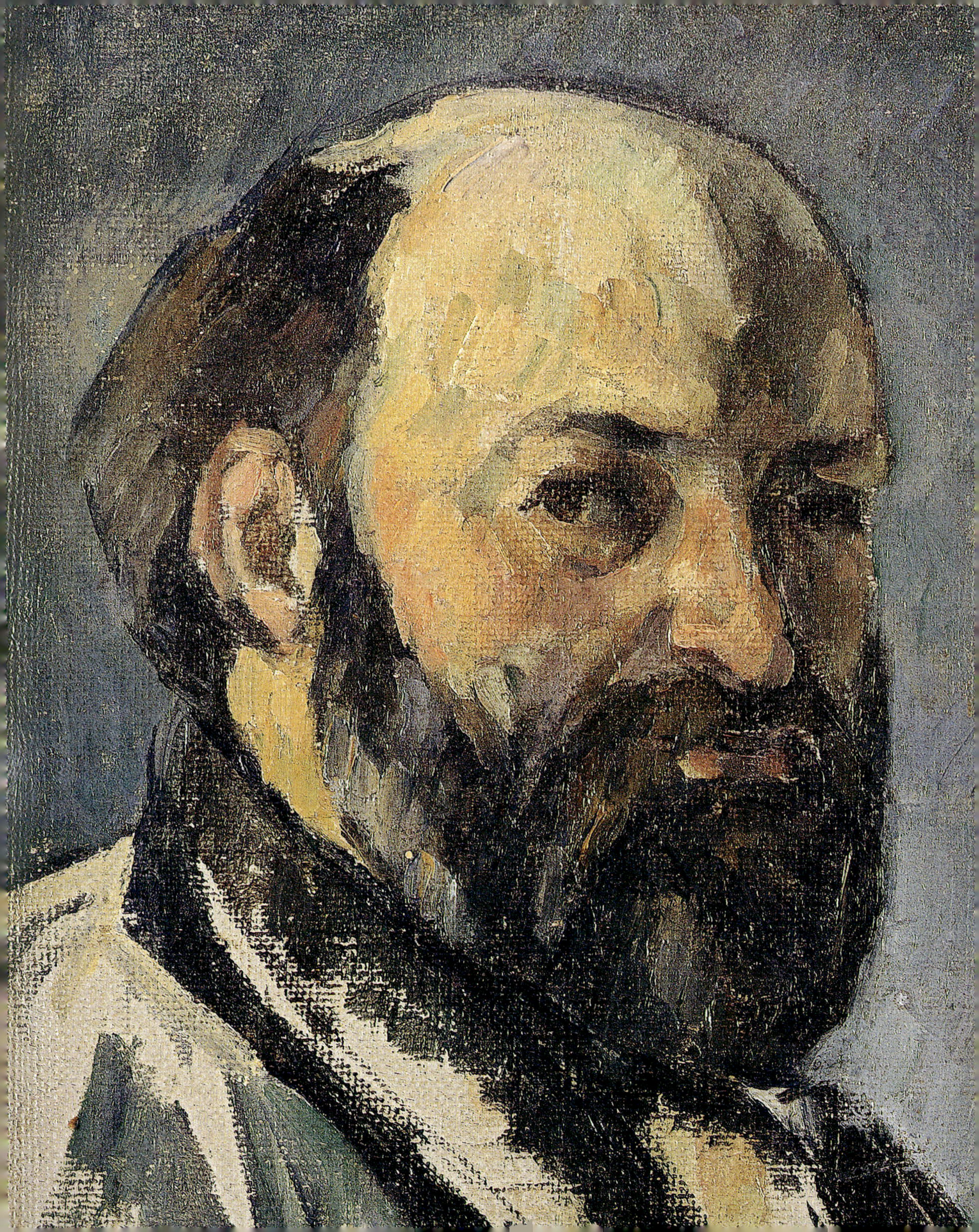

Masters of Art

Cézanne

Roberta Bernabei

PRESTEL
Munich · London · New York

Front cover: *Still Life with a Curtain*, c. 1899, The State Hermitage Museum, St. Petersburg (detail), see p. 117
Frontispiece: *Self-Portrait*, c. 1877, Musée d'Orsay, Paris (detail) see p. 47
Back cover: *Self-Portrait Before Rose Background*, c. 1875, private collection (detail)

British Library Cataloguing-in Publication Data: a catalogue record for this book is available from the British Library; Deutsche Nationalbibliothek holds a record of this publication in the Deutsche Nationalbibliografie; detailed bibliographical data can be found under: http://dnb.dnb.de
The Library of Congress Number: 2012954701

Prestel Verlag, Munich
A member of Verlagsgruppe Random House GmbH

Prestel Verlag
Neumarkter Strasse 28
81673 Munich
Tel. +49(0)89 4136 0
Fax +49(0)89 4136 2335

www.prestel.de

Prestel Publishing Ltd.
14–17 Wells Street
London W1T 3PD
Tel. +44 (0)20 7323-5004
Fax +44 (0)20 7323-0271

Prestel Publishing
900 Broadway, Suite 603
New York, NY 10003
Tel. +1 (212) 995-2720
Fax +1 (212) 995-2733

www.prestel.com

Prestel books are available worldwide. Please contact your nearest bookseller or one of the above addresses for information concerning your local distributor.

Editorial direction: Claudia Stäuble, assisted by Franziska Stegmann
Translation from German: Jane Michael
Copyediting: Chris Murray
Production: René Fink
Typesetting: Andrea Mogwitz, Munich
Cover: Sofarobotnik, Augsburg & Munich
Printing and binding: Elcograf S.p.A., Verona, Italy

FSC
www.fsc.org
MIX
Paper from responsible sources
FSC® C018290

Verlagsgruppe Random House FSC® N001967
The FSC®-certified paper *Respecta Satin* is produced by Burgo Group Spa, Italy.

ISBN 978-3-7913-4825-4

Contents

Introduction

In both appearance and character, Paul Cézanne resembled the silhouette of Mont Sainte-Victoire, his favorite landscape subject: immovable and constant, he doggedly remained true to himself, regardless of the weather and at all seasons of the year. In depicting the mountain, he was able to record the imperceptible changes in the light, the relationship between the different surfaces, interpreting their geometry and quietly measuring out every space. Cézanne's imperturbable steadfastness led him to disagree with everyone: not only with writers and artists, but also with his friends and family. We need only study his self-portraits in order to recognize immediately the character of this obstinate, determined Provençal painter.

He put in an appearance in Paris, but never liked the city. He chose a simple, circumscribed environment consisting of familiar places. He preferred the patiently tamped pipe to the ostentatious cigar of the Impressionists; rather than attending a noisy *bal-musette*, he would play cards in a country tavern; and he liked to spend his time in a simple rural house in the middle of the country rather than among the entertainment establishments in Montmartre and along the Seine.

It is interesting to study Cézanne's representation of the sea on the French Riviera, which he painted as a plain, not very attractive, blue expanse with an incongruous factory chimney dominating the shore. Moreover, Cézanne's subjects are never associated with the events of everyday life, something that mattered deeply to the Impressionists, but rather with a timeless universe. In his unrelenting remoteness from all fashionable trends, Cézanne was without doubt the greatest and the most introspective artist of his generation. He rigorously analyzed all aspects of art, light and color, form and drawing, perspective and artistic freedom, reducing them to essentials. He intuitively recognized the limitations of Impressionism and foresaw the end of a movement that for him was too concerned with merely depicting the ever-changing appearance of the world and so could not develop further. He returned to a deeper understanding of art history, revisiting subjects, artists, and compositions that had been declared passé. He anticipated the views and practices of the avant-garde artists of the early twentieth century not only with his apt observations on art, but above all with his paintings, which were seen as astoundingly modern. With the exception of a few early works, Cézanne was never interested in pleasing the art critics or the public at large by adapting his style to whatever was fashionable.

And yet, in spite of all the solitude and struggle, Cézanne's private life was far removed from that of an artist condemned to a life of misery—it was quite unlike the relentlessly tragic life of Vincent van Gogh, for example, who also lived and worked in Provence but who was soon defeated by financial cares and his own melancholy. Cézanne's life was lived out against a background of comfortable middle-class prosperity; nevertheless, it was he who, almost singlehandedly, created the basis for twentieth-century art. He was, in fact, extraordinarily intelligent. He was able to recognize the rules governing art and to dismantle them, one after the other, before putting them back together again. Though he repeatedly painted still lifes and portraits, he returned obsessively to certain landscape subjects, and it was in this genre that he principally worked through his investigations into the nature of painting, uncovering the mysterious interplay between geometry and nature.

This process culminated in the introduction of figures into the landscape, in the remarkable *Bathers* of his last creative years. But even though Cézanne often painted the same views or the same compositions, his pictures are never hackneyed or monotonous. The same applies when he focused his attention on the human figure, be it in portraits or in representations of anonymous people from his everyday surroundings. Each time he lifted his brush he discovered a new aspect, a new interplay of light, a new perspective, a more effective juxtaposition of colors, without allowing himself to be carried away by excessively loud stylistic proclamations or grandiose demonstrations of artistic innovation. Far from the glittering highlights of Paris, the "City of Light," and the attention of the critics, Cézanne retained the character of a painter who regarded himself as a "craftsman." He did not adapt his approach to the conditions of the Paris art market of the time, and so he worked away almost unnoticed. It was only after his death, when a major memorial exhibition was devoted to his work, that the young artists Pablo Picasso and Henri Matisse realized their debt to the great master, to this "classic" who had shown modern art a new direction.

Stefano Zuffi

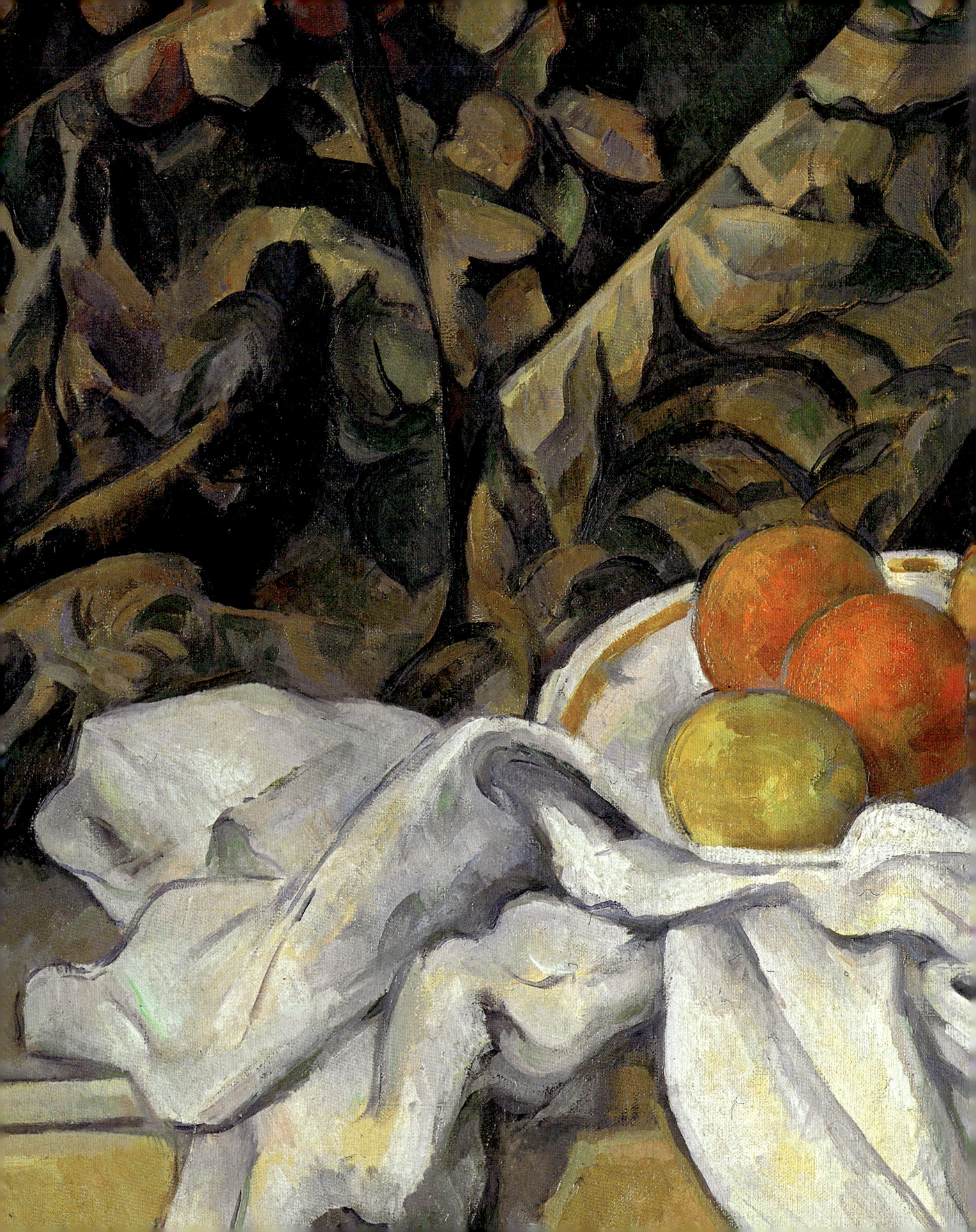

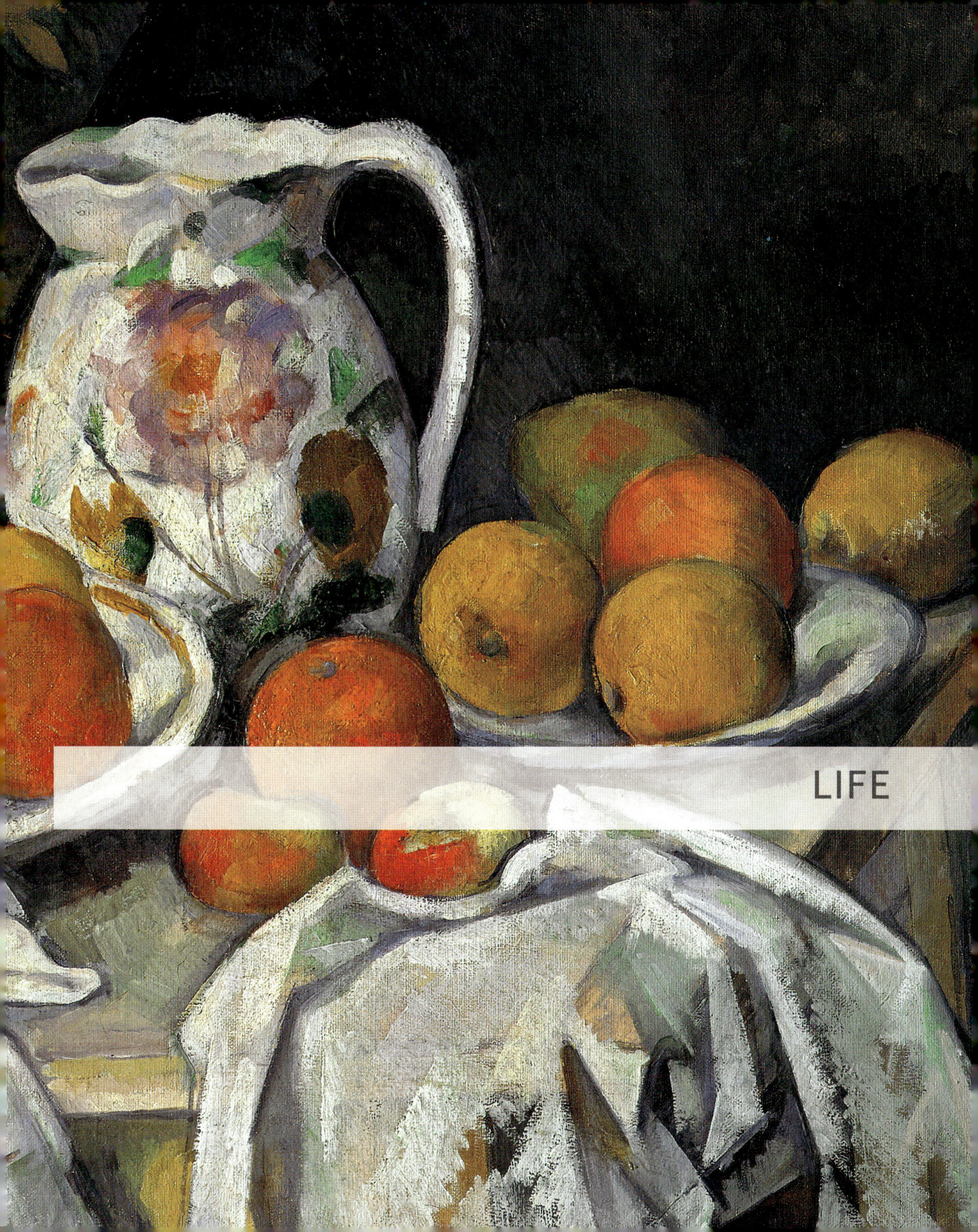

LIFE

Cézanne: a life for art

Opposite: Portrait of Madame Cézanne, c. 1885, Museum Berggruen, Berlin

Paul Cézanne was born on 19 January 1839 in Aix-en-Provence. His father, Louis-Auguste Cézanne, had moved to Aix in 1825 at the age of 25, where he had set up a hatter's shop. A successful businessman, in 1847 he took over the insolvent Barges bank, and the following year he and an associate founded their own bank, Cézanne & Cabassol. In 1859 he was able to purchase the imposing country villa Jas de Bouffan, which lay some distance outside the town of Aix-en-Provence and which had been the property of the provincial governor of Provence, whose family had spent their summers there.

It was this prosperity that would later permit Cézanne to live a retiring life in Aix, without the urgent financial worries that dogged the lives of many of his fellow-artists.

Education and training (1852–1871)

In 1852 Cézanne became a pupil at the Collège Bourbon, where he met Émile Zola. Before long he and the future writer had become close friends; their friendship was to last for many years, as we can see from the regular correspondence between them. In 1856 Cézanne began taking drawing lessons under Joseph Gibert at the École de Dessin in Aix-en-Provence. After leaving school, he followed his father's advice and began to study law at the University of Aix. After the first examination, however, Cézanne came to the firm conclusion that he was not cut out for a legal career: his greatest wish was to become an artist and he thought it was essential to go to Paris, the art capital. This marked the start of an acrimonious disagreement with his father, in whose bourgeois opinion art was an occupation that was neither very useful nor very profitable. Zola encouraged his friend to be more determined: "Is painting to you no more than a whim, which you suddenly decided to study one day when you were bored? Is it just a hobby, a subject which makes a good topic of conversation, a pretext, so that you need no longer spend your time studying law?"

Cézanne's mother and his sister Marie finally persuaded his father to agree to Paul's request, and so in 1861 he accompanied his son to Paris. Cézanne rented a studio and attended courses at the Académie Suisse, where he met Claude Monet, Camille Pissarro, and Armand Guillaumin. He visited the Salon exhibition, the most important official art exhibition of the time, which was held every year. Above all, his study of the Old Masters was of fundamental importance for his artistic development. He spent long afternoons wandering through the collections at the Louvre, where he was deeply moved by the works of Caravaggio, Zurbarán, Rubens, Velázquez, Tintoretto, Titian, and Veronese. At the same time, when confronted by the works of these acknowledged masters, he felt so discouraged that in a moment of crisis he was convinced that he was incapable of painting anything at all. He accordingly decided to leave Paris and to return to Aix-en-Provence.

Cézanne's emotional state was governed by his sensitivity and restlessness. Throughout his life he experienced such moments of uncertainty at regular intervals. Back in Aix,

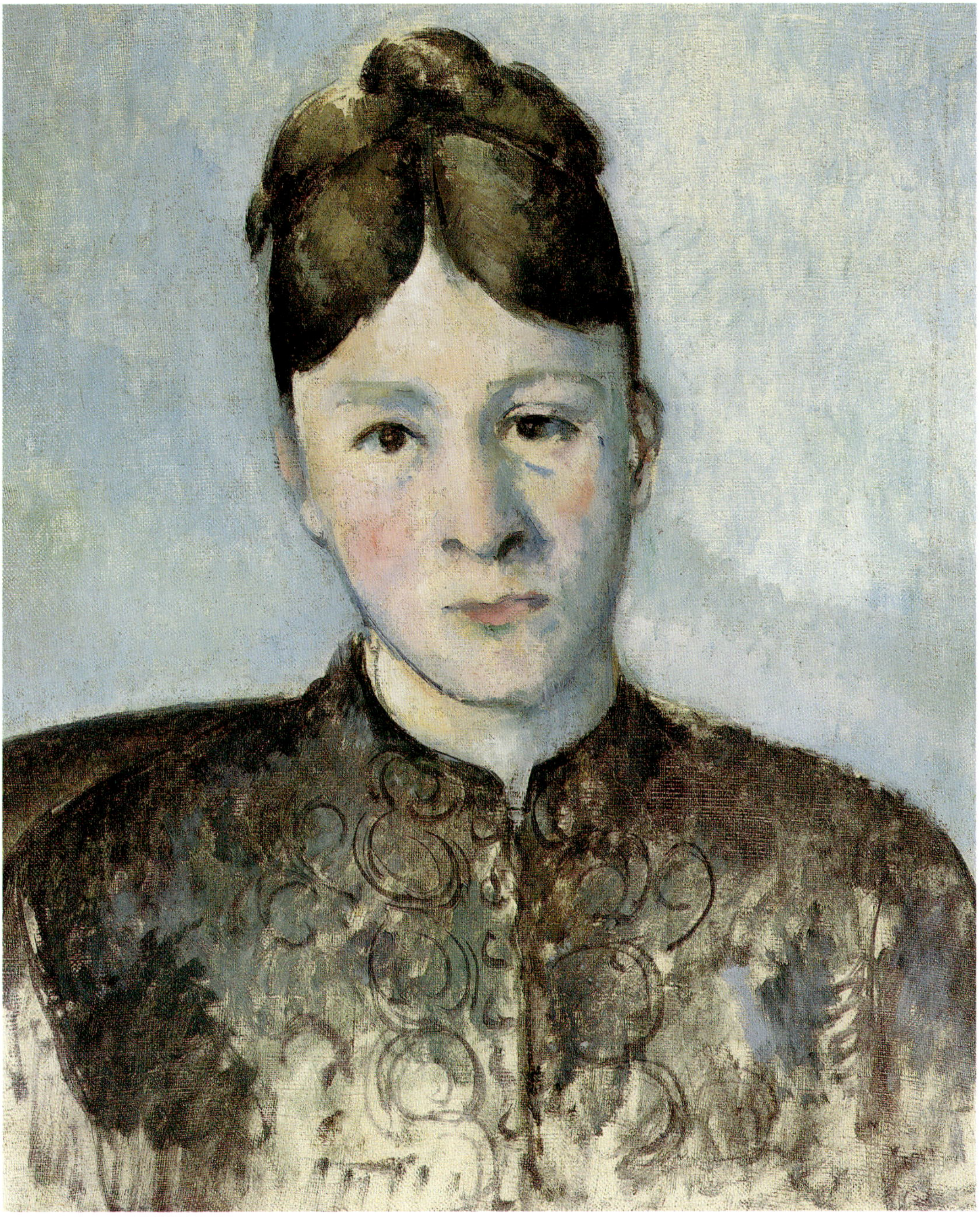

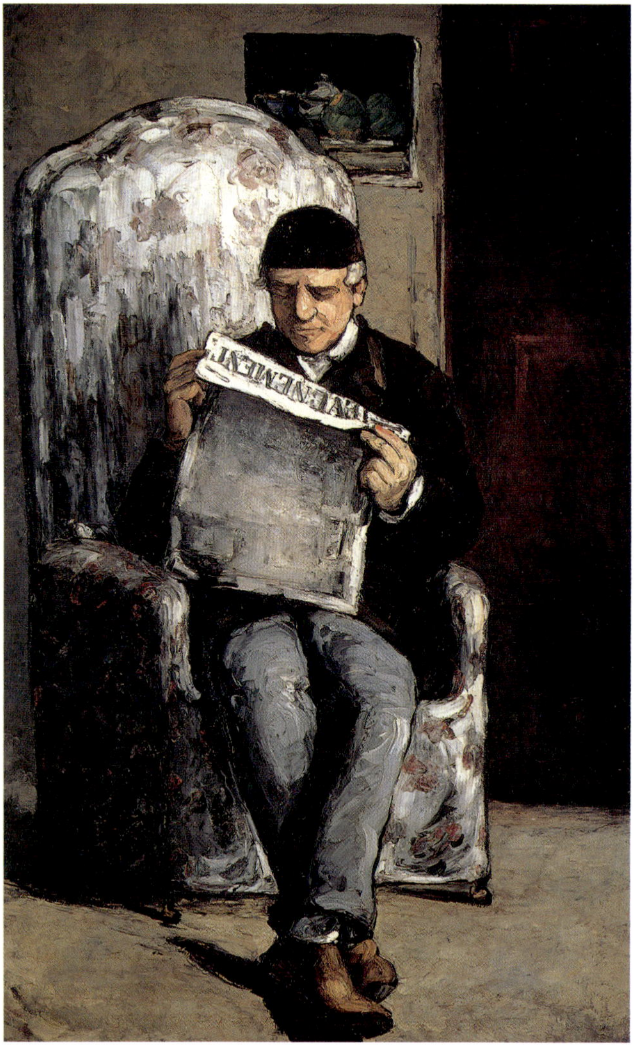

Portrait of Louis-Auguste Cézanne, 1866, National Gallery of Art, Washington

he was prepared to work for his father; however, a few months later, in 1862, he returned to Paris and applied for entry to the Académie des Beaux-Arts. Once again he failed the entrance examination, and so he returned to the Académie Suisse, where he saw Monet and Pissarro again and made the acquaintance of Alfred Sisley, Frédéric Bazille, and Auguste Renoir. From time to time he sat with his friends in the Café Guerbois, the favorite rendezvous of the artists who would later become known as the Impressionists; or he spent his time copying the works of the Old Masters in the galleries of the Louvre. In 1863 the famous Salon des Refusés took place at the instigation of Emperor Napoléon III. It showed the works of artists who had been turned down by the jury of the official Salon of that year. The event marked an important stage in the development of contemporary, and indeed modern, art. One of the works shown at the Salon des Refusés that year was the famous *Déjeuner sur l'herbe* by Édouard Manet. It was a painting that provoked a huge scandal when it was exhibited; not only because of the choice of subject—two dressed men having an outdoor meal with two women, one nude and one scantily dressed—but also for its innovative painting style. Manet was supported above all by artists of the younger generation; they were the only ones who were able to understand the revolutionary aspects of his painting.

Cézanne attended the Salon with his friend Zola and was impressed by the works of Manet. The works of Gustave Courbet and Eugène Delacroix in particular also made a lasting impression on him. During these years Cézanne lived alternately in Provence, on the family's Jas de Bouffan estate, and in the capital, where he frequented the circles of the Impressionists. He repeatedly—but always unsuccessfully—entered his pictures for the Salon.

In 1869 Cézanne met Hortense Fiquet in Paris and soon started living with her, but without telling his father. During this time he painted works of great emotional power, revealing both a passionately Romantic inclination and a marked predilection for the spectacular. Most of them were portraits, still lifes, or landscapes, but he also turned his attention to subjects full of violence of eroticism. In them, he referred back to the works of the Old Masters or took up literary sources. The paintings he produced at this time include *The Orgy*, *Pain*, *Scipio*, *The Negro*, *In the Rooms (Interior)*, *Preparation for the Funeral*, *The Murder*, *The Strangled Woman*, *The Temptation of St. Anthony*, *The Thieves and the Donkey*, and *Man in a Cotton Cap*. He painted such early works with a sketch-like but highly expressive technique, using dark colors to create dramatic lighting effects. In the choice of his subjects as well as in their artistic execution, Cézanne was clearly governed by turbulent emotions.

At this stage Cézanne surrounded his figures and objects with prominent dark contours, creating spatial structures by using paint applied in thick layers that contrasts with the background against which the figures move. Though he still displayed a Romantic disposition in these works that can be traced back to his admiration for Delacroix, that was already being tempered by the realism of artists like Gustave Courbet and Honoré Daumier.

His discovery of light and color (1872–1877)

When the Franco-Prussian war broke out in 1870, Monet and Pissarro fled to England. Cézanne, however, returned to Aix-en-Provence with Hortense, and later continued to L'Estaque, a fishing village on the Gulf of Marseilles, where he spent several months. After the end of the war he returned to Paris, where his son Paul was born on 4 January 1872. In the spring Cézanne went with his family to Pontoise to join Pissarro and other artist friends; that fall he moved to Auvers-sur-Oise, near Pontoise, where he was a houseguest of the same Dr. Gachet who would provide shelter for Vincent van Gogh 17 years later, during the last months of his tormented life.

The period in Auvers-sur-Oise was crucially important for the development of Cézanne's pictorial language. Between 1872 and 1873 he followed Pissarro's example and began painting *en plein air*, in other words outdoors. This enabled him to immerse himself in his subject entirely, and to study landscapes with fresh eyes and not as depicted by others. Influenced by his friend, Cézanne learned to capture changing effects of light; to observe his subjects with greater detachment; and to be concerned less with expressing his emotions and passions and more with recording the spectacle of nature. In a letter, Pissarro reported to the painter Antoine Guillemet, another of Cézanne's friends, that Cézanne was making progress: "Our dear friend gives me reason for hope ... I have seen one of his paintings ... which is definitely remarkable for its energy and power. Yes, as I hoped, he will stay in Auvers for a while. He wants to settle there, and he will yet surprise the other artists, who were all too quick to write off his work."

Working outdoors, Cézanne studied the wide range of effects that light creates at different times of day, the fine gradations of color and atmospheric effects. His views acquired a new freshness and light-filled brightness. He approached reality "objectively," with a fairly distanced attitude, wanting to observe as accurately as possible the structures and colors of nature. In order to reproduce the subtle effects of light and atmosphere on objects, Cézanne abandoned the dark color palette and the mostly thick paint application of his previous works. He also gave up the dark contours with which he had previously outlined his subjects. Instead, he now applied paint to the canvas using small brushstrokes. *The House of the Hanged Man*, which he painted in 1873 in Auvers, is one of his first masterpieces. It shows how close he had come to Impressionism as a result of Pissarro's influence. In this picture, the dark and somber palette of the early years has been completely abandoned. He no longer outlines individual shapes; he indicates the spatiality of his subjects solely through variations in tonality, while the technique of using tiny brushstrokes convincingly conveys the impression that light is being refracted on surfaces. During this period Cézanne also painted *The House of Dr. Gachet in Auvers*, *The House of Père Lacroix in Auvers*, and *View of Auvers from Above*. The paintings were created directly from nature; they are flooded with light and filled with a subtle, vibrant chromaticity, while at the same time conveying a sure feeling of space.

In 1874 Cézanne moved back to Paris. It was in this same year that the first group exhibition of works by the Impressionist painters took place in the studio of the photographer Nadar at 35 Boulevard des Capucines. It was an open provocation to the traditional approach to art. The exhibition was organized by the Société anonyme des artistes, peintres, sculpteurs et graveurs. On Pissarro's insistence, Cézanne finally agreed to take part in the exhibition. He showed *The House of the Hanged Man in Auvers* and the ironic picture *A Modern Olympia*, a direct and ironic response to Manet's large-format painting that had caused a scandal at the Salon des Refusés in 1865. Cézanne's works, like those of the other artists represented, were the subject of ribald comments in the press. In *L'Artiste* on 1 May 1874, one critic wrote that the artist seemed to him to resemble "some madman who paints while suffering from delirium tremens." And he added: "... as for the landscape, Cézanne clearly thinks it better not to take us right up to *The House of the Hanged Man* ... he abandons us half-way there." This first exhibition was followed by another seven, but Cézanne took part only once more, in the third Impressionist exhibition in 1877, where he showed 16 works, mostly still lifes and landscapes.

Following this exhibition, Cézanne increasingly distanced himself from the other artists who had exhibited, and in the following year he moved back to L'Estaque. The subjects on which he concentrated during this period would be the same ones he would continue to study throughout his entire creative life: landscapes, still lifes, bathers, and portraits. This recurring focus on the same subjects can be explained by his determination to study reality as thoroughly as possible; to penetrate external appearances and so to advance towards the very essence of things, towards discovering their inner structure. In doing so he created a new, synthetic appearance on the picture surface. It is less illusionistic than that of the Impressionists, more concrete and also more compact. "The object of painting is itself. The painter paints: an apple or a face—it is, for him, merely a pretext for the interplay of lines and colors—no more. Indeed, the artist concentrates at all times on the balance in the structure of his picture, on the correct relationship between color values; irrespective of the subject he is depicting—a portrait, a view of nature, or a basket of apples—he always investigates all possibilities of perception with the same intensity."

In the painting *Bathsheba*, painted between 1875 and 1877, Cézanne analyzed the relationship between man and nature. For him this theme, to which he would return frequently during the last years of his life, opened up the possibility of pursuing his explorations of structure and color. These works reveal a

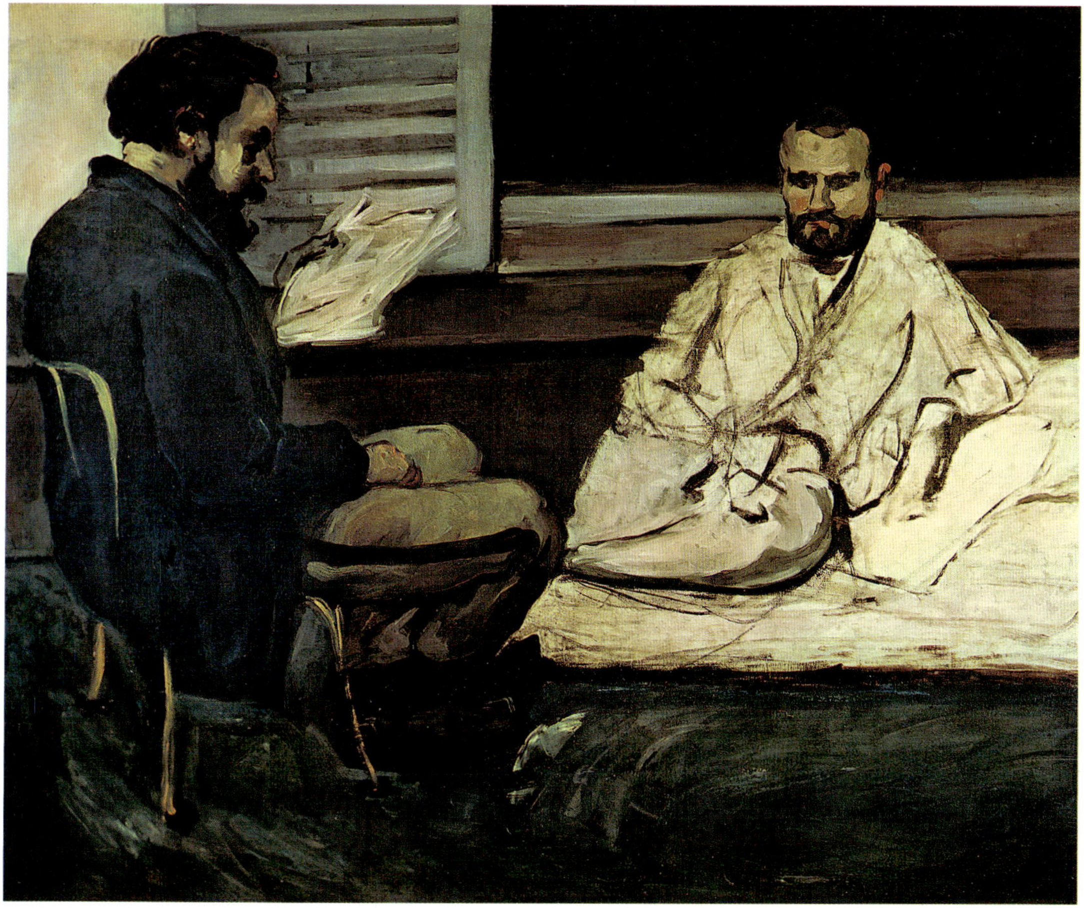

particular compositional balance. Stereometric relationships are increasingly evident here, and the human figures are treated in exactly the same way as trees, water, the entire natural environment. In *Still Life with Apples and Biscuits* of 1877 Cézanne concentrates on the representation of objects in an interior. He analyzes the stereometric structures of the objects, the spatial and color relationships that exist between the individual elements of the composition as a whole, and the different ways in which objects absorb or reflect light. All this lends the picture in its entirety a highly concrete cohesiveness.

During the same year Cézanne also completed his *Self-Portrait with Hat*, *Madame Cézanne in a Red Armchair*, *Landscape near Pontoise*, *Trees and Houses*, *Roofs*, and *Plate and Painted Vase*—all works that show very clearly the painterly investigations that obsessed him. The plastic presence, the careful composition of the picture, and the links between the object and space, "which gives things a feeling of eternity"—all this eventually

Paul Alexis Reading Aloud to Émile Zola, 1869–1870, Museu de Arte, São Paulo

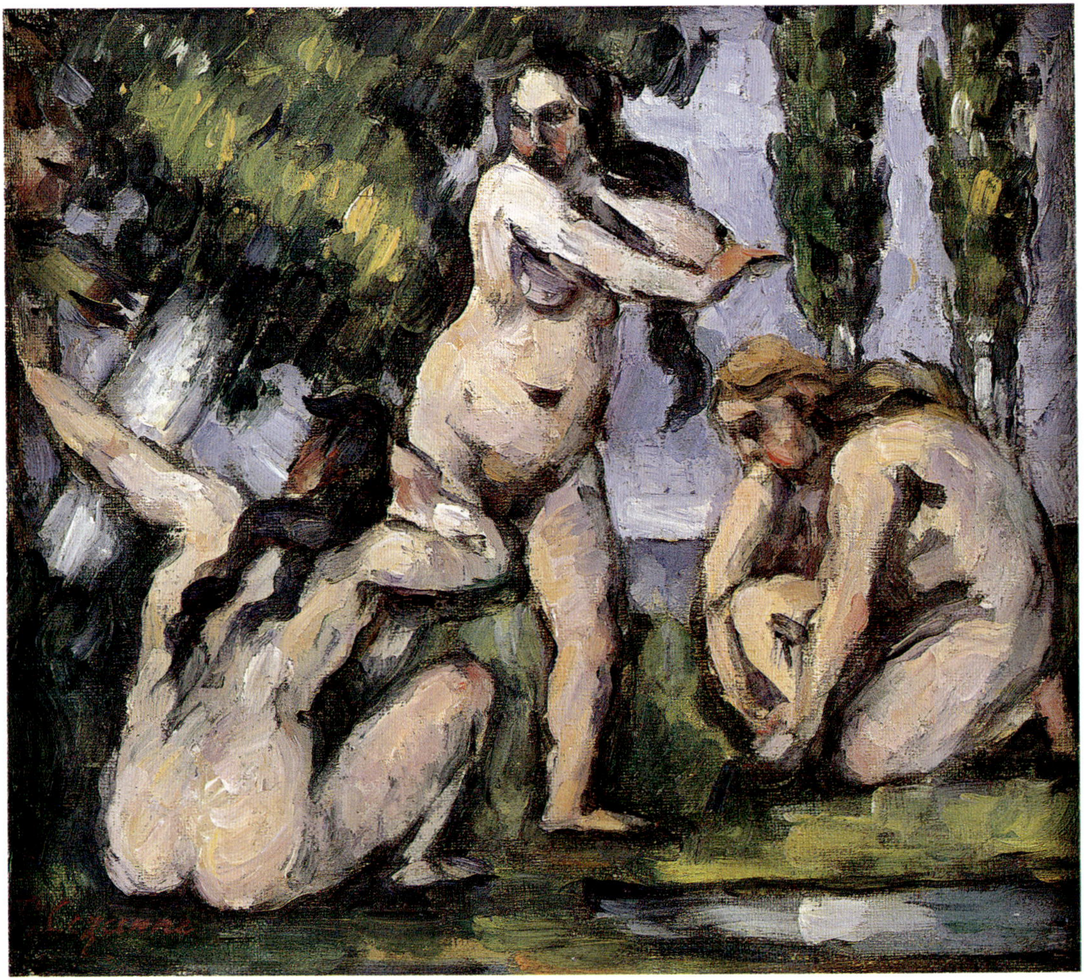

Three Bathers, 1874–1875, Musée d'Orsay, Paris

led Cézanne to painterly solutions that were often diametrically opposed to those of Impressionism. Cézanne was not satisfied with merely observing, with the visual impression that we experience when looking at nature. "A mind which organizes with energy is the most valuable assistant of sensibility in the creation of a work of art ... There are two things in painting: the eye and the mind; each of them should aid the other." The emotion, the subjective impression that we gain of the visible world, thus needs the support of thought, of a rational approach that analyzes the sensory impressions and gives them a structure.

The search for structural coherence (1878–1887)

At this stage of his life Cézanne was restless, still searching for the right place and the right subjects. During the whole of 1878 he continued to work in L'Estaque, traveling only occasionally to Aix to visit his sick mother. In the meanwhile his relationship with his father became increasingly strained, especially since the latter had learned of Cézanne's relationship with Hortense and that they had a son, also called Paul. The following year Cézanne made frequent trips to Medan, where his friend Zola had bought a house. Among the works produced during this visits was *The Castle of Medan (The Home of Zola)*, a light and lively painting of great expressivity. Cézanne then spent the whole of 1880 in Paris, where he had the opportunity of seeing his Impressionist friends again, and also made the acquaintance of more artists and intellectuals, including Joris-Karl (real name: Charles Marie Georges) Huysmans. He next stayed for a while with Pissarro in Pontoise, but then returned to Paris in 1882. At last one of his paintings was accepted for the Salon exhibition, largely thanks to Antoine Guillemet. In 1883 Cézanne traveled through Provence, staying for a while in the picturesque little town of Gardanne. The following year he met Monet and Renoir again in L'Estaque, and from time to time he also visited Aix. In 1885 he painted with Renoir in La Roche-Guyon before returning to Gardanne.

When his father died in 1886, Cézanne found himself in possession of a considerable fortune, whereupon he married Hortense. In that same year an event took place that was to have far-reaching consequences for Cézanne's future life: Zola published his novel *L'Œuvre* (The Masterpiece), the fourteenth volume in his Rougon-Macquart series. In it the author tells the story of the unsuccessful artist Claude Lantier, a "failed genius" who is incapable of finishing a painting and who eventually commits suicide. Cézanne immediately recognized himself in the portrait of the artist. In fact, Zola, who had initially supported the young Impressionist painters, had later distanced himself from them. His novel shows exactly what he thought of them. In a final cool letter from Gardanne, Cézanne put an end to their 30 years of friendship. The two men would never meet again.

In 1887 Cézanne returned to the family home in Aix, where he continued to work away feverishly. The paintings he produced over the next ten years reveal an intense concentration on the structural texture of his subjects. He analyzed them meticulously and thereby arrived at compositions characterized by tremendous solidity and harmony. During this period Cézanne largely lived in isolation and devoted his entire attention to his work *sur le motif*, in front of the object. He was seeking to give the painted picture more structural cohesiveness, and developed his painting style accordingly. Although the public and the majority of art critics failed to understand his aims, he continued to paint after nature. "Talking about art is largely useless," he wrote to Émile Bernard some years later. "The work, which allows one to make progress in one's own field, is sufficient compensation for the incomprehension of idiots." Landscape, his preferred genre during this period, contained its own inherent constructive order. For Cézanne, the varied colored elements that formed a landscape were the concrete equivalent of the colored elements he wanted to create with his precise brushstrokes, their careful juxtaposition creating the painterly structure of the painting.

This technique can be seen very clearly in works like *Maincy Bridge*, *Poplars*, *Village Behind Trees*, and *Basin and Washhouse at Jas de Bouffan*. Cézanne's highly individual style is evident above all in the two paintings *Mont Sainte-Victoire* and *The Gulf of Marseilles Seen from L'Estaque*. In the latter, our gaze roams from a bird's-eye perspective across an expansive view. The surface of the sea is an intense blue. In contrast to Claude Monet, who was interested in the refraction of the light on the water and the scintillating effect of the choppy surface, Cézanne increased the blueness of the sea as if he wanted to capture the "density" of the water. In the first picture, Mont Sainte-Victoire rises in the distance, forming the horizon. From now on this mountain became a genre of its own in Cézanne's work. In his painterly exploration of the rocky massif, Cézanne carries through the constructive synthesis of the picture arrangement down to the last detail in an attempt to arrive at the "second nature" he was striving for.

The years of constructive synthesis (1888–1906)

After Cézanne had spent almost the whole of 1887 in Aix-en-Provence, he returned to Paris, undertaking a number of excursions to the Île-de-France. He eventually returned to the family home, Jas de Bouffan; Renoir was his guest there for a while. In 1891 he interrupted his sojourn in Provence to travel to Switzerland—his only journey outside France during his entire life. It gave him the opportunity to broaden his artistic horizons through the new impressions of landscapes. In 1895 Cézanne visited Monet in Giverny, where he also met the sculptor Auguste Rodin. His first solo exhibition was held at the Galerie Ambroise Vollard in Rue Lafitte in Paris. The critics had not yet recognized the stature of this artist from Provence, though the younger artists already saw in him a role model. Cézanne left Paris in June and returned to Aix. For health reasons he visited the resort of Vichy and later went to Talloires on Lac d'Annecy. Returning home, in 1896 and 1897 Cézanne focused his attention entirely on landscape painting. He produced numerous views of the Arc valley, dominated by Mont Sainte-Victoire. In 1897 the National Gallery in Berlin was the first museum to purchase one of Cézanne's works. After his mother's death in 1898, Cézanne was compelled to sell Jas de Bouffan in order to settle the estate. He retired to a house in the center of Aix-en-Provence with his old governess, Madame Brémond. From this point onwards, his wife and son spent most of the year in Paris.

In 1900 Maurice Denis painted his famous group portrait *Homage to Cézanne* to express his admiration of the Provençal master. Gathered around a still life by Cézanne, placed prominently on an easel, can be seen Denis himself and a number of other artists, including Odilon Redon, Édouard Vuillard, and Pierre Bonnard. Denis also used his influence to ensure that Cézanne was permitted to exhibit his works at the Salon des Indépendants in 1902. By this stage, Cézanne had achieved a certain degree of fame, and a number of artists made their way to Provence to see him. During this time he regularly met the artists Charles Camoin and Émile Bernard, and conducted a lively correspondence with them. In his letters Cézanne

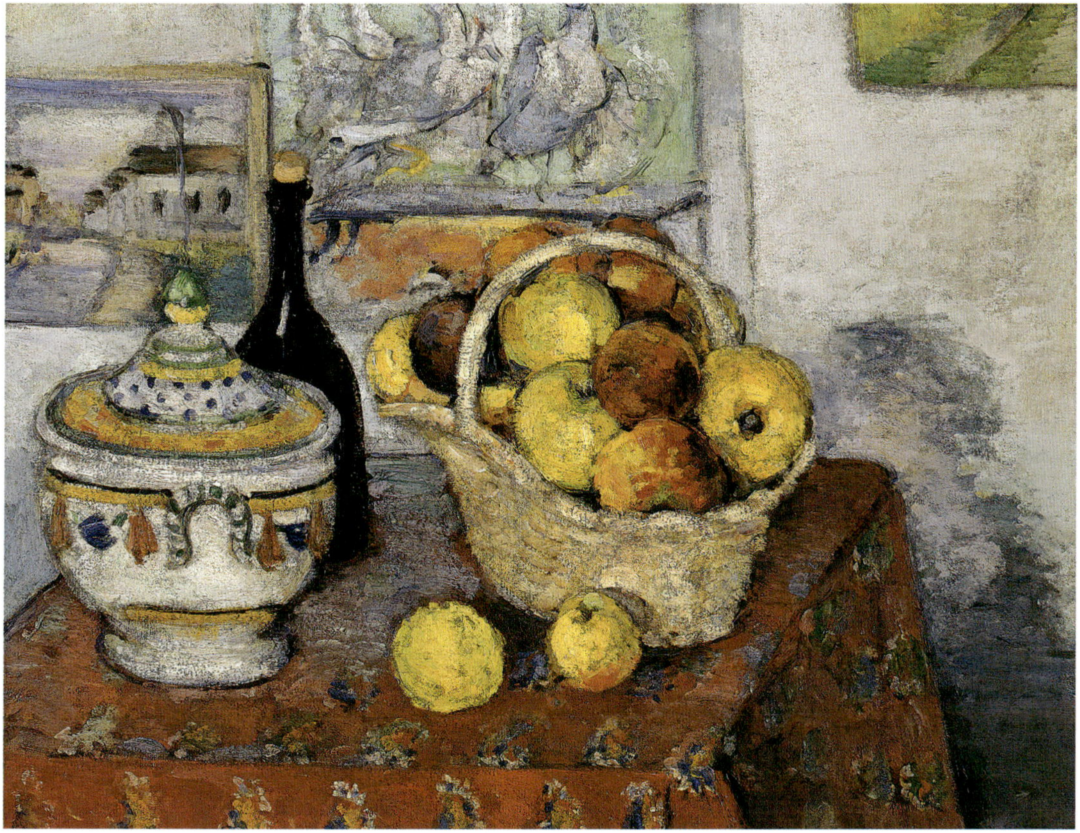

exhorted his younger colleagues to focus on the study of nature. He wrote to Camoin: "Couture used to say to his students: 'Spend your time with the right people,' which meant: 'Go to the Louvre.' But after you have seen the great masters whose works are hanging there ... you must see that you come out again quickly in order to enliven your own instincts through contact with nature, the artistic sensibility that lies within us." In a letter to Bernard we find a famous comment by Cézanne that the Cubists would later take up to justify their positions. It is a comment that is very revealing for our understanding of the development which Cézanne's pictorial language would finally take: "Please allow me to repeat to you what I have already told you: treat nature as a cylinder, a sphere, a cone, everything in proper perspective so that each side of an object or a plane is directed towards a central point."

In the pictures produced during this period, Cézanne attempted to work logically through his sensory impressions in a rigorously systematic way: the forms are 'cubed,' in other words simplified according to the laws of geometrical perfection. Despite the rigor of construction with which they are arranged and structured, these compositions retain a certain lightness that can be traced back to the

Still Life with Terrine, c. 1877, Musée d'Orsay, Paris

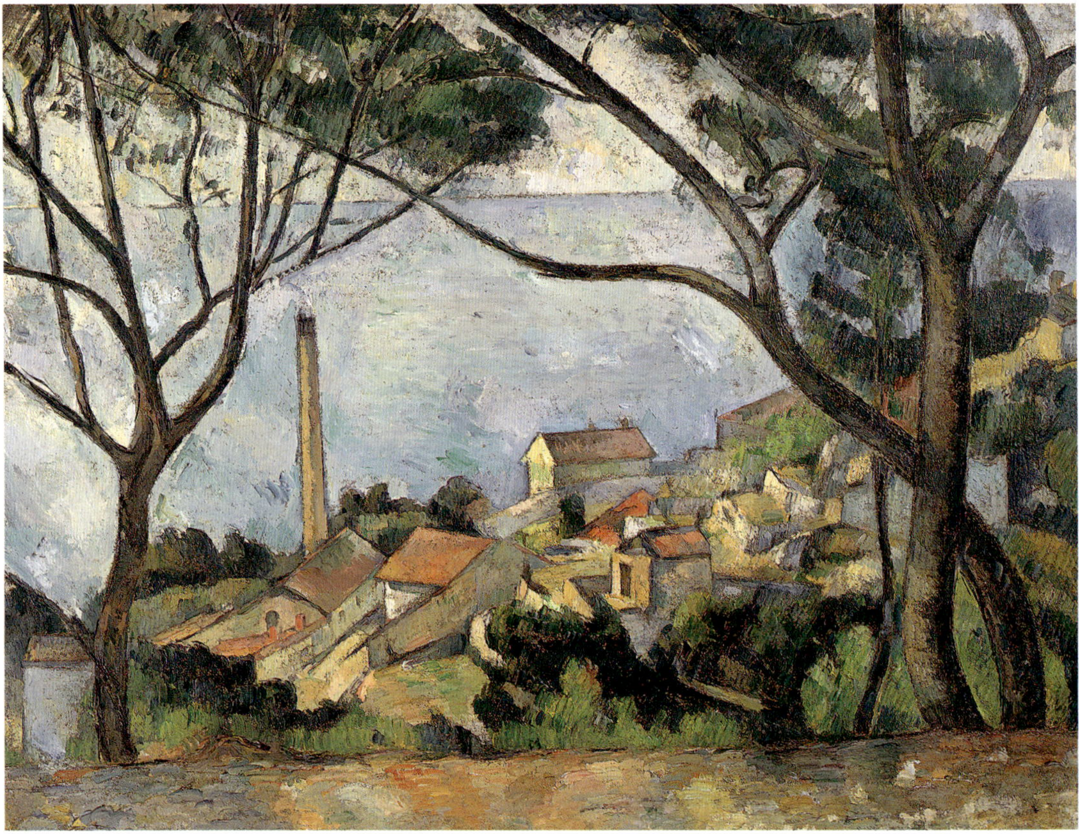

L'Estaque, View Through the Trees, c. 1878, Musée National Picasso, Paris

artist's deep-seated affinity with nature, the only sure element in the rapid and inescapable passage of time. In the landscapes of the last years—*Rocks in the Forest*, *Lake Annecy*, *Forest*, *In the Park of Château Noir*, and *The Forest Stream*—Cézanne lends the picture a vibrant liveliness through colors and forms that *hint* at mass and surface, and in doing so create the structure he felt was essential in a painting. Thus Cézanne gives the pictures a unique monumentality, a feeling of "eternity," creating an ultimate sanctuary for the agitated emotions. In these compositions, developed using short, lightly placed brushstrokes, landscape and vegetation are depicted in the same carefully composed way. He does not record the impressions as on a screen, but progresses beyond the fleeting impression, attempting to make of Impressionism "something solid and permanent like the art in museums." This lyrical aspect is open to "the delicacy of the sky and the light, its shades of blue and green, to the expanse of air, to the nostalgia of nature as a refuge of enchanting purity."

Although he had achieved a certain degree of fame by this stage—at the Salon d'Automne of 1904 an entire room was reserved for his works—Cézanne's doubts and insecurities never left him. In 1906, shortly before his death, he wrote to Émile Bernard: "Shall I achieve the goal which I have searched for so hard and pursued for so long? I do so wish it, but as long as I have not achieved it, a certain state of discomfort remains, which will disappear only when I have reached the harbor, in other words when I have achieved something which is better developed than it is so far, and can therefore prove the theories ... What causes serious difficulty is actually proving what one believes. So I continue my studies."

In 1905 Cézanne exhibited works once more at the Salon d'Automne and also at the Salon des Indépendants. Around this time he completed his painting *The Bathers* (Philadelphia Museum of Art), on which he had been working for seven years. This picture, "a masterpiece of his architectural fantasy," is considered one of the most perfectly balanced works he ever produced. The picture embraces everything in one grand, expansive panorama: the bodies, the plants, the water's surface, and the sky. Tall trees incline towards the middle of the composition, creating a protective space that the bathers organize through the spatial structure of their bodies. Everything in the picture is in equilibrium, well structured, sound. The viewer's gaze is led toward the distance, between the trees and across the water toward the horizon. In *The Bathers*, Cézanne progressed beyond his own theories, driven by a rage for order and an insatiable desire to create.

During these last years of his life, Cézanne's preferred subject was Mont Sainte-Victoire. In *Mont Sainte-Victoire* and *Plain with Houses and Trees*, the masses dissolve so that only dashes of color remain, like an infinite number of facets. In the latter painting, he left small areas of the canvas without paint, thereby lending the whole a glowing brightness. "The chaos is no longer ordered by God in accordance with the laws of nature, but by the artist in accordance with the requirements of painting." To that very end, Cézanne worked indefatigably outdoors before his subject. On 8 September 1906, one month before he died, he wrote to his son Paul:

"I cannot reach the intensity that develops before my senses; I do not possess that wonderful wealth of colors that enlivens nature. Here, on the banks of the river, the motifs multiply; the same subject, seen from another angle, offers an object of study of the greatest interest and of such diversity, that I believe I could occupy myself for several months without moving, merely by looking sometimes more to the right and sometimes more to the left."

On 15 October, while he was completely absorbed in his work, he was caught unawares by a violent storm. He suffered a seizure and lost consciousness; he was finally brought home by a passer-by. His health, already weakened by diabetes, deteriorated rapidly.

The following day, Cézanne decided to get up in order to complete a portrait of his gardener, Vallier, but after a short time he felt unwell again. He died in Aix on 22 October. His wife and son set out in haste from Paris but arrived too late to see him again alive. The following year, 56 oil paintings and a number of watercolors by Cézanne were exhibited in the Salon d'Automne. It was his first retrospective, and a belated act of homage to his extraordinary achievement.

His legacy: "Cézanne is the teacher of us all" (Matisse)

"I work very slowly, because nature presents itself to me in great variety and it is my unremitting aim to make progress," wrote Cézanne shortly before his death in a letter to Émile Bernard. During his entire life he had pursued a single goal with great tenacity: to penetrate the innermost secrets of creation in his representation of nature, and thereby to progress beyond simple, fleeting sensory

Opposite: Self-Portrait with Hat, c. 1879–1880, Kunstmuseum, Bern

impressions in order to discover the firmly established, the concrete, the eternal. Cézanne himself was restless and anxious, but he attempted with his powerful pictorial language and his cubic forms to create something permanent, something everlasting, with which he could counter the vicissitudes of life, the turbulence of emotions. He always pursued this goal with great determination, while living more or less in isolation in Provence in the south of France, far away from the big cities and their distractions. To the very end he remained faithful to nature, his model, working outdoors "in front of the subject." "Everything that we see is dispersed, disappears, don't you agree? Nature is always the same, but of its visible appearance nothing remains constant," was how Cézanne explained his view of nature. "Our art must give it the nobility of permanence, with the elements and the appearance of all its changes. Art must give it eternity in our imagination. What is behind nature? Perhaps nothing. Perhaps everything."

Cézanne lived in an age of transition. The rigorousness of his method seems like a final attempt to counter the new feelings of existential unease regarding the apparent loss of order. It is the expression of an indeterminate feeling of being unable to adapt to reality. In fact, during the last two decades of the nineteenth century, the supposedly unswerving faith in technical progress, the positivist conviction that it was possible to explain and control the whole of nature, slowly gave way to feelings of unease and doubt. The crisis in spiritual values during the nineteenth century helped art to achieve a breakthrough by concentrating entirely on the subject. In a time of uncertainty, of an inability to adapt to reality, a time of unease, Cézanne's methodical and rigorous approach seems like a desperate attempt to introduce order into the chaos of existence.

Impressionism helped Cézanne to abandon the dark color palette of his early years. It showed him the way to a light-filled and carefree painting style, in which he worked with pure colors applied with small, precise brushstrokes. But his artistic search continued; he sought the perfection of geometry. He aimed to give the fleeting immediacy of what he had seen the dignity of eternal validity.

Cézanne has been called the "Father of Modern Art." He was the artistic personality who had the greatest effect on the development of painting for at least half a century. He was the first consciously to revise the traditional system of perspective and to develop a new understanding of pictorial space—one that was no longer based on the rational constructions of linear perspective, but on the sensibility of the artist, on his own personal way of perceiving reality. Space, for Cézanne, was a complex phenomenon that was linked to a new canon of values. The result is a compositional structure in which a highly individual worldview is expressed, one that is fragmentary but no less significant.

Cézanne's fame as the "artist-hermit of Aix-en-Provence" began to grow rapidly shortly after his death. The exhibitions that took place even during the first few years clearly prove the extent to which his work was valued. In his study *The Art of Cézanne*, Kurt Badt wrote that Cézanne's uniqueness lies in the way that, with the appearance of a carefully preserved objectivity, he nonetheless captures both his own personality and the tenor of his era. Cézanne's pictorial language and artistic aims are so distinctive that they can be seen as one of the boldest achievements in modern art, as evidenced by the countless critical appraisals that his work received immediately after his death.

In 1910, 68 works by Cézanne—paintings and watercolors—were exhibited in the Galerie Bernheim Jeune in Paris. During the

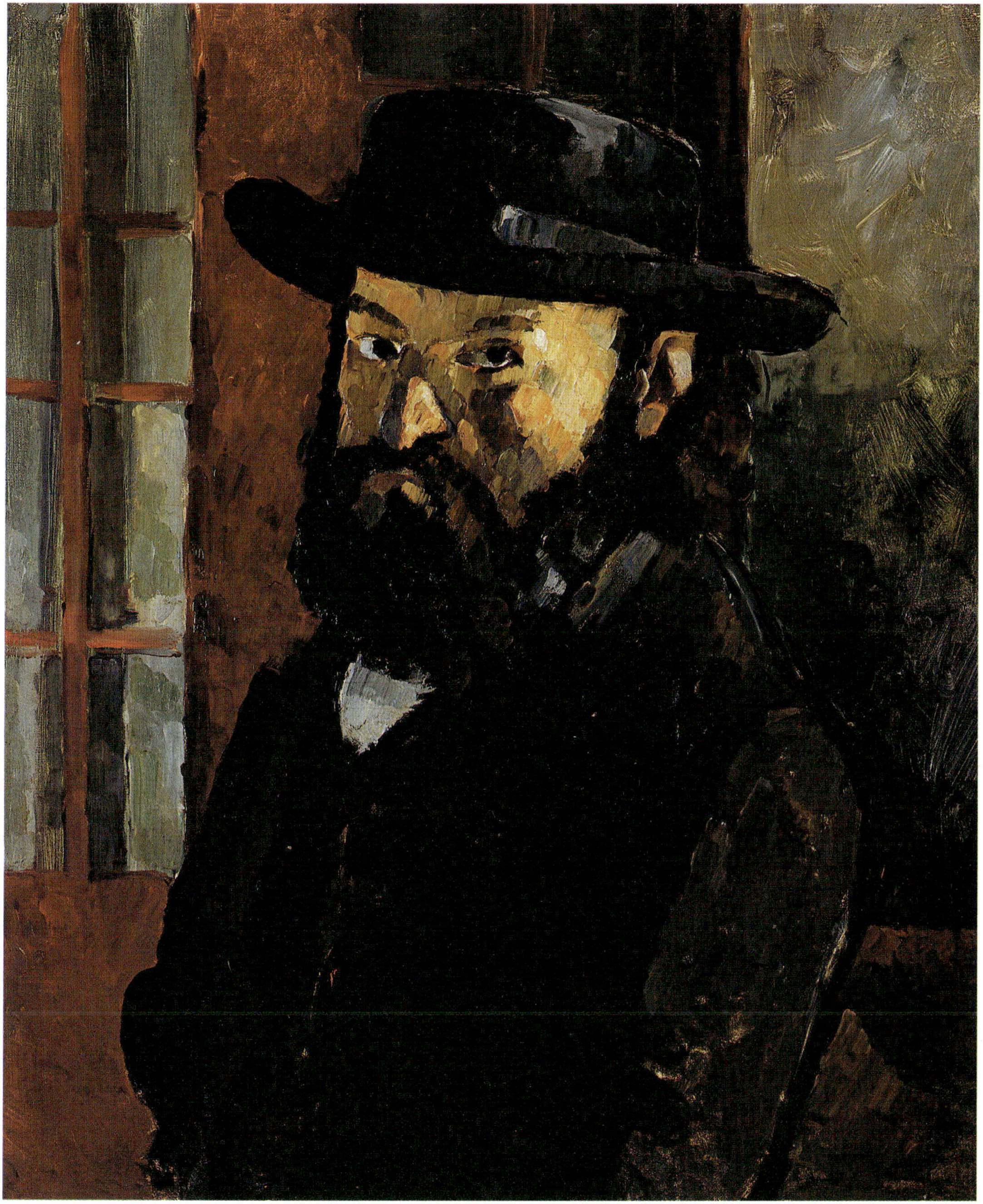

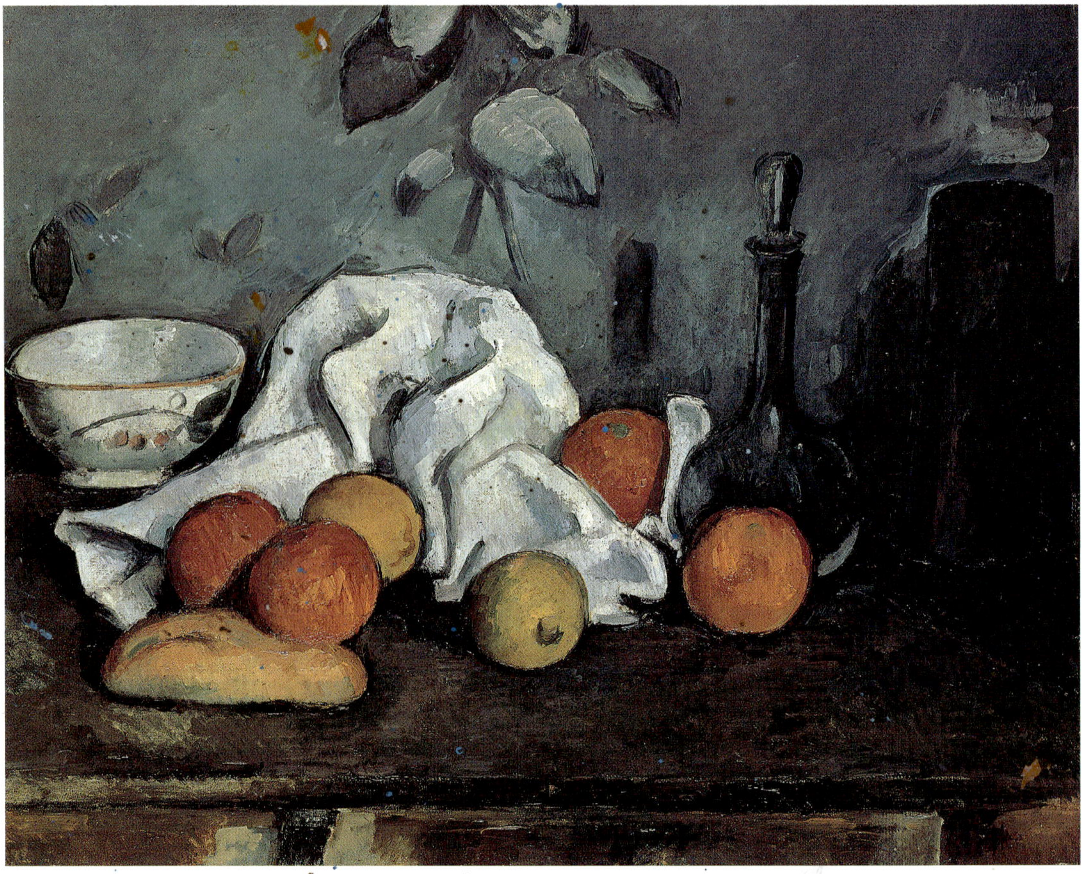

Still Life with Dishes, Fruits and Drapery, c. 1879–1880, The State Hermitage Museum, St. Petersburg

following year the Louvre acquired *The House of the Hanged Man*, *The Card Players*, and *The Blue Vase.* Exhibitions were held in 1921 in the Kunsthalle Basel and in the Galerie Cassirer in Berlin. In 1926 Bernheim Jeune staged an important retrospective; two years later, a Cézanne exhibition was held in the Galerie Wildenstein in New York. During the 1930s, works by Cézanne were on show in various museums, and to mark his centenary in 1939 France issued a special postage stamp. The Galerie de France in Paris celebrated him in 1947 in a major exhibition with the telling name *L'influence de Cézanne 1908–1911*; in 1951 the Louvre expanded its collection of Cézannes with the addition of works from the estate of Dr. Gachet. The following year, the Art Institute in Chicago also staged a Cézanne exhibition, which was subsequently on view at the Metropolitan Museum in New York. In 1954 the Orangerie in Paris presented the exhibition *Hommage à Cézanne*, and the Tate Gallery in London arranged a Cézanne exhibition during the same year. In the meantime, the prices that Cézanne's works commanded had reached astronomic heights. Museums and collectors hastily bought up all the paintings and watercolors they could find.

"If a tradition develops during our time, which I very much hope, then it will be derived from the works of Cézanne," wrote Paul Sérusier in 1905. Countless artists have based their paintings on his ideas and works, including Pablo Picasso and Georges Braque, Henri Matisse and the Fauves, the German Expressionists, Kazimir Malevich, Umberto Boccioni, and Piet Mondrian. For all these artists, Paul Cézanne was an important role model, especially because of the consistency and total commitment with which he searched for a grammar of visual construction. If Paul Gauguin is an example of exoticism, the escape from reality into a faraway ideal world in the face of the collapse of traditional values, then Cézanne is the exact opposite. He devoted himself with tremendous passion to the study of nature, focusing entirely on the appearance of reality.

Cézanne's classicism was based precisely on his notion of art as a "second nature," which is eternal and constant and which he recreates daily through his hard work: a sort of paradise before the Fall of Man, a sphere of purity that gives people the possibility of finding a place to escape from all that is unsettling. Cézanne's work looked to the future, and the outstanding quality of his artistic means of expression proves that he fully understood the problems of his age, and at the same time was, to a remarkable extent, was able to anticipate the issues that future generations of artists would face. "Cézanne would never have interested me," commented Picasso, "if he had lived and thought like Jacques-Émile Blanche, even if the apple which he painted was ten times more beautiful. What interests us is Cézanne's restlessness, van Gogh's agonies. In a word: the human drama."

Émile Bernard was one of the first artists to recognize the value of Cézanne's painting, even though his own tendency toward mysticism and a strongly marked Symbolist vein led to an understanding of art far removed from that of the Master of Aix. Henri Matisse was also one of the first to express his high esteem for Cézanne's artistic objectives. It was Pissarro, whom he had met together with Henri Manguin in Rodin's studio, who encouraged the young Matisse to study the oeuvre of the Provençal artist. Although Matisse greatly admired Cézanne, he never met him; this was, perhaps, a conscious decision meant to preserve the aura and the fascination that surrounded the great artist who lived and worked in isolation in a rural area of southern France. Pissarro explained to Matisse that Cézanne was not an Impressionist, but a classical painter, because he had ultimately always painted the same picture his entire life long: *The Bathers*. In an interview for the magazine *L'Art Vivant* of 15 September 1925, Matisse declared:

"If only you knew how much moral strength, how much courage his wonderful example has given me throughout my life. In moments of doubt, while I was still searching, when at times I was shocked by my own discoveries, I thought to myself: 'If Cézanne is right, then I am right, too.' And I knew that Cézanne had not been wrong. You see, one finds in Cézanne's oeuvre certain principles that are very useful to a young painter. Among his greatest achievements was his attempt to make the shades of color in a painting powerful, which represented a supreme challenge to his claims as an artist."

In 1899 Matisse purchased a painting by Cézanne from Vollard, *Three Bathers*. He would keep it for the rest of his life. "I could most certainly have sold it, but I hung on to it," explained Matisse, "because I loved the painting passionately." In 1937 he donated the picture to the Musée du Petit Palais in Paris. In a letter to Raymond Escholier, the curator of the collection, Matisse wrote: "Yesterday I gave the *Bathers* by Cézanne to your messenger ... Allow me to point out that the picture is of outstanding importance in Cézanne's oeuvre ... Since it has been in my possession for 37 years I know it pretty well, albeit, I hope, not yet in its entirety; in difficult moments of my artistic career this painting was a moral support for me; from it I drew confidence and staying power. So please allow me to request that you give the work the space it needs, so that it can convey all its possibilities. To do so it needs light and a certain amount of space, so that the sweep of its lines and the extraordinary simplicity of the compositional relationships can be shown to best advantage. I know that there is no need for me to tell you this; but nonetheless I feel I have a duty to do so; so please accept it as a sentimental expression of my admiration for this work, an admiration that has continued to grow since I have owned it."

In 1907 the Salon d'Automne dedicated an important retrospective to Cézanne, who had died the previous year. Fifty-six works were shown; Braque and Picasso attended the exhibition, and from their impressions they developed the fundamentals of what would later become Cubism. Also among the visitors was the German poet Rainer Maria Rilke, who was visiting Paris for the third time. Rilke's thoughts about Cézanne's work provided him with an opportunity to examine his own position and to formulate the artistic principles to which he would remain true throughout his life.

When Rilke left the exhibition in the Grand Palais on 6 October 1907, he was a different person, and the letters he subsequently wrote—mostly to his wife, Clara Westhoff—bear witness to this rebirth. During the days of the exhibition, Rilke read the memories of Cézanne that the artist Émile Bernard had published in a two-part article in the *Mercure de France*. They fueled his admiration for the great artist from Provence and confirmed his intention to explore the roots of Cézanne's painting. Rilke was in close contact with a number of artists and made a study of their works (at one stage he was secretary to the sculptor Auguste Rodin), but the revelation he experienced when he saw Cézanne's paintings was unique in its profundity: "But I then finally came across the colorful picture market, which, though it taxed me with all its impressions, nonetheless did not frighten away my inner mood. ... Cézanne is ... moving and important. He has also (like Goya) painted the walls of his studio in Aix with fantasies." (6 October 1907)

The following day, Rilke returned to the Grand Palais: "This morning I went to the Salon d'Automne again ... You know how I always find the people walking around at exhibitions so much more noteworthy than the paintings. That is the case at the Salon d'Automne, too, with the exception of the Cézanne room. There all the reality is on his side—in that dense, quilted blue of his, in his red and his shadowless green, in the reddish black of his wine bottles. How humble all the objects are in his pictures! The apples are all cooking apples and the wine bottles belong in baggy old jacket pockets." (7 October 1907) He wrote to his wife again two days later: "...Today I want to tell you a little about Cézanne. Where work is concerned, he claims to have lived the life of a bohemian until the age of forty. It was then, he says, that through his acquaintance with Pissarro he discovered the joys of work. So much so that he did nothing but work for the next thirty years of his life. ... even when he was old, sick, sucked dry to the point of exhaustion every evening by his regular, everyday work (so much so that he often went to bed when the sun set at six, following an unconsciously consumed meal), irascible, suspicious, always laughed at, ridiculed, abused on his way to his atelier ... and very

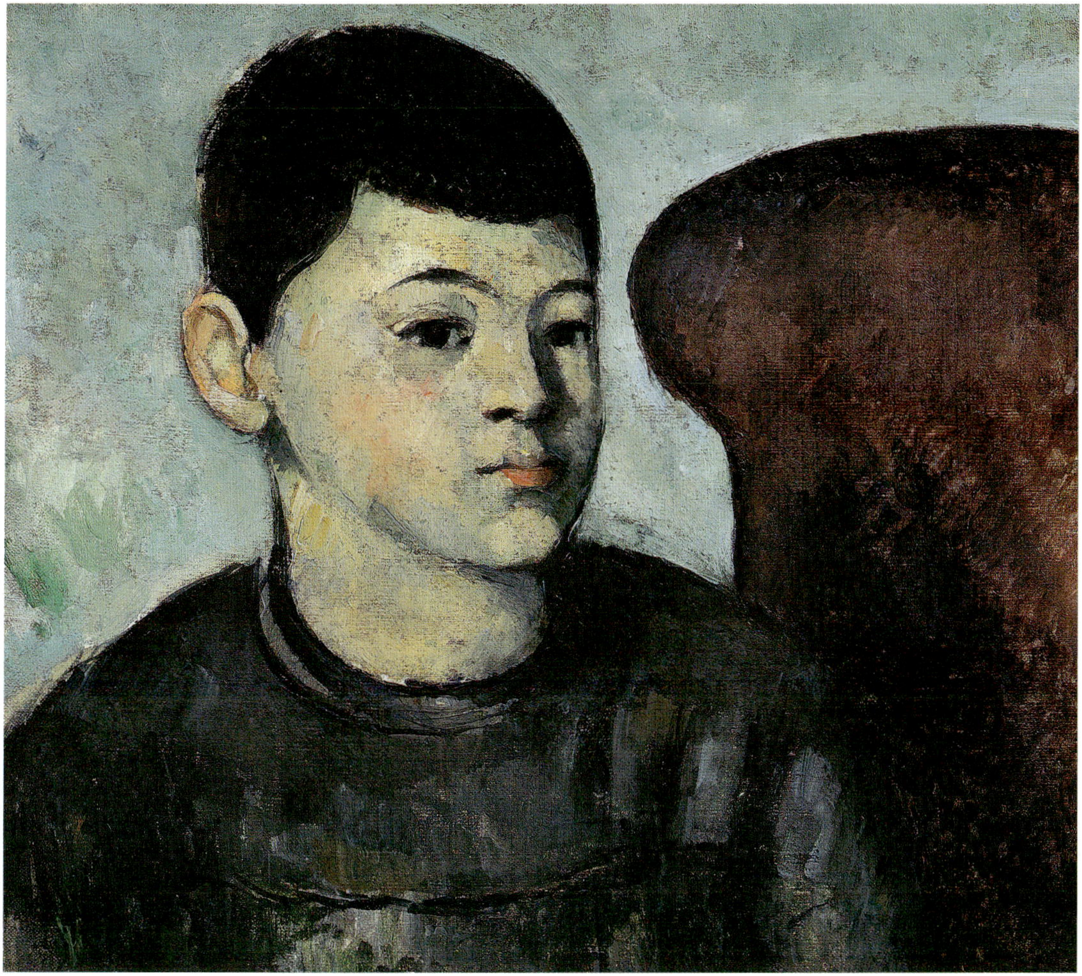

Portrait of Paul Cézanne, the Artist's Son, c. 1882–1885, Musée de l'Orangerie, Paris

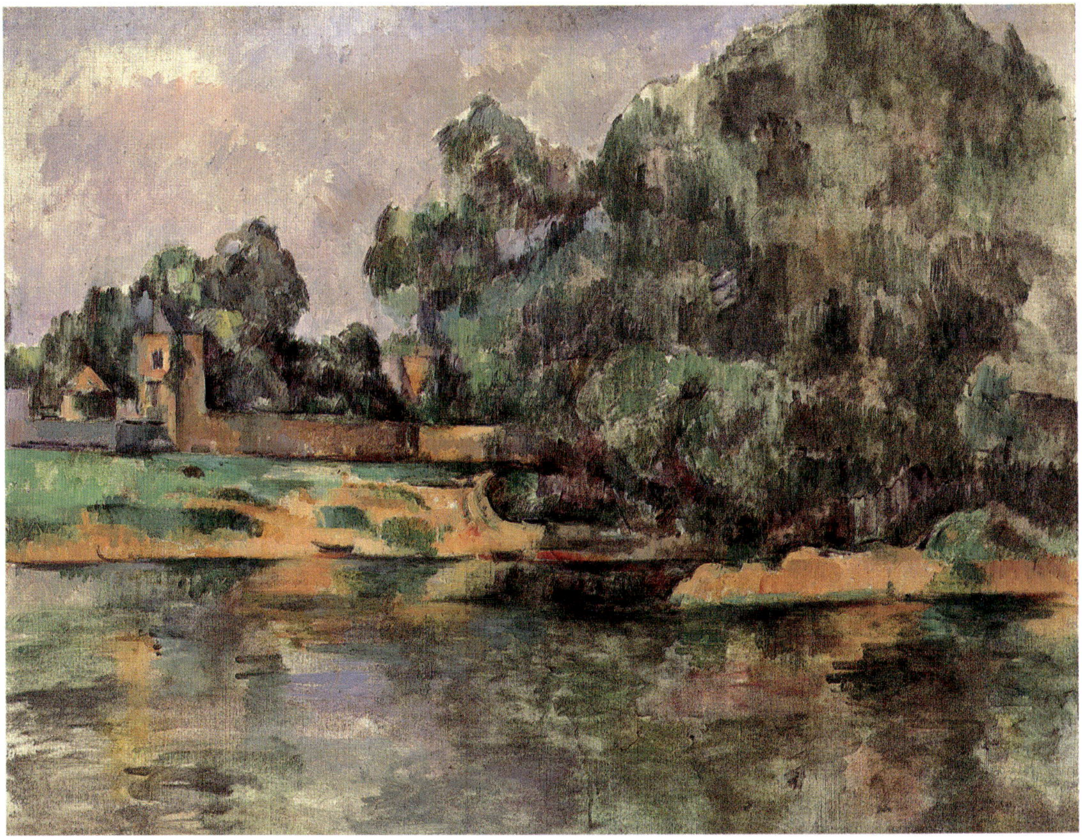

Riverbank, c. 1895, National Gallery of Art, Washington

politely requesting a slightly better meal from his housekeeper, Madame Brémond. Perhaps he did live in hope from one day to the next that he would achieve the only success that he considered important. ... But the next day he would start yet again in his attempts at success. He got up every morning at 6 o'clock, walked through the town to his studio and stayed there until ten; then he walked back along the same route to go home to eat; he ate and then set off again. Often he walked for half an hour beyond the studio, 'sur le motif' in a valley; before him the peaks of Sainte Victoire rose indescribably with all its one thousand challenges. There he sat for hours..." (9 October 1907) A little later: "I notice how much Cézanne now gives me to do, how different I have become ... I went to see his pictures again today; it is remarkable what an environment they create. Without looking at a single one, standing in the middle between the two rooms, you feel their presence gathering together to form a colossal reality. As if these colors were taking away one's indecision, once and for all. The good conscience of these reds, these blues, their simple authenticity teaches one a lesson; and if you stand at the ready beneath them, it is as if they were doing something for you." (13 October 1907) Finally, on 22 October, he wrote: "The Salon is closing today. And already, as I head for home from there for the last time, I should like to return to look for a violet, or a green or specific shades of blue again, which I feel I should have looked at more attentively, more unforgettably."

On several occasions, Rilke considered writing an essay on Cézanne, but ultimately his letters remain the only testimony to his deeply felt admiration for the work of the French artist. For Rilke the discovery of Cézanne was a decisive milestone in his development as an individual and as a poet. "In my sensibility, the awareness of its presence has been heightened in a way that I experience even when I am asleep."

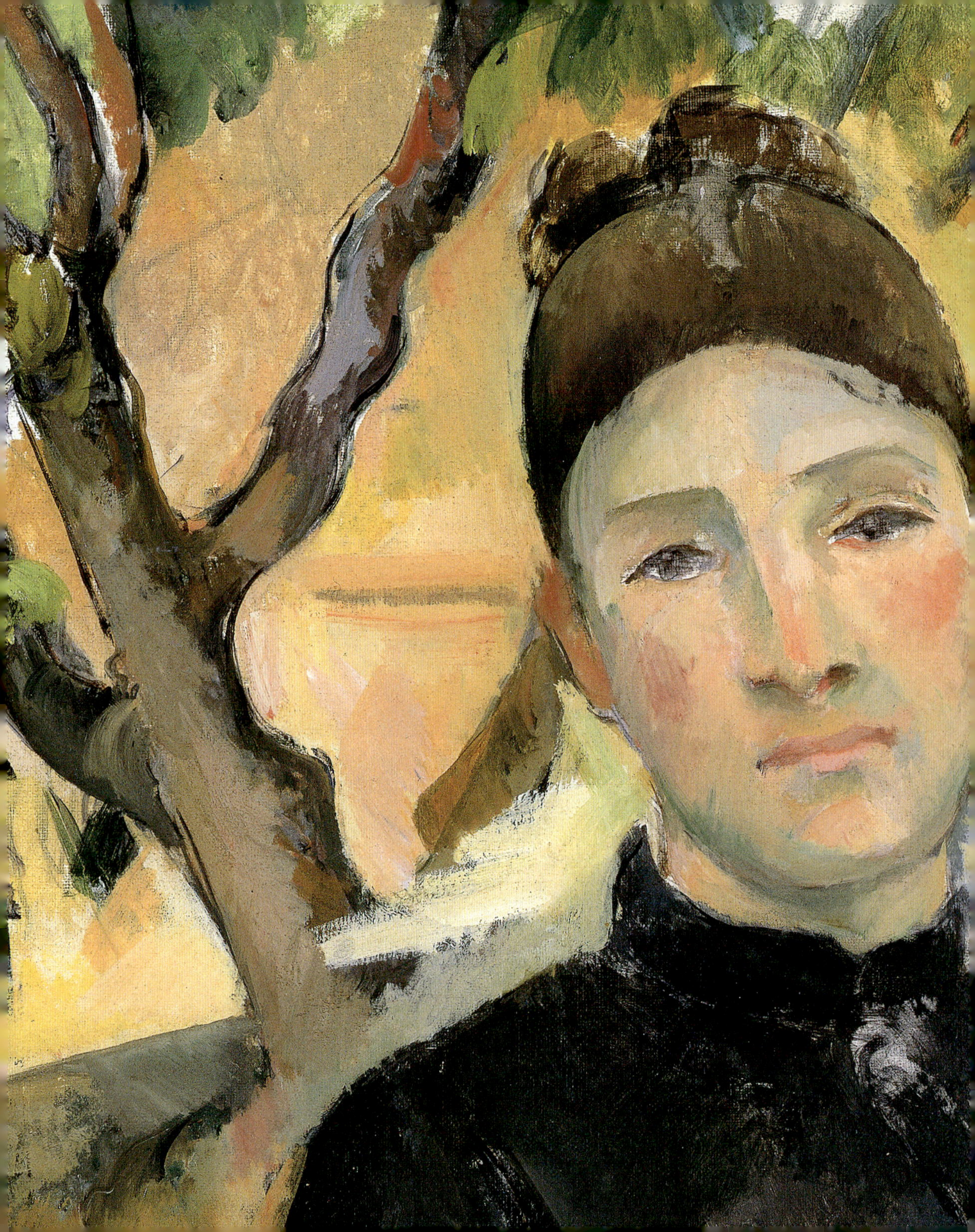

WORKS

Girl at the Piano (Overture to "Tannhäuser")

c. 1869

Oil on canvas, 57 x 92 cm
The State Hermitage Museum, St. Petersburg

Despite depicting a cozy bourgeois interior in which a girl is playing the piano while a woman sits on a sofa and sews, this painting can be seen as a homage to the music of Richard Wagner, which particularly fascinated Cézanne; the title refers explicitly the opera *Tannhäuser* by Wagner, which was first performed in 1861 in Paris. Like a number of other French artists and intellectuals, Cézanne loved Wagner's stirring music, and he occasionally attended the evenings organized by Commandant Lejosne, one of the composer's most important patrons. In this painting, which is thought to show his sister Rose and his mother, Cézanne pays particular attention to the decorative details of the interior. The patterned cover of the armchair in the foreground, the carpet, and the floral wallpaper: these elements enhance the cozy atmosphere radiated by the scene. His first painting on this subject was executed in 1866, entitled *The Overture to "Tannhäuser."* He later painted a second version, but left it unfinished. He wrote to Zola: "I have tried to reproduce an evening among family members, but I have not been entirely successful." The painting illustrated here is the third, and final, version. It is characterized by a distinctive, energetic style, a robust application of paint, with dark tones thickly painted, which lends the scene a distinctive immediacy. In this powerfully composed interior with a double portrait, Cézanne liberated himself from the demands of correct drawing in favor of an expressivity through which a passionate intensity finds expression.

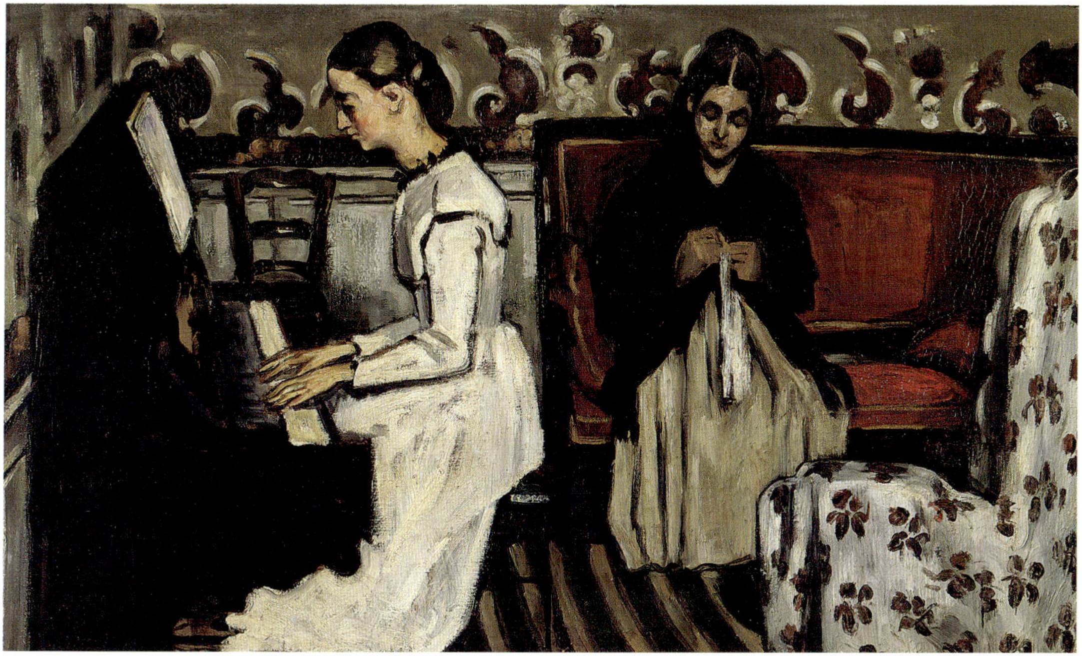

The House of the Hanged Man, Auvers-sur-Oise

1872–1873

Oil on canvas, 55 x 66 cm
Musée d'Orsay, Paris

This painting marks an important turning point in the development of Cézanne's pictorial language. It was at this time that he met Camille Pissarro, who introduced him to Impressionist painting, showing him how to build up a scene in terms of light and of complementary contrasts of colors, and advising him to observe nature with a certain detachment in order to better capture its structures and colors. One of a small number of artworks signed by the painter, this landscape was shown in 1874, at the first Impressionist exhibition, which took place in the studio of the photographer Nadar (Gaspard-Félix Tournachon). Visitors to the exhibition reacted with surprise and even anger to the various paintings, while the critics were scathing. The collector Armand Doria bought the painting for 300 francs, making it one of only a few paintings to be sold at this exhibition. Despite the fact that the application of paint is again fairly thick, Cézanne was here able to transcend the heaviness and immobility of his earlier compositions. His stay in Auvers-sur-Oise, starting in 1872, where he worked side by side with Pissarro, marks a crucial stage in the development of his pictorial language. Cézanne discovered a new world through his older colleague, as well as a more objective approach to nature. Both artists worked closely together, and often painted the same landscapes. Cézanne's palette became progressively lighter, and he now achieved a synthesis of objects and space through the subtle use of light and the glow of the colors, lending his art an extraordinary freshness and closeness to nature. Objects are clearly and succinctly rendered, the houses are of an almost palpable materiality, and yet the light falls gently on the scene, giving the ensemble an aura of airy lightness.

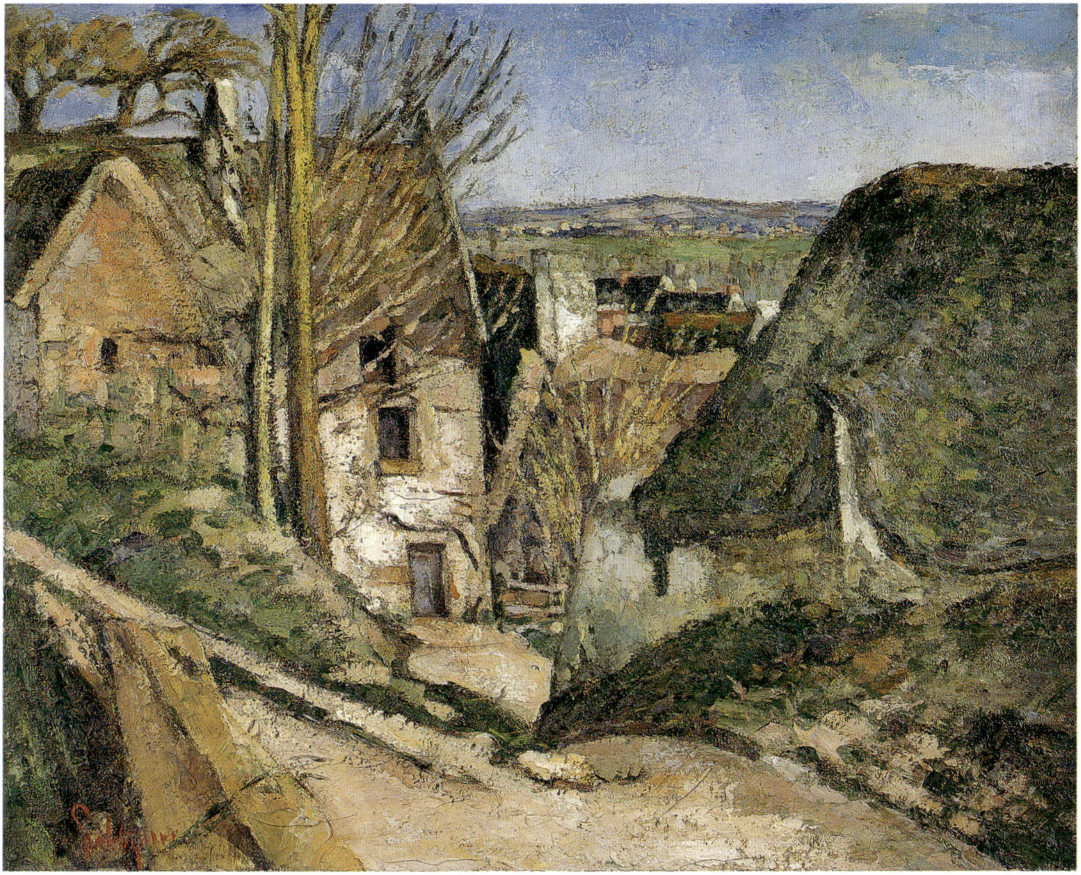

A Modern Olympia

1872–1874

Oil on canvas, 46 x 55 cm
Musée d'Orsay, Paris

"On Sunday, the viewers saw fit to ridicule a fantastical figure that presents itself to a drug addict underneath an opium sky. This apparition of light-pink naked flesh that a sort of demon or incubus chases ahead of himself like a lascivious vision in a heavenly cloud—this niche of an artificial paradise made even the boldest feel lost for words. Monsieur Cézanne has simply created the impression that he is some sort of madman, who paints while suffering from delirium tremens." This scornful description of Cézanne's painting, written by the art critic Marc de Montifaud, appeared in *L'Artiste* in 1874, in a review of the first Impressionist exhibition. This painting is the second version of the subject and draws directly on the famous *Olympia* of 1863 by Manet, a work that is now also in the collection of the Musée d'Orsay. Cézanne painted it during his visit to Dr. Gachet in Auvers-sur-Oise. Exaggerated and ironic, Cézanne's painting was dashed down on canvas using rapid brushstrokes and bright colors. But it was not meant merely as a provocation; it is a vision, a symbolic reference to the female body as the object of desire. Cézanne depicted himself in the man seated on the right. A little dog next to him provides a humorous note, equivalent to the black cat in Manet's painting. Unrobed by her black servant as if to be openly displayed to the male figure in the painting, and to the viewer, the woman lies stretched out on a mass of brilliantly white sheets. The painting was also a homage to Manet, whom Cézanne knew and greatly admired.

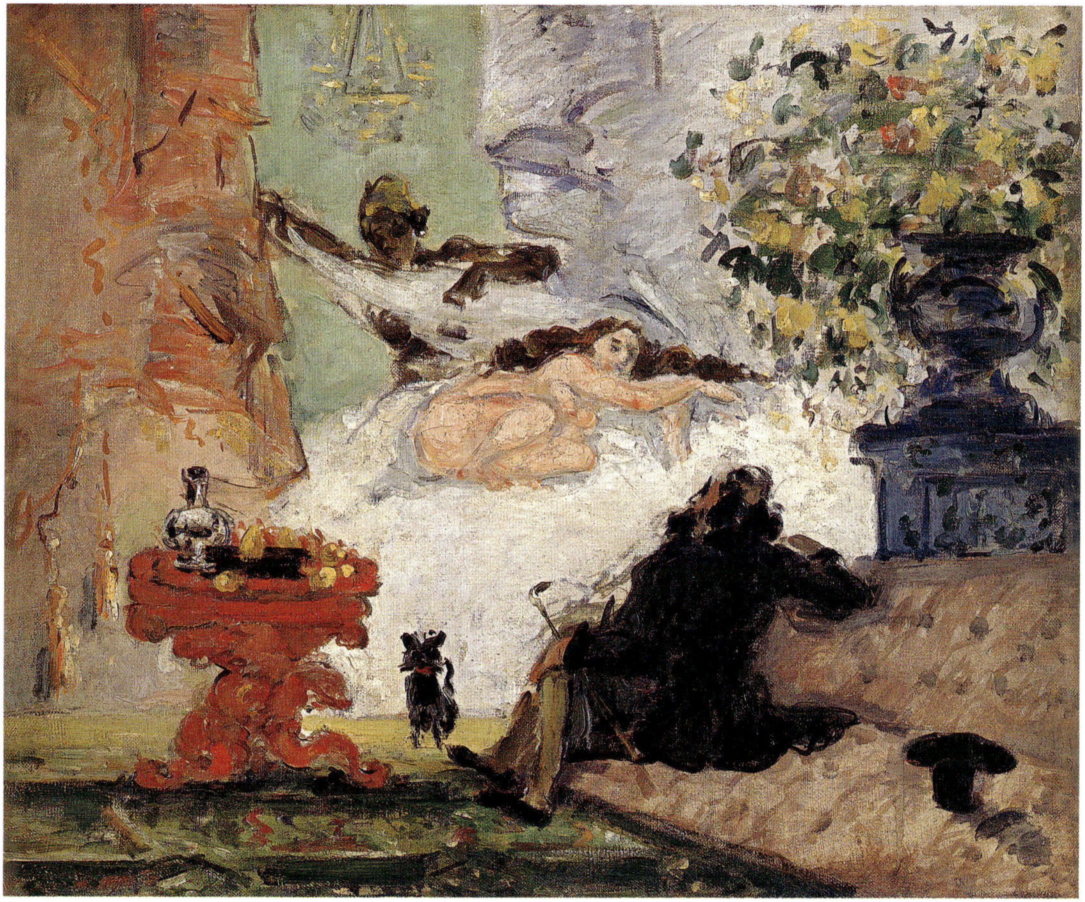

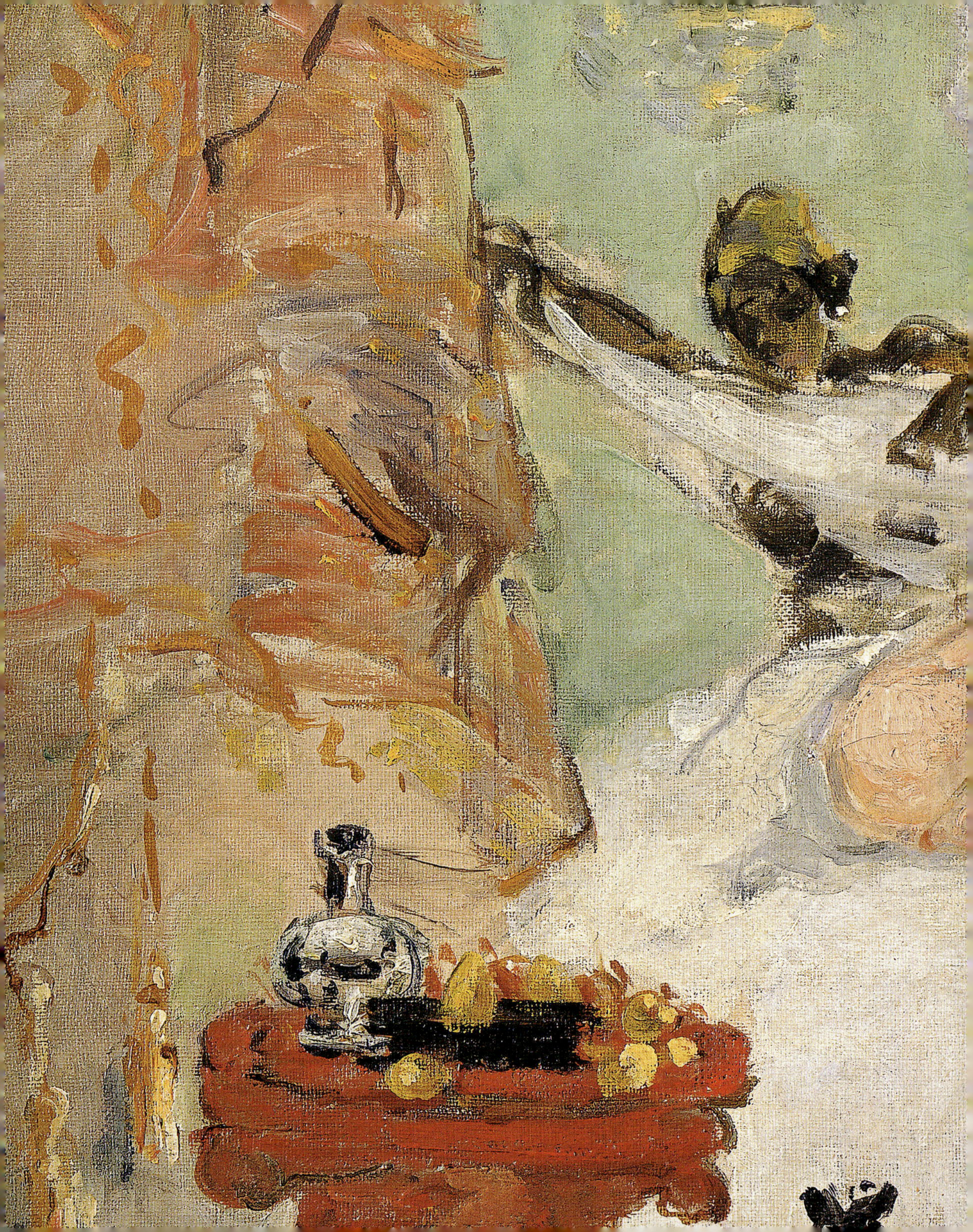

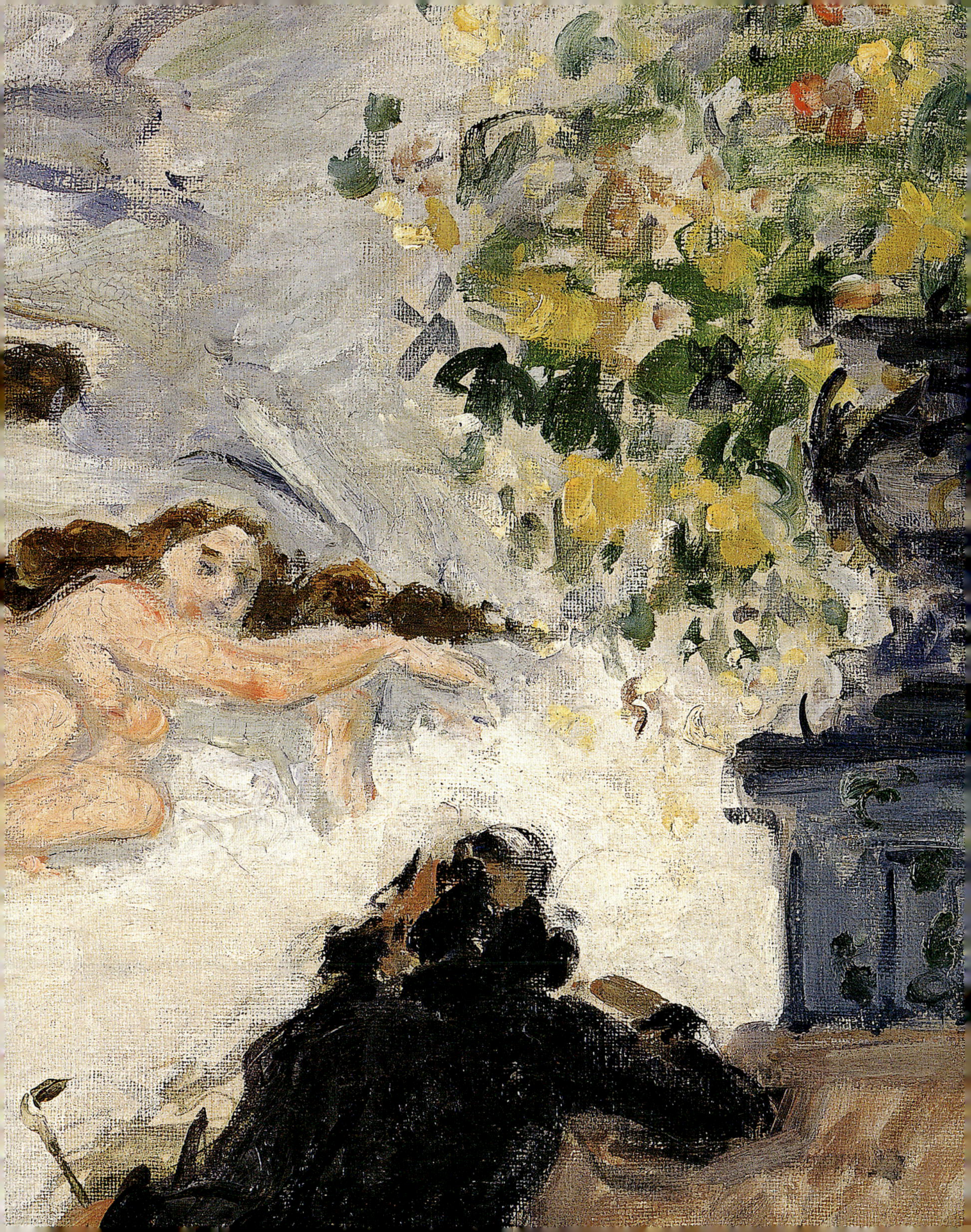

The House of Père Lacroix in Auvers-sur-Oise

1873

Oil on canvas, 61.5 x 51 cm
National Gallery of Art, Washington

In 1872 Cézanne accepted Pissarro's invitation to paint with him in the countryside surrounding Pontoise, and traveled there with Hortense and his son Paul. At first, he lived in a hotel close to Pissarro's apartment, and then, from early 1873 onwards, in Auvers, in a house near that of Dr. Paul Gachet. The latter was a medical doctor with a fairly unconventional external appearance, who was interested in homeopathic medicine, a committed socialist, and who treated the poor residents of the town without payment. He, too, painted, and was a great supporter of "modern" artists. Painters working outdoors in the area, attracted by the delightful landscape of the Île-de-France region (which also enchanted Cézanne), were often guests at his house. Cézanne came into his own in Auvers, in the company of Pissarro. He worked tirelessly *en plein air*. He freed himself of the broad and somber brushstrokes of his early years, and started to use more fragmented dots of color, better suited to capturing the artist's impressions when painting directly from nature. The cheerful and lively composition shown here works with a spectrum of yellows and greens that suggest the luscious natural landscape surrounding the little white house in Auvers-sur-Oise. Cézanne was always skilled at reproducing his subjects in a manner so true to life that it is sometimes even possible to determine the precise point at which his easel once stood. In many of his landscapes, as in this painting, Cézanne depicts houses surrounded by dense vegetation. This motif allowed him to base the composition on geometric forms, thus imbuing the arrangement of pictorial elements with solidity and structure. This also portrays a symbiosis of man and nature, though people are never shown in his landscapes.

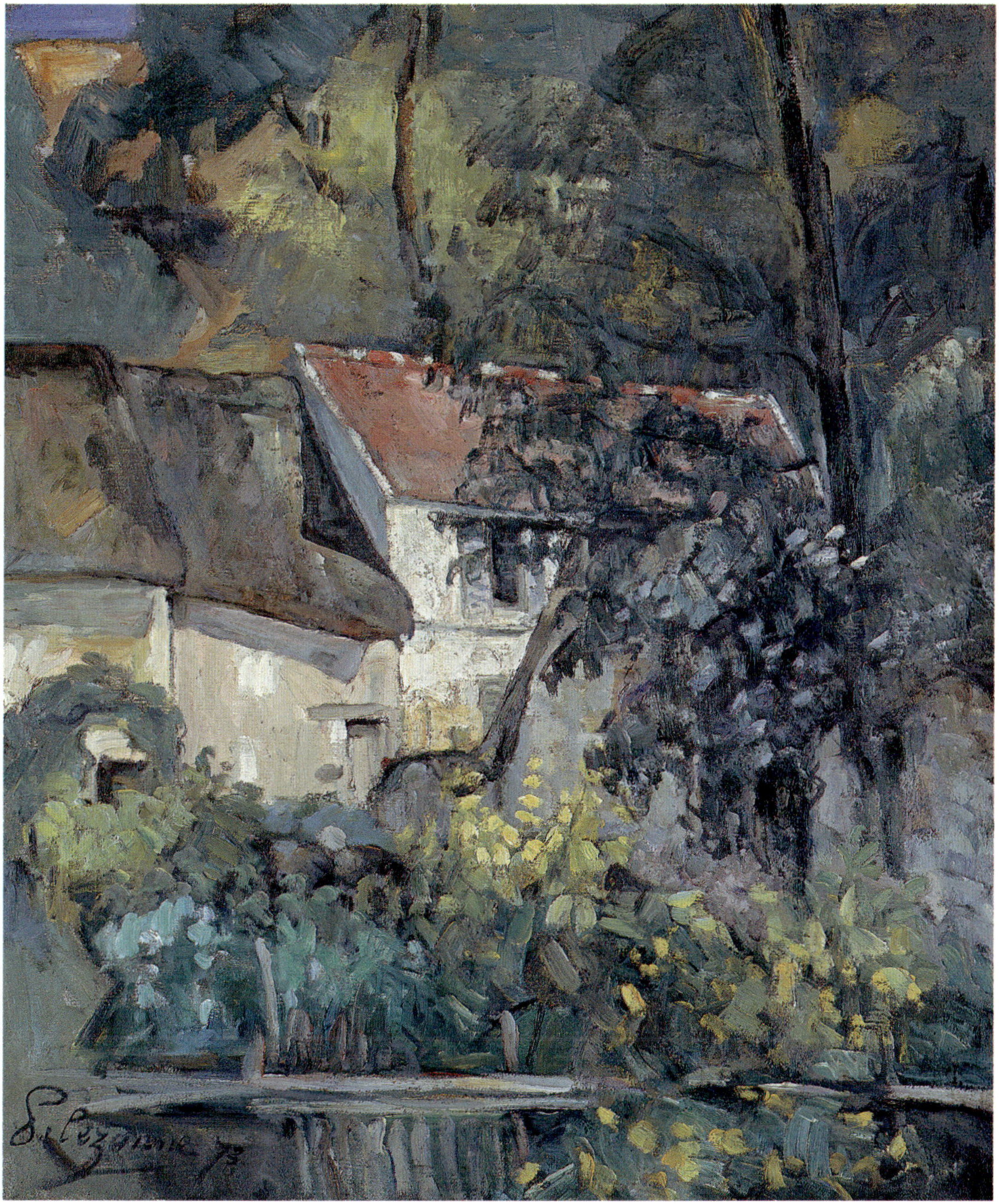

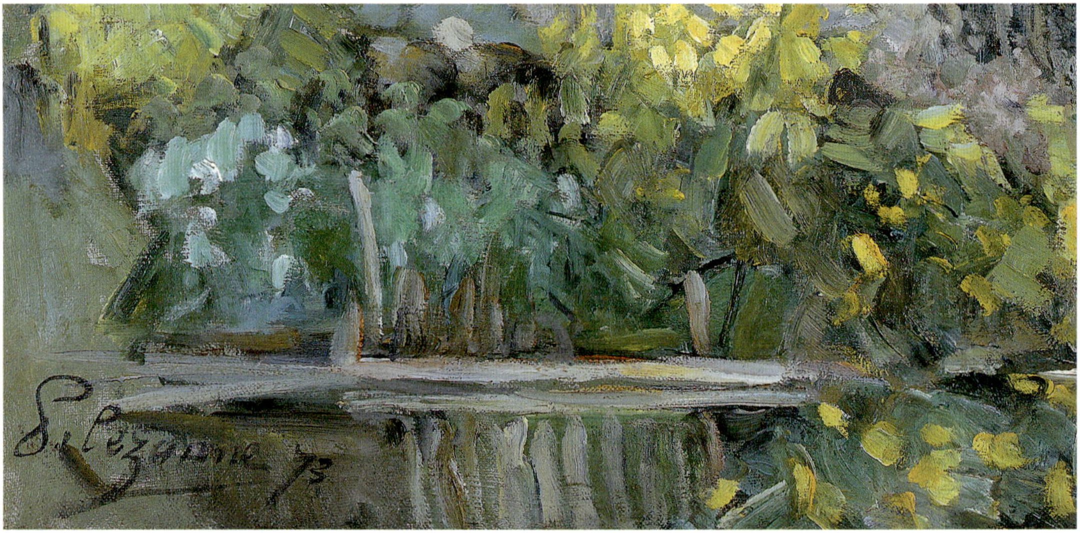

The House of Père Lacroix in Auvers-sur-Oise (details)

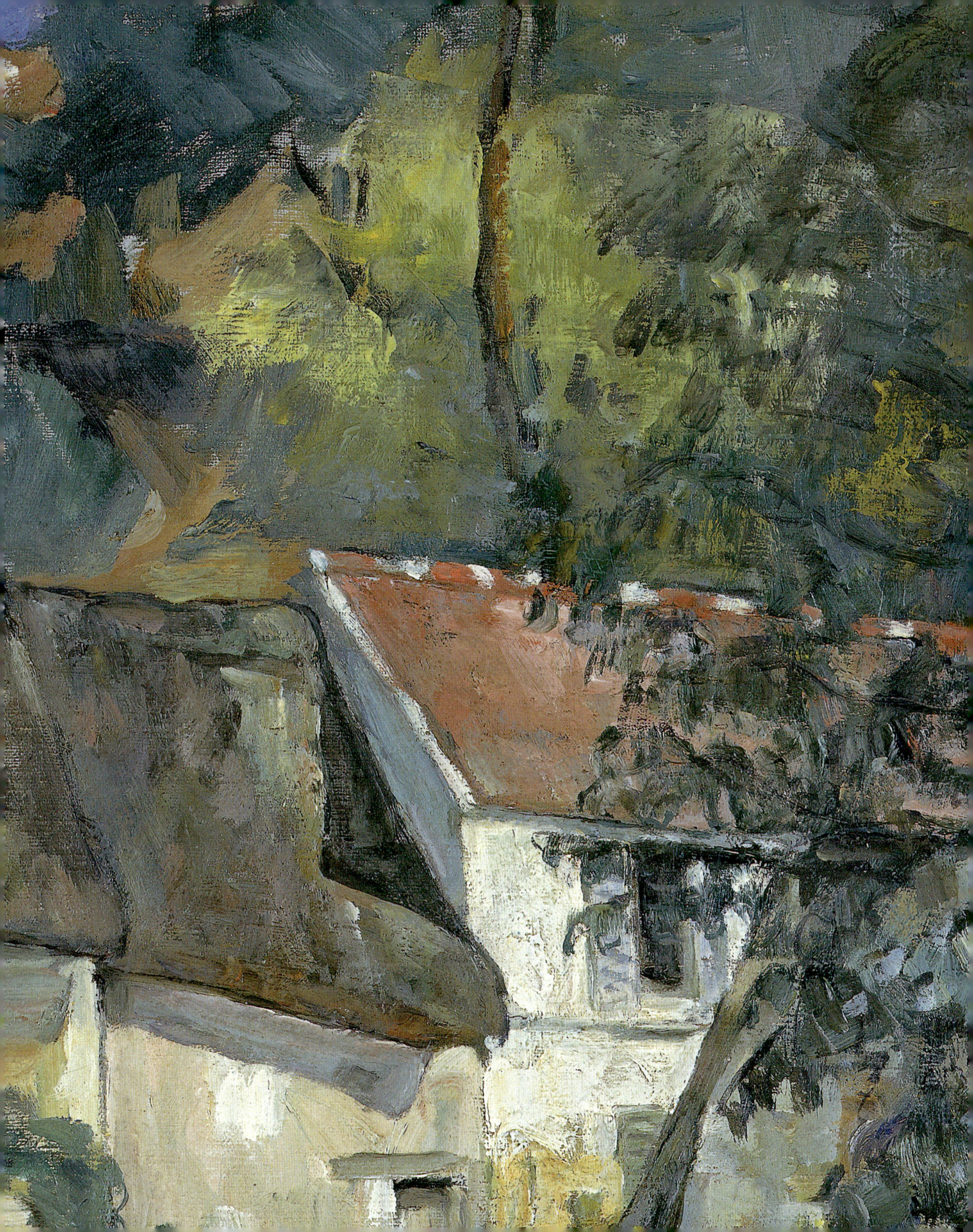

Madame Cézanne in a Red Armchair

c. 1877

Oil on canvas, 72.5 x 56 cm
Museum of Fine Arts, Boston

Cézanne produced several paintings of his wife. He met Hortense Fiquet, a beautiful young woman with chestnut-brown hair and dark eyes, in 1869 in Paris, where the 19-year-old worked as a model. Cézanne, who was at the time financially dependent on his father, did not tell him about his relationship with Hortense, or about the birth of his son Paul on 4 January 1872. The situation was not easy to manage for Cézanne, and the father soon accused the son of having "relationships in Paris." When he discovered the situation, Louis-Auguste Cézanne went so far as to try separate his son from Hortense and her child, but finally gave in to the mother's pleas and accepted the situation. It was not until his father had died in 1886, however, that Cézanne married Hortense.

In the portraits of this period, Cézanne abandoned the intense expressivity of his early work. He began to pay more attention to his subjects, as he had been taught by Pissarro. The symbolically monumental figure of the young woman is depicted from the front, in an interior. The painting as a whole constitutes a palette of shades of green: Madame Cézanne's elegant gown is green, as is the wallpaper in the background and the shadows of the flesh tones. This somewhat subdued palette of colors complements the intense red of the armchair in which the woman has made herself comfortable and which offsets her contour and her plump body. Cézanne's brushwork is powerful, the painting well structured. Here, he applied the paint in small patches that lend the painting as a whole a remarkable cohesiveness and compactness, an ingenious solidity that gives expression to his search for a more generous, innovative concept of pictorial space.

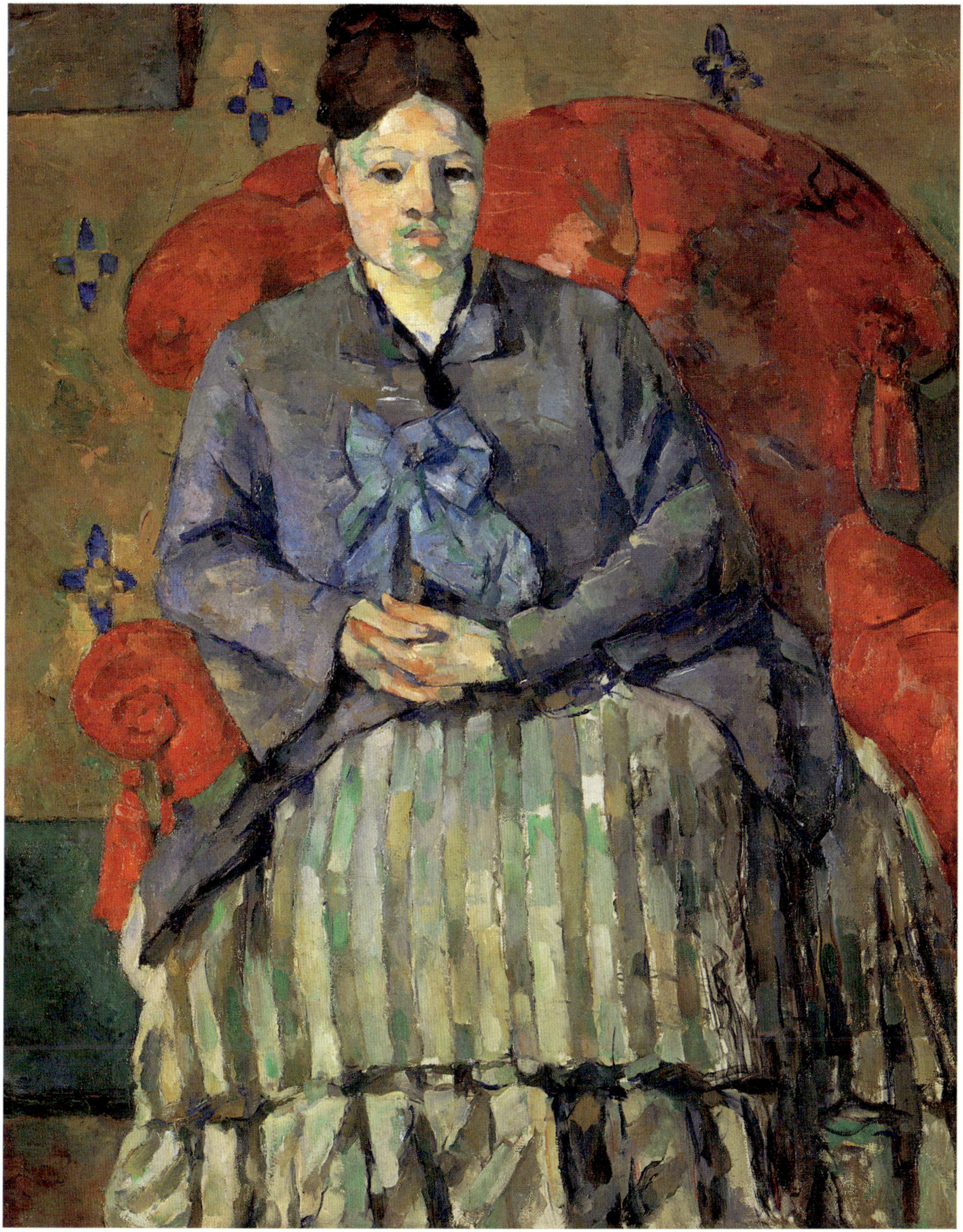

Self-Portrait

c. 1877

Oil on canvas, 26 x 15 cm
Musée d'Orsay, Paris

This unfinished self-portrait was once in the collection of Cézanne's friend, Camille Pissarro, who described Cézanne's "unfinished and spectacular," incredibly expressive half-length portraits with great enthusiasm. The painting makes a powerful impression on viewers thanks to the strong modeling and the artist's expressive gaze. Studying his appearance closely, and capturing the essence of his features in just a few brushstrokes, Cézanne created a work of great emotional intensity. The painting technique with which Cézanne constructs—one might even say sculpts—his paintings is clearly visible in this unfinished work. He first transferred the basic structure directly to the canvas using fine pencil lines and brushstrokes in various colors, and then started to apply paint with a palette knife. His jacket is hinted at in green, against which the yellow of the lighter sections and the blue of the lapel stand out. In front of the blue background enlivened with subtle color contrasts, the almost completely fleshed-out head is illuminated by light from the viewer's left. The brightness of the high, bald forehead contrasts with the left-hand side of the figure's face, which is almost completely in shadow. The tightly closed lips under the beard, and the eyes that look inquisitively at the viewer, give the impression of a proud and questioning artist who has recently experienced the failure of the third Impressionist exhibition.

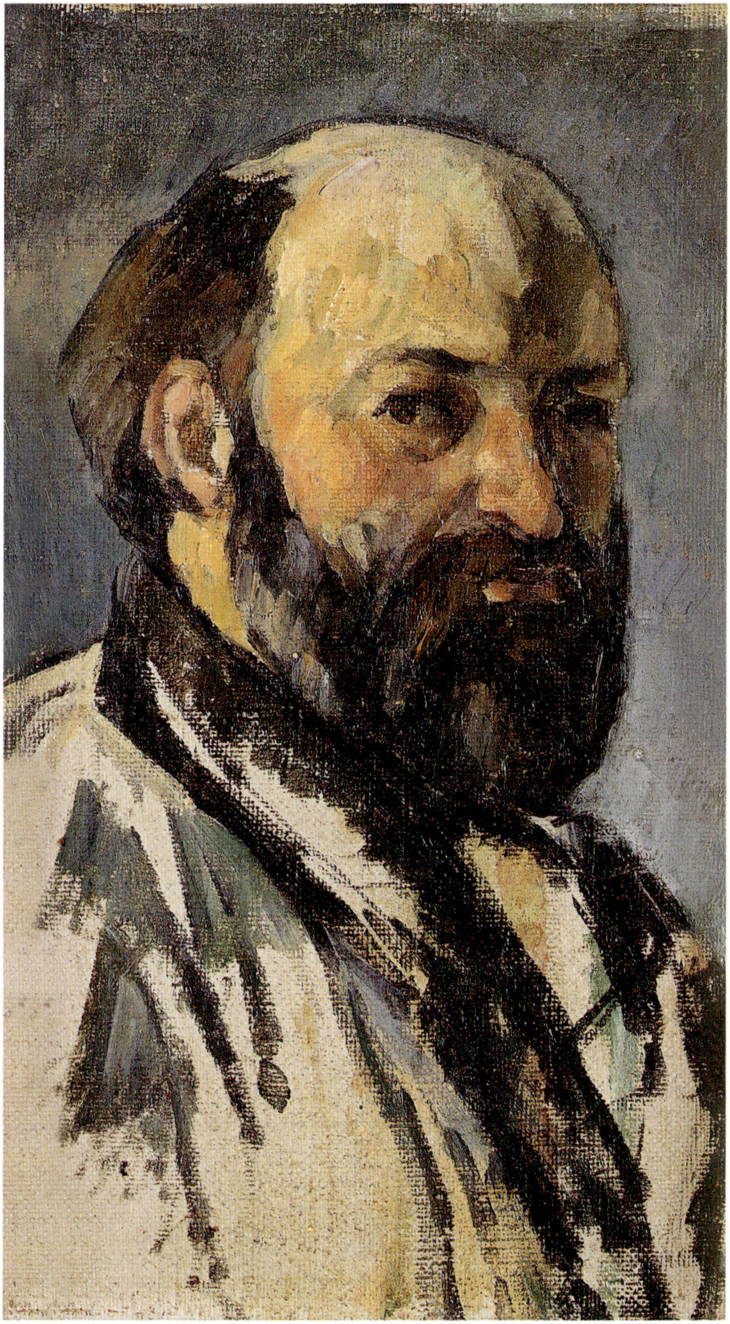

The Gulf of Marseilles from L'Estaque

1878–1879

Oil on canvas, 59.5 x 73 cm
Musée d'Orsay, Paris

Cézanne left Paris with Hortense and their son Paul in 1878, withdrawing to a small fishing village on the bay of Marseilles called, L'Estaque, where Renoir, too, stayed. The intensity of the Mediterranean light, which causes the silhouettes of objects to be cast in clear lines, led him towards a painting style based increasingly on geometric structures. He soon became fond of L'Estaque, and would return to it often. Cézanne, whose painting was now characterized by the dense and compact application of paint, wrote to his friend Pissarro: "I have started work on two little motifs with the sea for Monsieur Chocquet, who spoke to me about this. – It is like a playing card. Red roofs in front of the blue sea ... The sun is so terrible here that it is as though all objects were silhouetted, and not only in black and white, but in blue, in red, in brown, in violet." In his *L'Estaque, View Through the Trees* (see p. 20) painted during the same period, the viewer's gaze travels from the pine trees on the hill, across the sea, and finally settles on the cuboid shapes of the sun-drenched houses. In the present painting there is also a chimney, in the foreground, but it is far less prominent, and there are no tree branches to frame the scene, which is therefore more open and expansive. The shades of green, brown, and blue have been applied to the canvas in small brushstrokes, the juxtaposition of the contrasting color values beautifully reproducing the liveliness of the natural colors of the landscape.

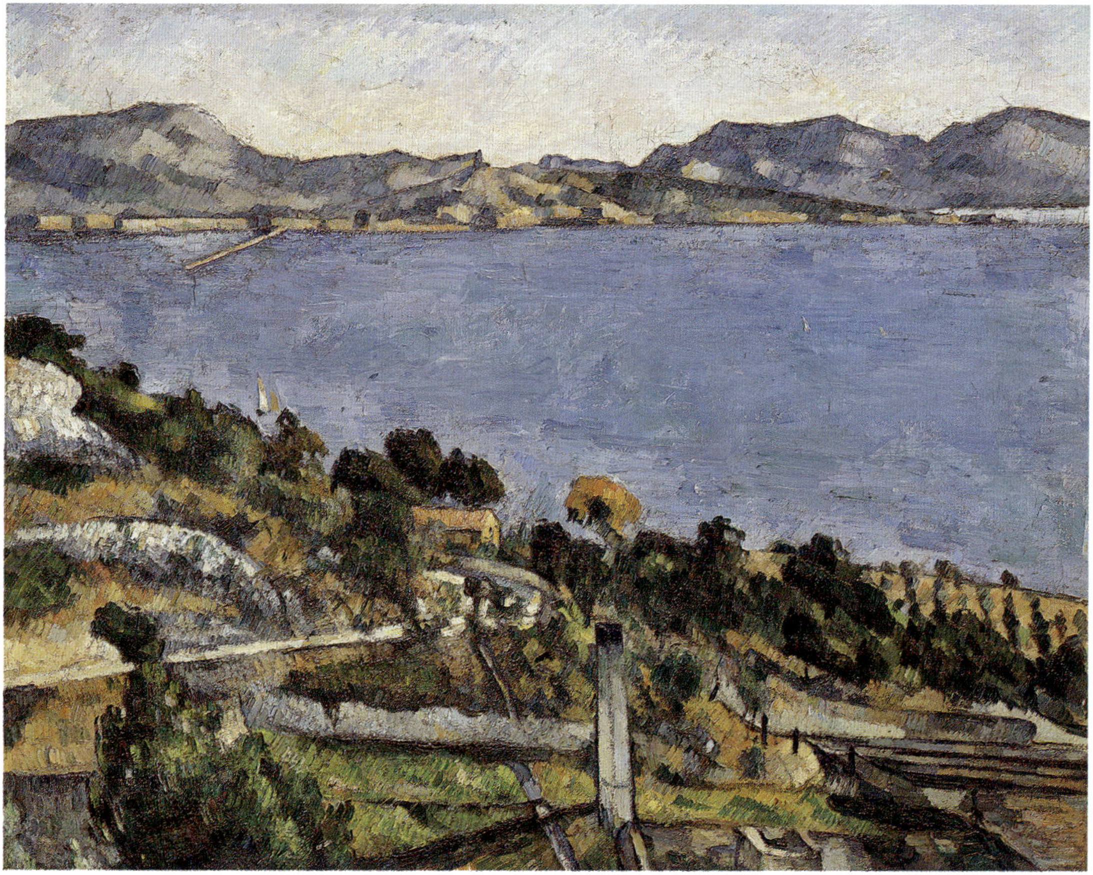

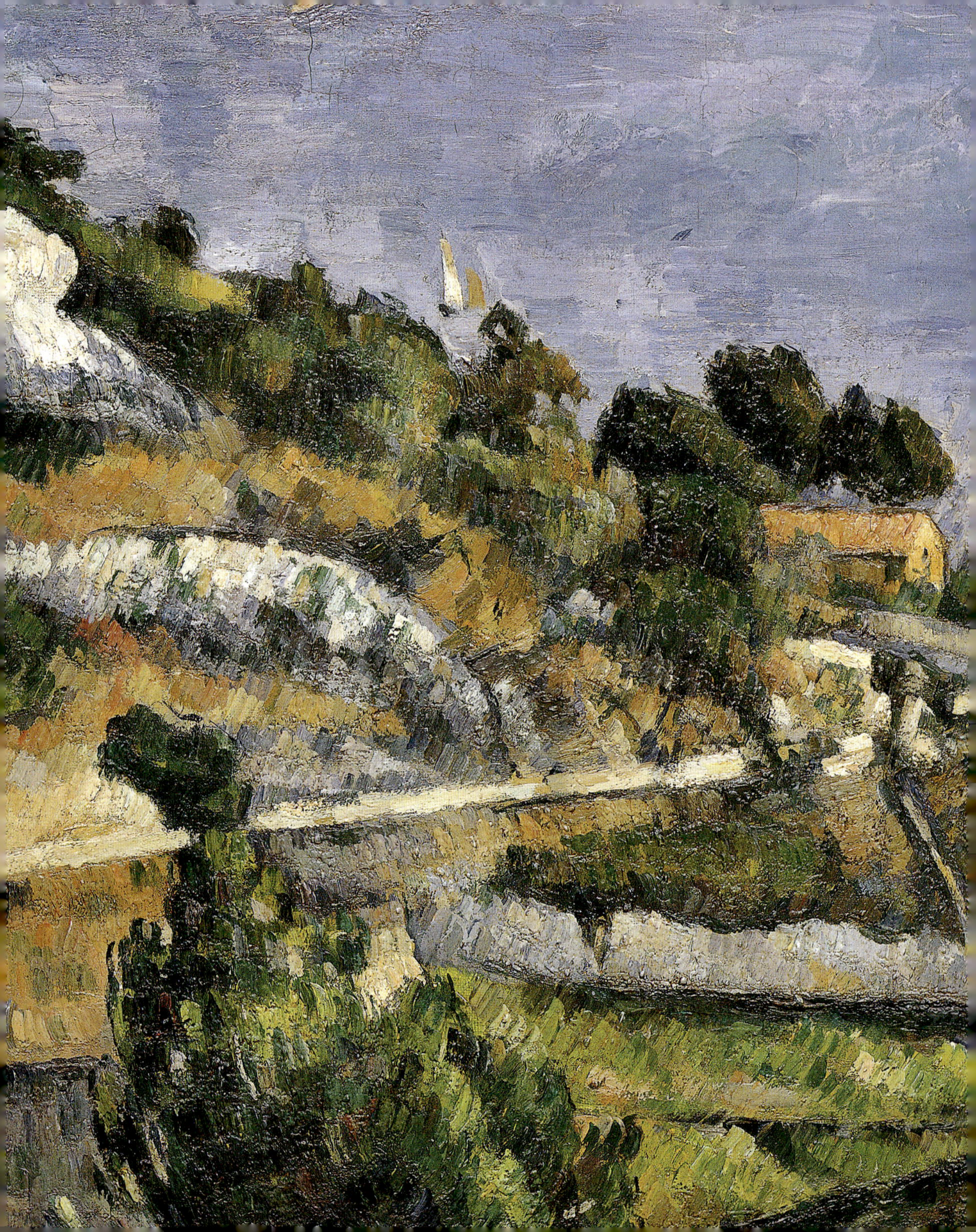

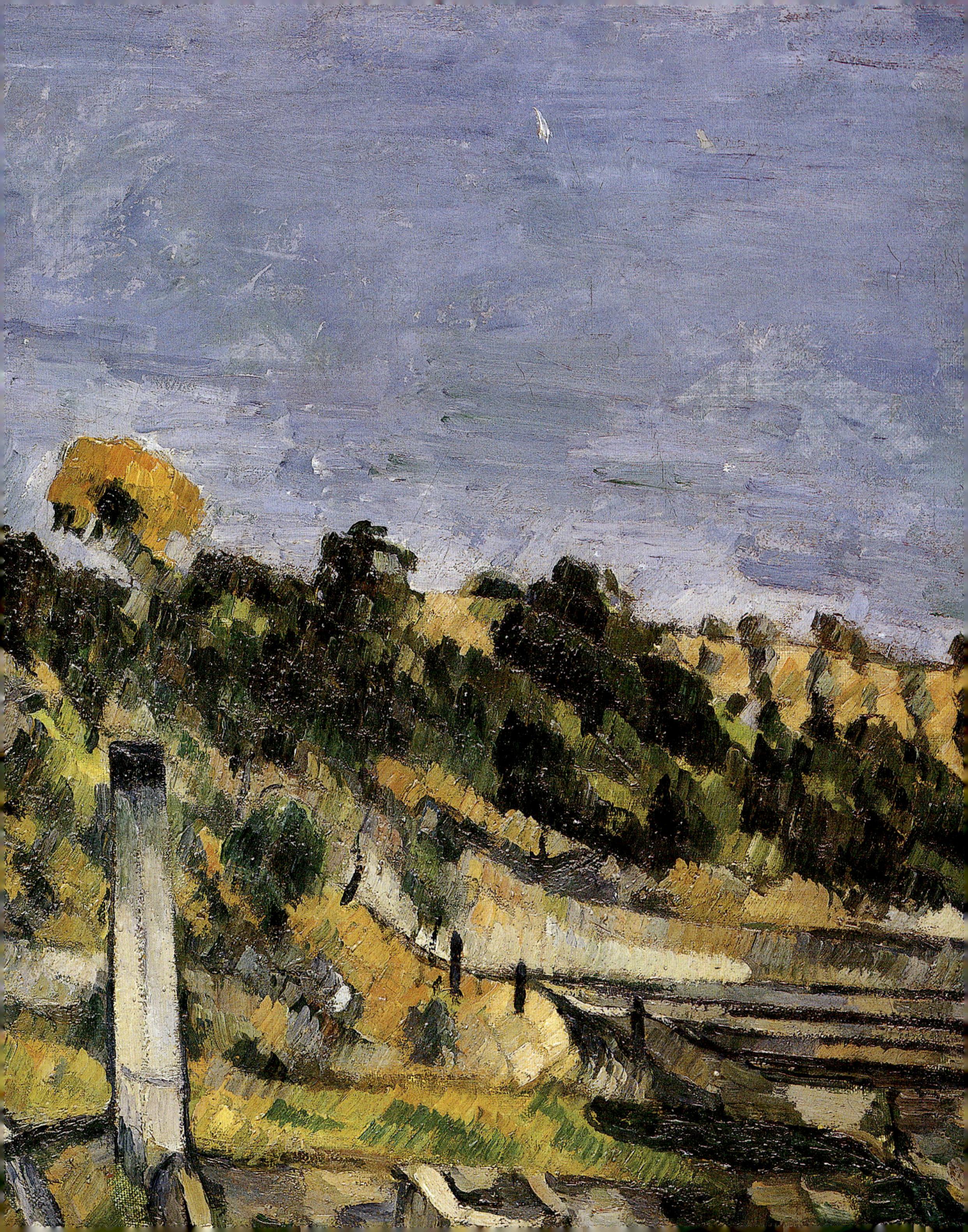

Maincy Bridge

1879

Oil on canvas, 58 x 72 cm
Musée d'Orsay, Paris

It has been possible to date this painting, which was created at the end of the artist's Impressionist phase, thanks to a coincidence: in the course of a walk, a schoolgirl recognized the bridge depicted in a reproduction of the painting that hung on the wall of her classroom. Cézanne spent the period between May 1879 and February 1880 in Melun, near Maincy. The spring-like or summery atmosphere of this painting thus suggests that it was executed between May and September 1879. *Maincy Bridge* is one of the small number of paintings that Cézanne was able to sell during his lifetime. The bridge is completely immersed in the green of the surrounding vegetation, creating an atmosphere reminiscent of the works of the painters of the Barbizon School, an artists' association that played an important role in the development of Impressionism. But with Cézanne, the bucolic is less important than a concern with the constructive aspects of a painting. This was driven by his desire to transcend the fleeting moment and to create something that is firmer and more absolute. In this landscape, the sky disappears completely behind trees. The result is a quiet, intimate scene, which Cézanne found "captivating and suggestive through the transitions between light and shadow, through the victory of the green and the magic of the effects of light." The foreground is dominated by a stretch of water in which the bridge is reflected, a compositional device that creates an elegant geometry. The architectural structure of the bridge, which is reproduced using confident strokes and a firm sense of the structural, is clearly defined against the compact mass of the trees in the background, which are executed in small brushstrokes in a variety of greens. As is sometimes the case, Cézanne positions a tall, thin tree in the foreground here, which structures the composition and draws the gaze of the viewer to the main subject, located slightly farther back.

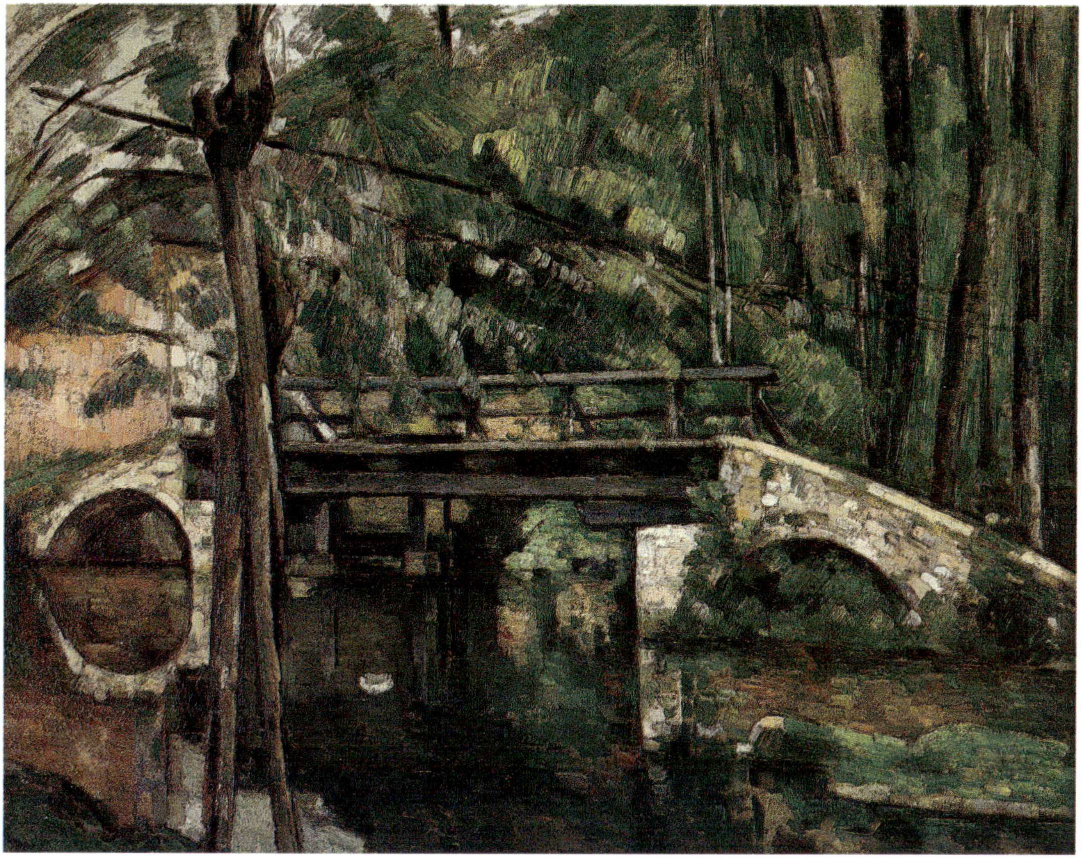

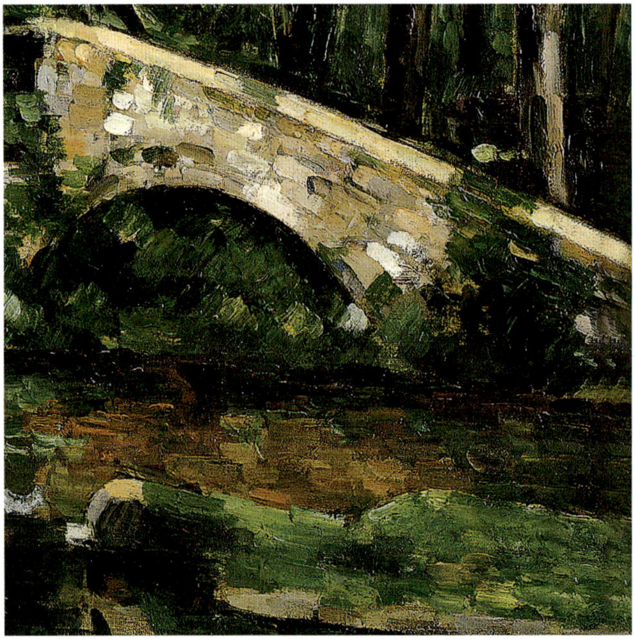

Maincy Bridge (details)

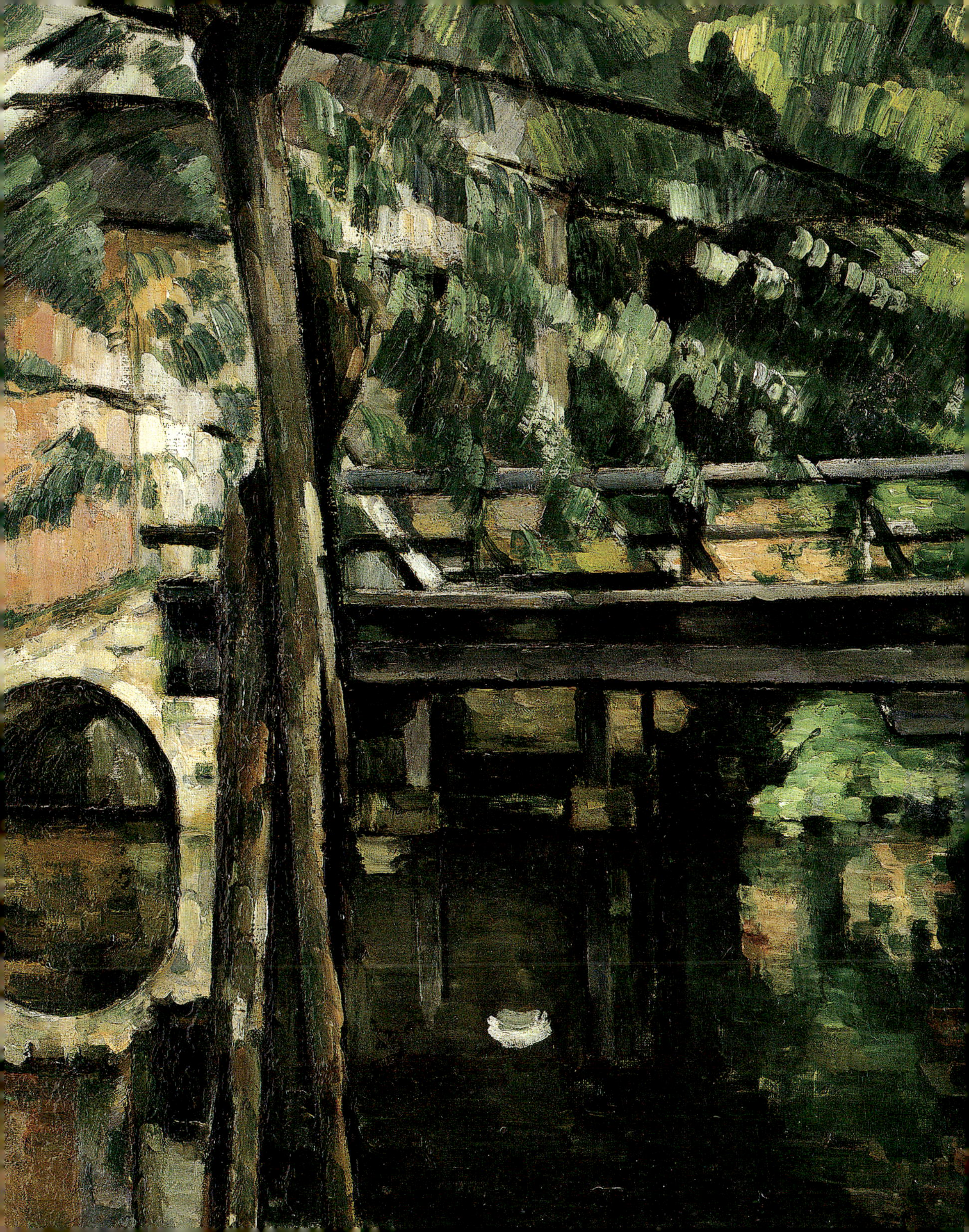

Poplars

1879–1880

Oil on canvas, 65 x 80 cm
Musée d'Orsay, Paris

In a letter dated 24 September 1879, Cézanne wrote to his friend Zola: "I continue to work hard on finding my way as a painter." His experiences with Impressionist painting caused him to advance his study of light and color effects so far that he was able to reproduce them as mere patches of color on the canvas. He also remained true to a number of the basic tenets of the movement, including working *en plein air*. Between the end of the 1880s and the first years of the following decade, Cézanne immersed himself entirely in the study of nature, capturing with great precision the various light effects of particular times of day and of various seasons of the year. *Poplars* reveals all of the characteristics of this period of his artistic development. The landscape looks firm and compact, and the composition appears to draw on the work of the great masters of landscape painting, including Nicolas Poussin (1594–1665). Cézanne once said he wanted to "redo" Poussin's paintings anew, "after nature," in order to give them "something solid and enduring ... like the art of museums." The eye of the Impressionist, which immersed itself in nature like that of a naturalistic photographer, looked for painterly angles from which to structure a painting according to the classic rules of composition. The only subject of this painting is a long row of poplars, which extends diagonally into pictorial space, the tree tops being silhouetted against a gray sky. The viewer's gaze touches lightly on the green meadow and on the small path that leads through the trees before trailing off in the dark mass of leaves, executed in small brushstrokes, in the background.

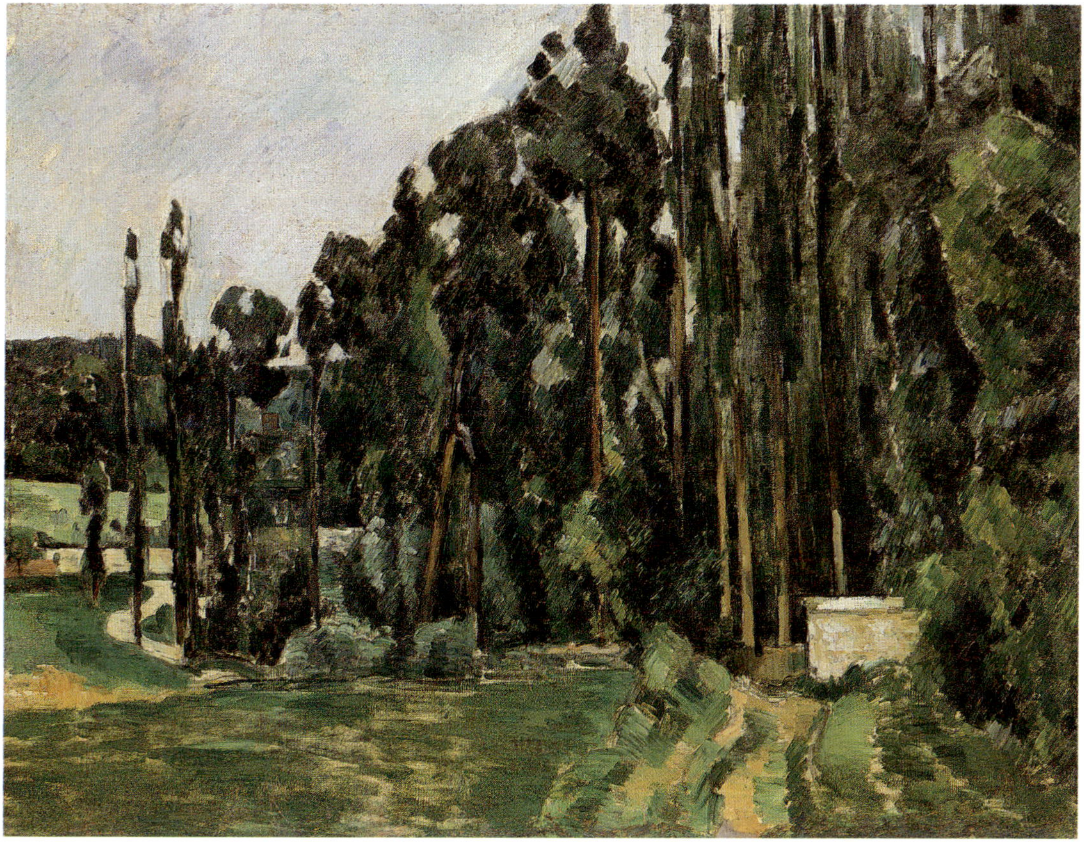

Bathsheba

c. 1800–1890

Oil on canvas, 29 x 25 cm
Musée Granet, Aix-en-Provence

Academic painters produced a vast number of male and female nudes painted in studios from models, and later incorporated them more complex compositions. They include all types of characters, from the mythological to the contemporary, and from allegories to sensual representations of nudity. Manet's *Le Déjeuner sur l'herbe* depicts naked people from his own time in a natural environment, constituting both a reference to and an undermining of the classical iconography of Diana bathing with her entourage. In painting bathers who were, presumably, as contemporary as the figures depicted by Manet, Cézanne ventured to follow this long tradition of depicting nudes in natural landscapes. *Bathsheba* is part of a transition to this new subject, which became one of the primary and recurring elements in the artist's oeuvre, and would later also inspire Picasso. The biblical heroine Bathsheba was the lover and—following the death of her husband, Uriah—wife of King David and the mother of King Solomon. She is here depicted undressed at the edge of a pool of water, accompanied by an obliging maid. The sensuous female figure lying on the blue cloth appears almost to melt into her environment, which mirrors her curves. The two women, their forms hinted at in a sketch-like manner, are completely absorbed by the landscape, a dreamlike and fantastical apparition beyond time and space. Here Cézanne does not pursue his search for the geometric, but rather creates a *paradis artificiel* steeped in sensuality.

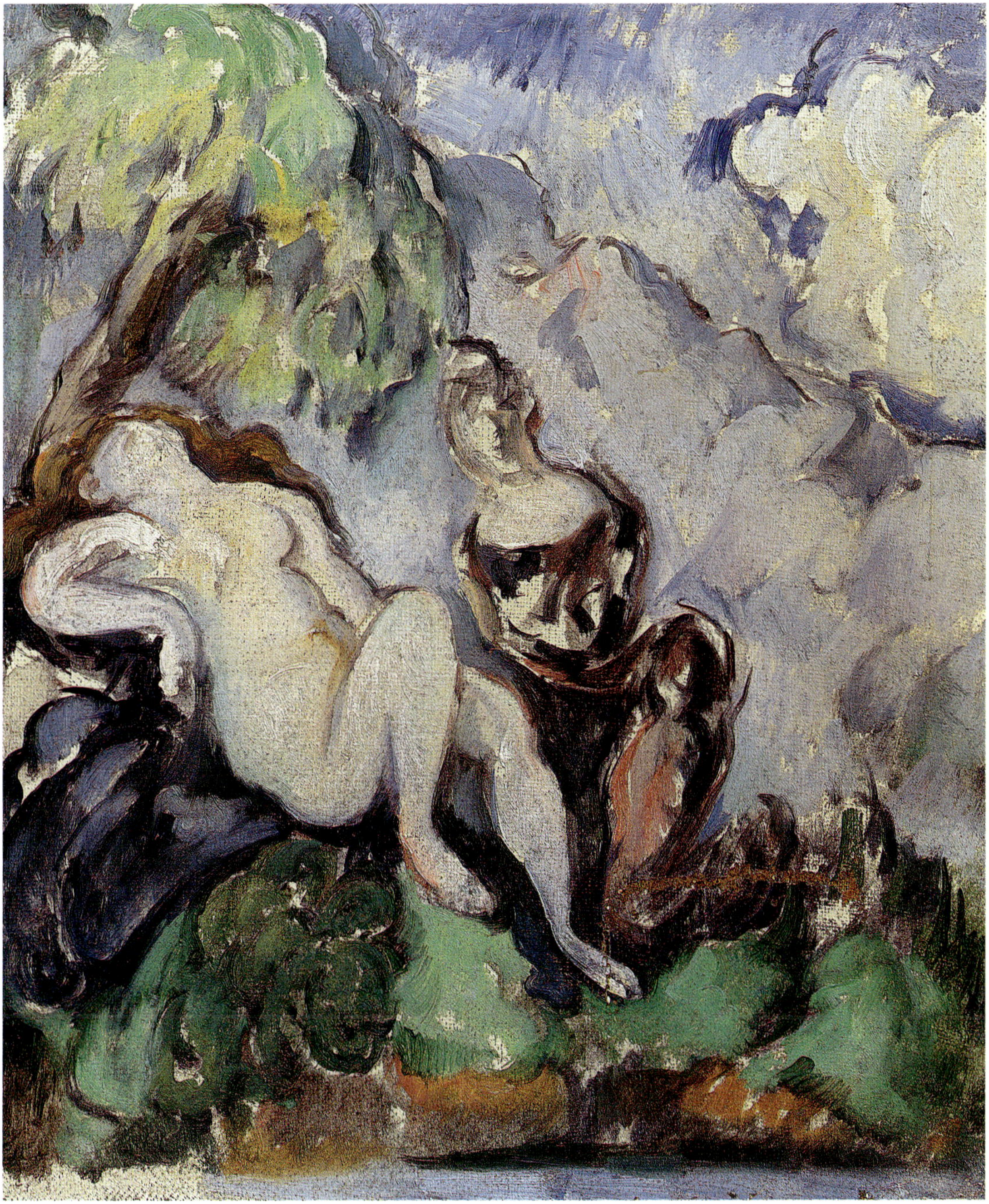

Self-Portrait

c. 1882

Oil on canvas, 46 x 38 cm
Pushkin Museum, Moscow

It was in the field of landscape painting that Cézanne developed his innovative technique. Starting from a particular subject, he typically (like several of the Impressionists) worked slowly on several canvases simultaneously, so that he could continue to work on any given painting when the natural light was just right. The still life and the portrait constituted the test of this method developed *en plein air*. For these, he was able to work in the studio, and could use unchanging, artificial sources of light. Cézanne arranged objects and figures in space and studied them carefully in order to fully grasp their volumes and structures. Though he also pursued such formal concerns in his self-portraits, they were more than mere opportunities to test his technical skills: they were also instruments of introspection. As he wrote in 1904: "If one wants to make progress, there is only one way: nature, through contact with which the eye is educated ... By this I mean that there is in an orange, in an apple, in a ball, in a head a culminating point, and this point is—despite the powerful effect of light, shadow, and color impressions—always closest to the eye." In this self-portrait, the "culminating point" is the high, wide forehead of the artist, who appears to be looking at himself attentively in a mirror at close range. Light enters from the left, illuminating the face and drawing attention to the angular eyebrows, the small eyes, the pointed nose, and the dense full beard. The gray of the suit is only slightly relieved by the white of the shirt, and otherwise appears almost to melt into the dark background.

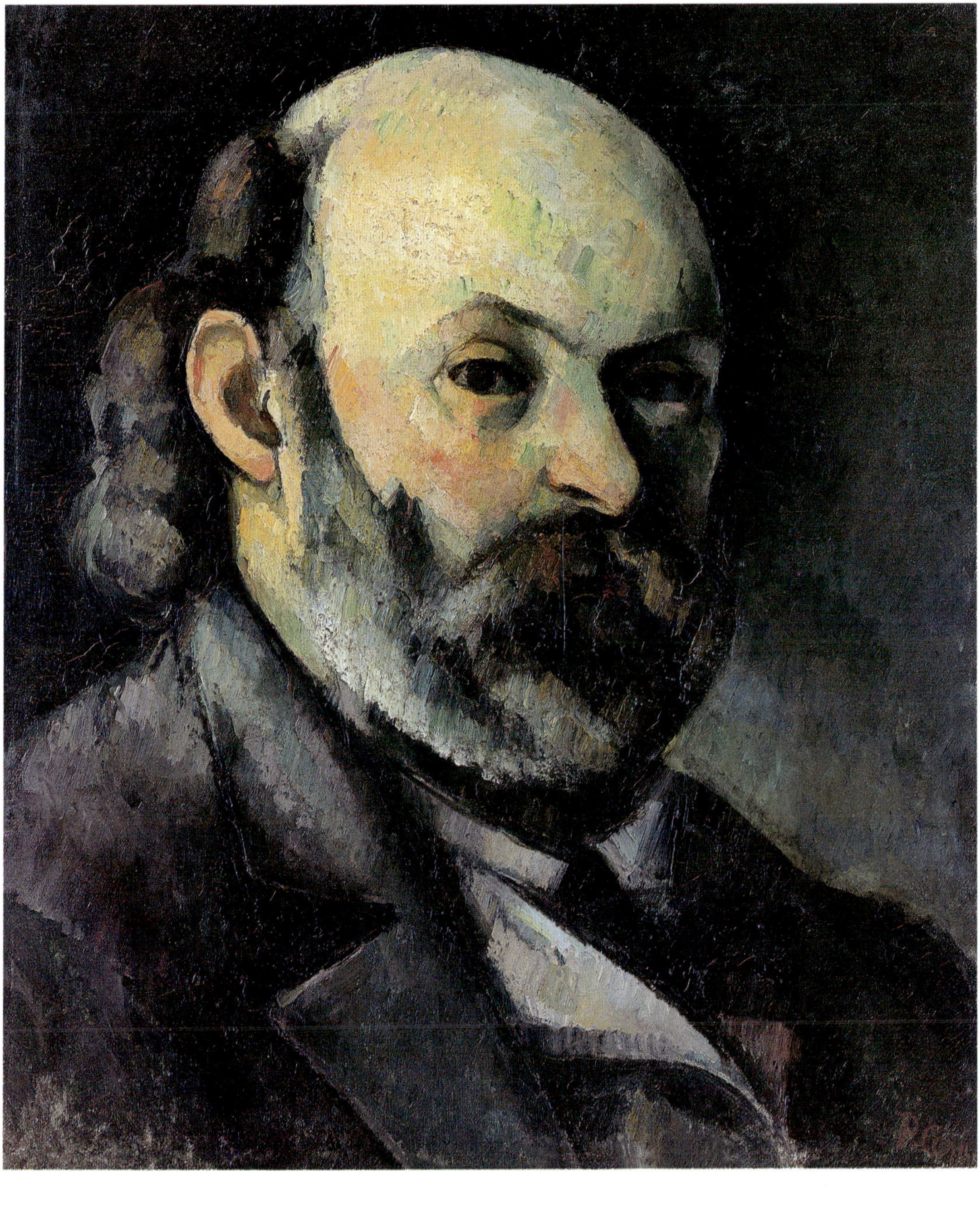

Mont Sainte-Victoire and the Viaduct of the River Arc Valley

c. 1882–1885

Oil on canvas, 65.5 x 81.7 cm
Metropolitan Museum of Art, New York

Like the Impressionists, Cézanne returned to the same subjects repeatedly in order to develop his painting technique. To this end, he used a serial method that Claude Monet would later adopt in his famous paintings of the cathedral of Rouen and of water lilies. Cézanne's most famous series is dedicated to Mont Sainte-Victoire, a limestone massif that rises to the east of the city of Aix-en-Provence. From 1880 onwards, he would paint the mountain again and again, capturing it from a wide variety of different angles. He got to know the massif in every detail and unlocked all of its secrets. In this version, the mountain is depicted from some distance, from the house of his brother-in-law Maxime Conil, on the hill of Bellevue. In the valley through which the River Arc flows, and which is straddled by a viaduct, we can see a few little houses; the rocky massif is visible on the left, framed by trees. The viewer's gaze is unlikely to rest on the pine tree in the foreground in the middle of the painting, finding itself drawn to towards the mountain, which undoubtedly plays the principal role in this painting. The colors form solid shapes and define the space with geometric clarity, in contrast to the paintings of Manet, who put his faith entirely in the interplay of light and color in his paintings. Cézanne was clearly fascinated by nature, and considered it to be the artist's duty to capture it in such a way that its beauty is everlasting. As he wrote to Émile Bernard in 1904: "The painter should dedicate himself entirely to the study of nature, and should attempt to create paintings that are instructive."

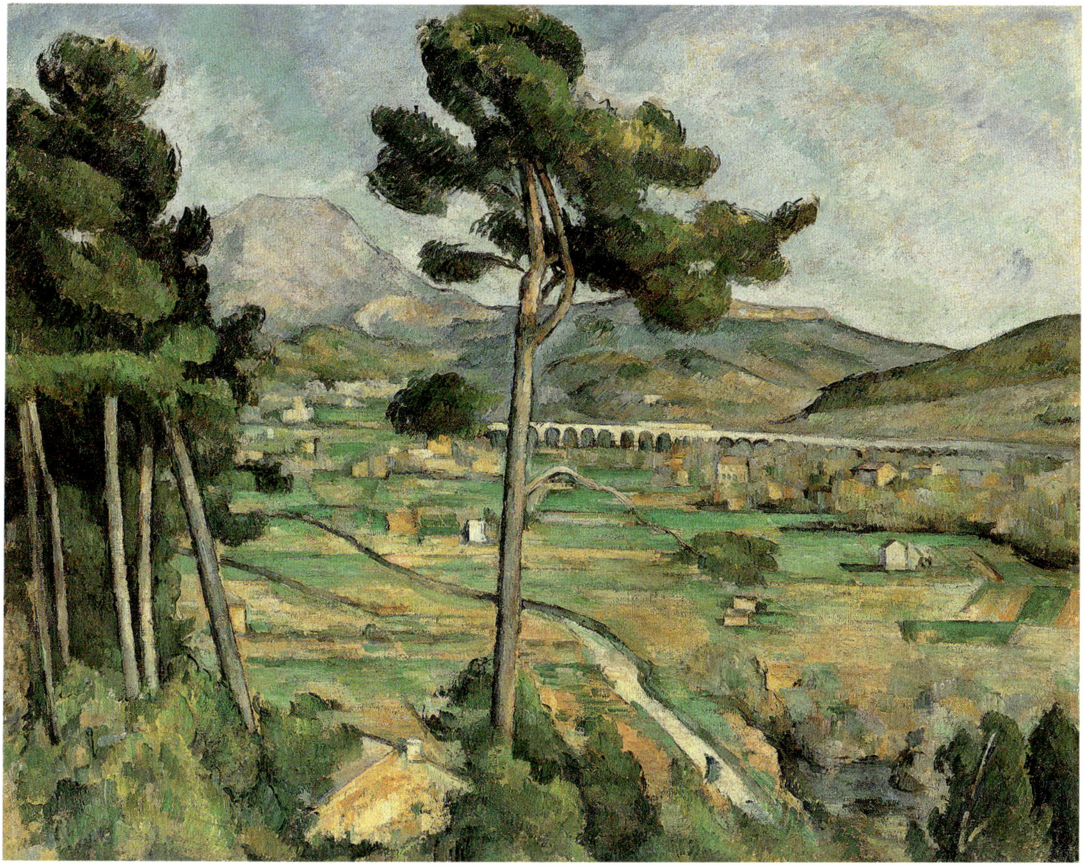

The Gulf of Marseilles Seen from L'Estaque

c. 1885

Oil on canvas, 73 x 100 cm
The Metropolitan Museum of Art, New York

The summers that Cézanne spent in L'Estaque, a small fishing village in the bay of Marseilles, would have a profound impact on the history of modern painting. In a letter to Pissarro, Cézanne described the panorama that he had the opportunity to admire every day during his sojourns: "It is like a playing card. Red roofs in front of a blue sea ... The olive trees and pine trees retain their foliage throughout the year. The sun is so terrible here that it is as though all objects were silhouetted, and not only in black and white, but in blue, in red, in brown, in violet." The painting is composed of four different zones. At the top is the light, virtually white sky, then the mountains, which close off the bay towards the horizon, next the sea, and finally the village in the foreground. Painting, Cézanne firmly believed, "means recording one's own color impressions." The sea is reproduced in brushstrokes that follow the horizontal lines of the roofs, and simultaneously set the rhythm for the composition. The color contrasts contribute to the harmonious effect of this landscape. The essence of the subjects of the painting has been captured; they appear to be at once very close to the viewer and far, far away. The artist loved to paint in the middle of the day, when sunlight develops its full potential, falling intensely on everything. Pissarro recommended to Cézanne that he should paint using only the three primary colors, and that he should give up the dark shades entirely, studying the landscape so carefully that he could grasp all of the subtle color effects that envelop every object.

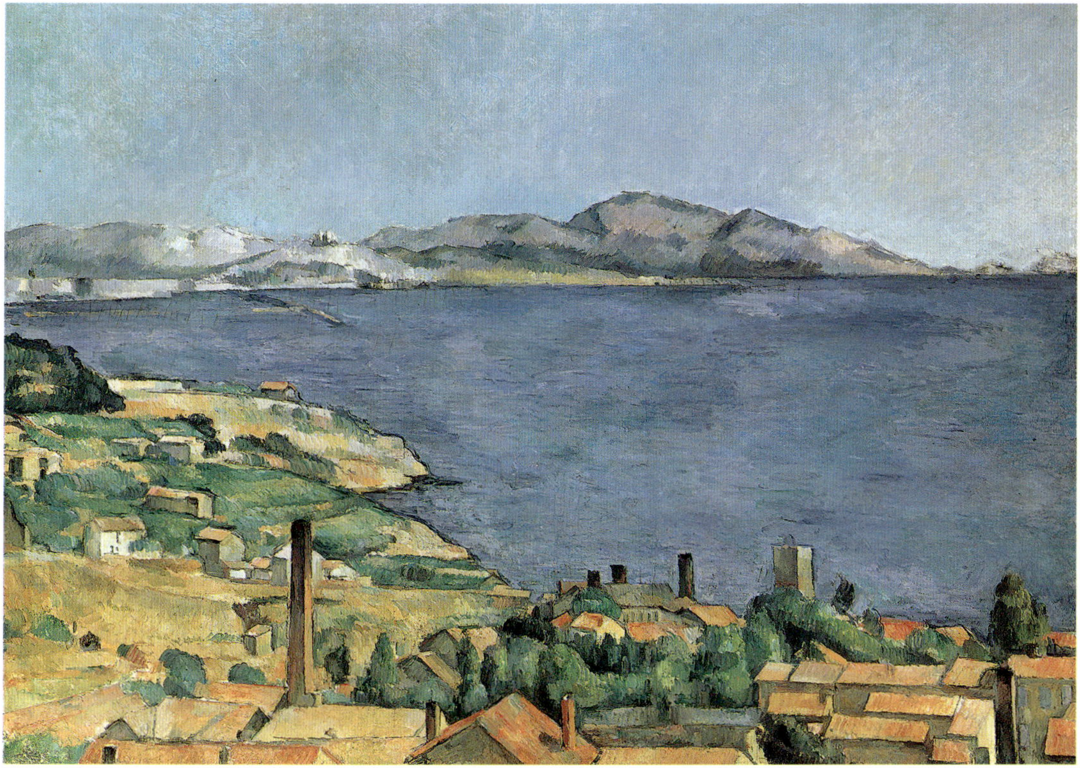

The Bather

c. 1885

Oil on canvas, 127 x 96.8 cm
Museum of Modern Art, New York

This male figure walking towards the viewer with an almost dancing step is among the most interesting and singular works in Cézanne's oeuvre. The imposing figure of the young man is offset against an undefined blue background in a pose almost certainly inspired by the sculptures of classical antiquity. Indeed, he seems to be part modern bather, part iconic apparition of antiquity. This painting is rich in learned references. Whereas the unstable balance of the pose is reminiscent of the works of the Greek sculptor Polykleitos, the clear, well-defined physical forms of the muscular male nude bring to mind Michelangelo: the figure of Duke Lorenzo, from the tomb of the Medici in the new sacristy in San Lorenzo in Florence, is a sculpture by Michelangelo with which Cézanne was certainly familiar.
It features the same unsteady stance, the same tension between contemplation and action, between static pause and movement. The bather, who is walking slowly and meditatively, becomes one with the surrounding landscape, whose colors are mirrored on his skin. Pink, blue, and violet are generously distributed in the foreground and middle ground, separated only by the dark contour of the body. Only the right leg, slightly behind, suggests movement, a calm yet confident stride. The head is slightly bowed; the thoughtful gaze appears to be entirely concentrated on the path ahead. In this painting, the dominant feature is the way in which the color harmonies, firmly based on blue, establish an intimate relationship between the figure and the setting; as so often, the subject seems little more than a pretext for experiments with color and form.

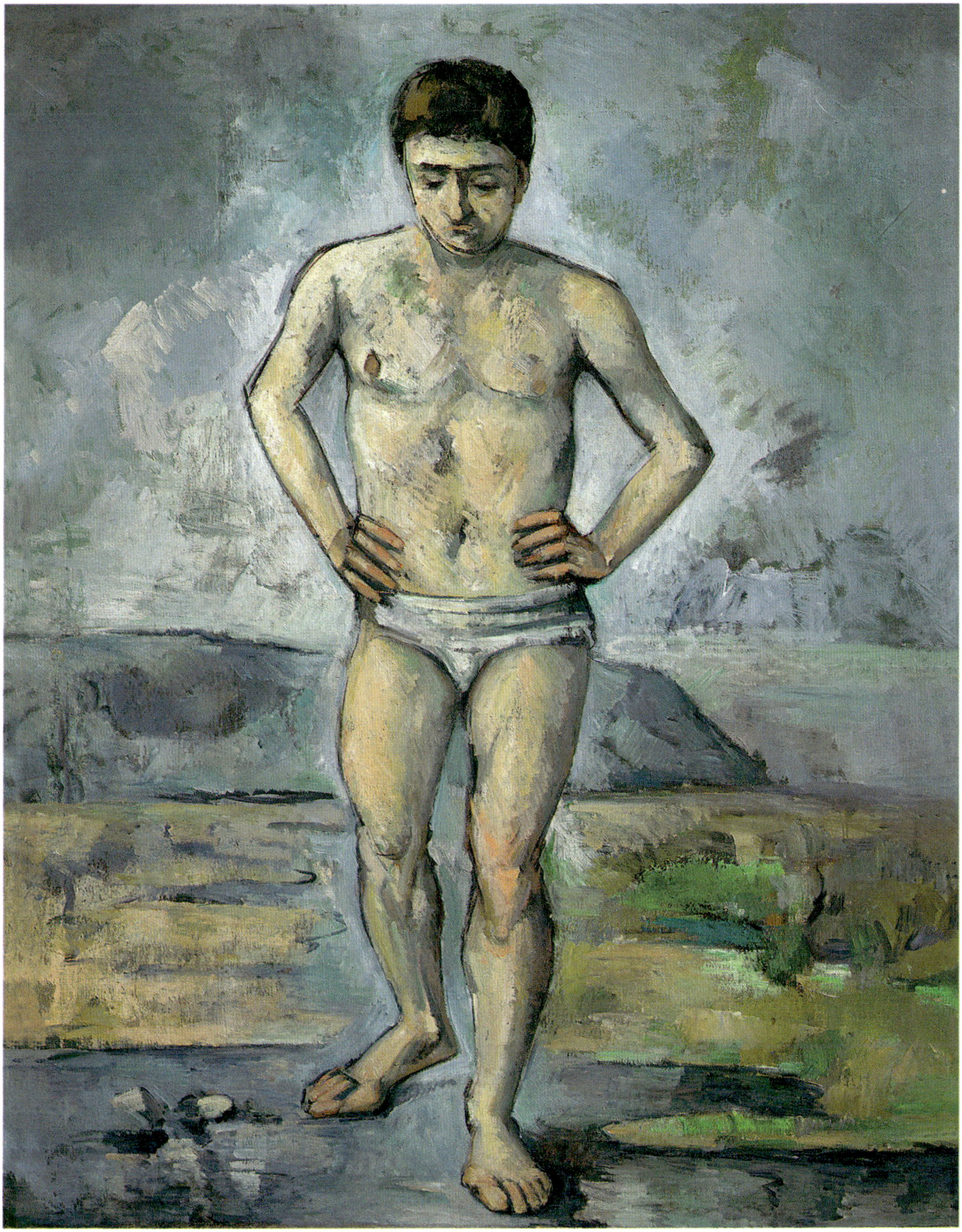

Mont Sainte-Victoire

c. 1890

Oil on canvas, 65 x 95 cm
Musée d'Orsay, Paris

Mont Sainte-Victoire is a subject that Cézanne painting repeatedly during this period. He went on long excursions to the mountain, carrying his paints and canvas with him. In the same way that he walked around an apple or a person in his atelier in order to grasp fully their form and structure, so he climbed to the top of the massif, and walked across every part of it to unlock every one of its secrets. He observed it up close and from a distance, painted it from all angles possible, in all seasons and under every imaginable weather condition. In this depiction, the mountain melts into its natural environment, forming a continuum with the plain and the gentle hills of the surrounding countryside. The sky is blue; the mountain rises above the horizon in shades of violet and above the plain in ocher and green. The various colors are clearly differentiated from one another and separated by colored contours, Cézanne's brushstrokes becoming more and more closely linked to the spatial structure of the subjects he depicted. A tall tree in the foreground constitutes a counterpoint in the expanse of the pictorial space. His young friend Joachim Gasquet describes how Cézanne went about completing one of his paintings of the mountain: "The canvas was slowly saturated with equilibrium. The image before his inner eye, perfectly thought through in its composition, and which he must have sketched out in rapid charcoal lines as was his wont, had already begun to emerge in colored patches that framed it from all sides. The landscape appeared to vibrate, for Cézanne had carefully circumscribed each object, testing each shade, so to speak. Every day, he imperceptibly balanced all of these values, connecting them to one another in their muted luminosity."

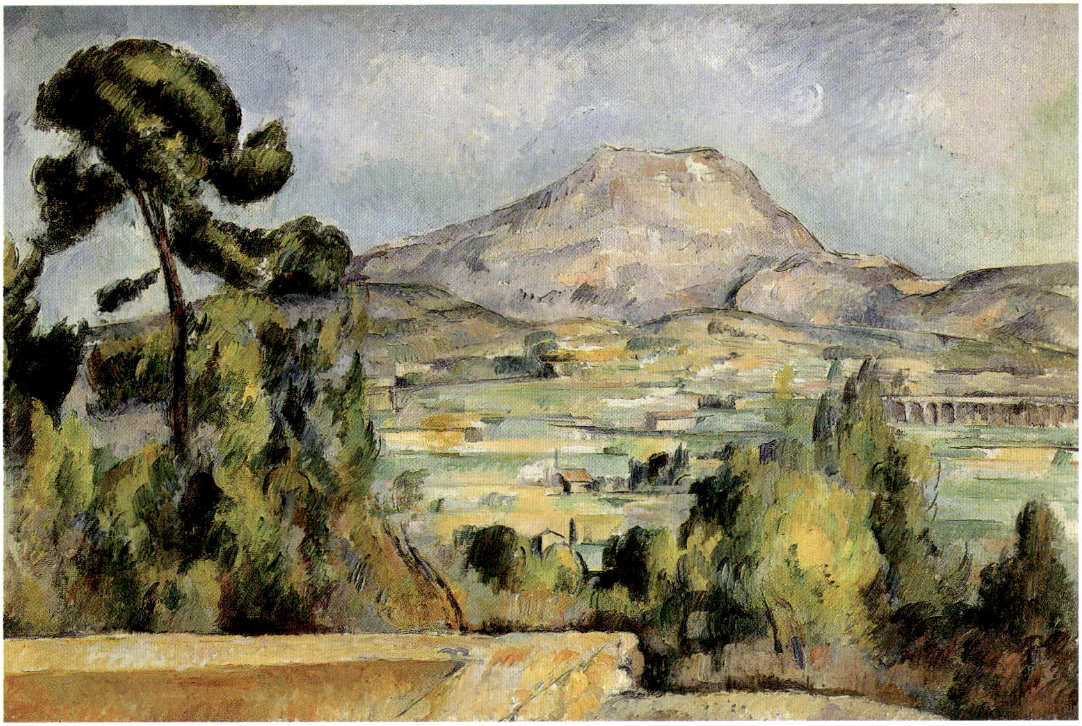

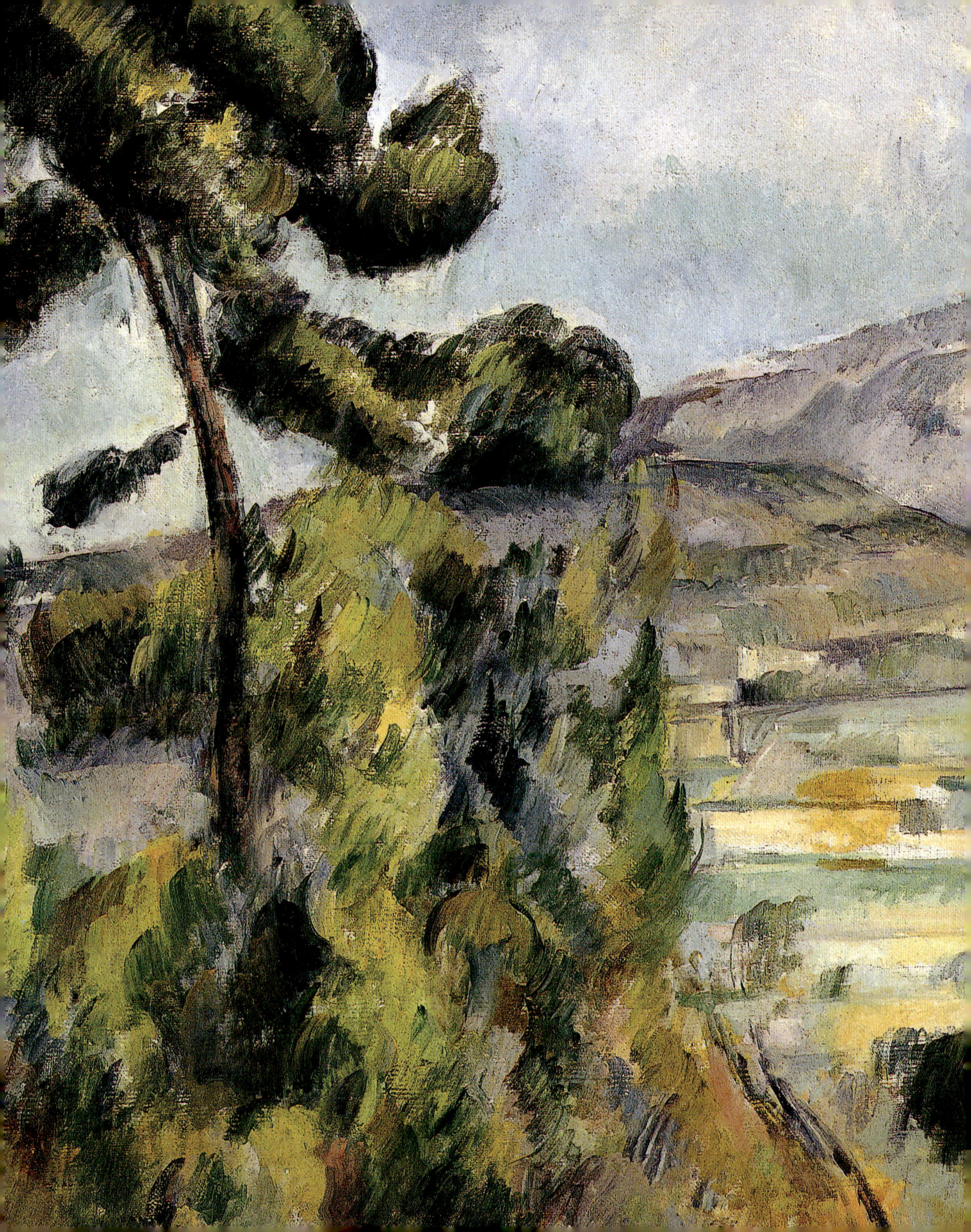

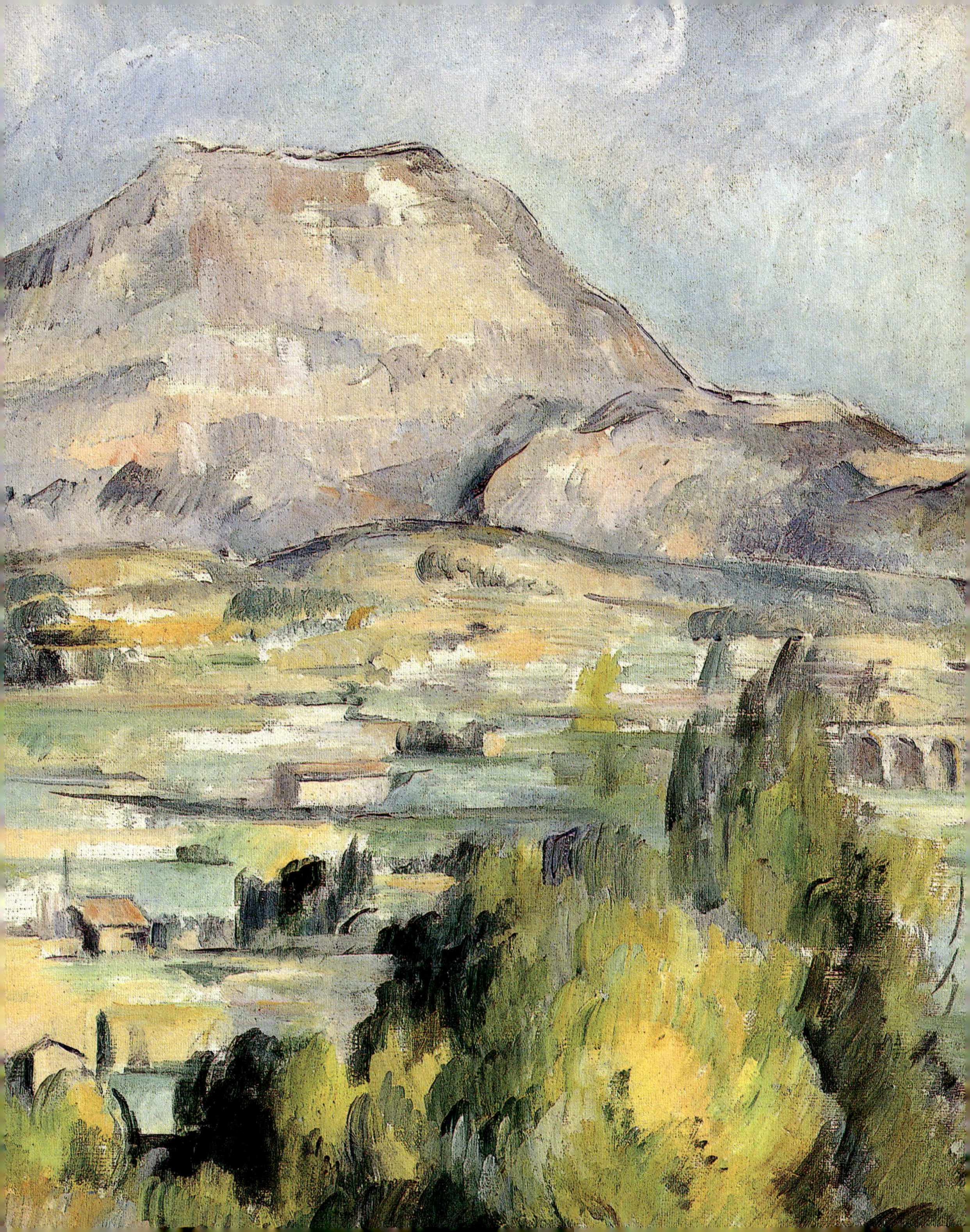

Bridge Over the Marne at Créteil

c. 1888

Oil on canvas, 71 x 90 cm
Pushkin Museum, Moscow

In the years 1888 to 1890, Cézanne lived with his family in Paris and worked primarily in his studio, his preferred subject being the human figure. In the summer in particular, however, he felt the desire to get back to nature, and so he returned again and again to the Marne, one of the rivers of the Île-de-France. During this period he painted a number of landscapes in which a cheerful natural scene is mirrored in water. The atmosphere is peaceful, summery, and fresh. The artist repeatedly painted what he saw on the other bank of the river: trees, but also bridges and houses, signs of the increasing urbanization of this rural area, a process that could be clearly observed in the environs of Paris at the end of the nineteenth century. The fleeting, ever changing glints and reflections on water were one of the Impressionists' favorite motifs. Cézanne, however, was not interested in the transience of what we perceive. For him, the river was a mirror, a device he could use to focus on the architecture of the picture. The trees and the bridges are matched by identical counterparts on the surface of the water. The lower section of the painting is divided in two by the line of the riverbank. The river essentially repeats the fresh and bright colors of the surrounding landscape. The white and red house on the right, which draws the attention of the viewer, is the only strong color accent. Two groups of trees form a frame of sorts for the composition, which culminates at the top with a cloud-filled sky that is suggested in blue and white brushstrokes.

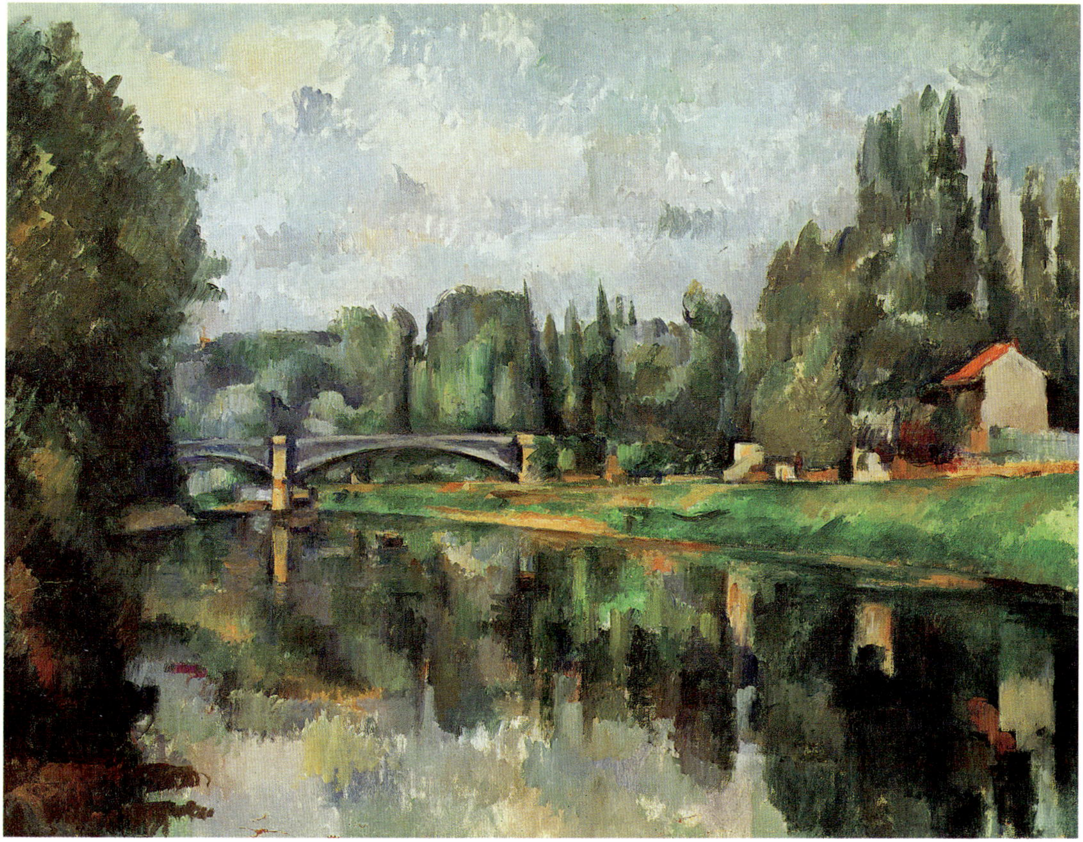

The Kitchen Table (Still Life with Basket)

c. 1888–1890

Oil on canvas, 65 x 80 cm
Musée d'Orsay, Paris

The still life, traditionally a favorite genre of Flemish painting, attracted Cézanne (and also Manet among his contemporaries) because of the challenges it presented. In landscape painting, the painters have to tackle the coincidences of the natural environment. In still lifes, by contrast, they must select the objects to be depicted, and arrange them on the canvas, which gives them complete control over the composition. One of the elements that makes the still life reproduced here so extraordinary is the multiplicity of angles combined in the painting. They allow the viewer to perceive a slightly altered, distorted reality. Nothing is left to chance, and the composition of the objects is bold and finely balanced. The kinds of objects shown here are certainly typical of this period: fruit, which has always been a reliable and faithful standby for painters, pots, bowls, a sugar jar, and other articles of daily use combine to form a multifaceted whole. Though the arrangement is complex, in the depiction and modeling of forms Cézanne aimed to achieve geometrical simplicity and a harmonious overall balance. The tablecloth brings together all the elements, its whiteness intensifying the colors. The furniture along the left edge of the painting creates a diagonal that suggests a different perspectival vanishing point from that of the table. This is as impressive as the magnificent fruit basket, which lends the painting a particular sense of order.

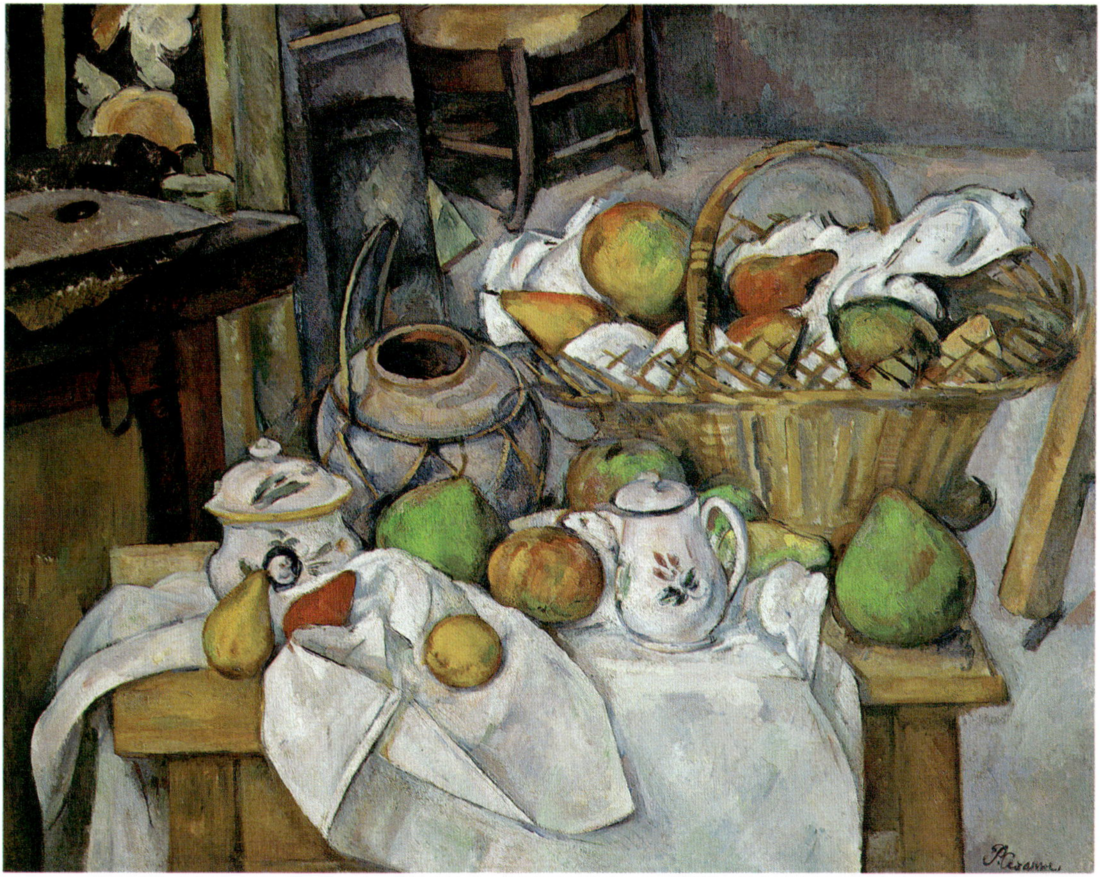

Madame Cézanne in a Yellow Armchair

c. 1888–1890

Oil on canvas, 116 x 89 cm
The Metropolitan Museum of Art, New York

Cézanne painted several portraits of his wife, Hortense Fiquet. She was something like a familiar icon, a still, calm, almost aloof model. Hortense was a remarkably docile woman, who patiently endured the endlessly drawn-out sessions that Cézanne put his models through, treating them like landscapes or still lifes. She appears in at least 24 paintings and countless drawings. Here she sits in the same yellow armchair and wears the same red dress as in the second version (1888–1890), which is now in the collection of the Art Institute of Chicago. Wearing a bright red bress, Madame Cézanne is sitting in a neat and tidy bourgeois interior, framed by a colored curtain and a landscape painting on the wall behind her. Her gaze is firmly trained on the viewer. Her slightly closed hands and her head, bent a little to one side, convey the impression of calm serenity, of gentle patience. The painting is characterized by the strong contrast between the red of the dress and the yellow of the armchair, which is sharply contoured against the wall behind it. This painting is testament to the cheerfully relaxed state Cézanne reached once again by 1890, thanks to the painterly confidence he had achieved in the meantime. Its well-ordered calm contrasts strongly with the dark and turbulent mood of his earlier works.

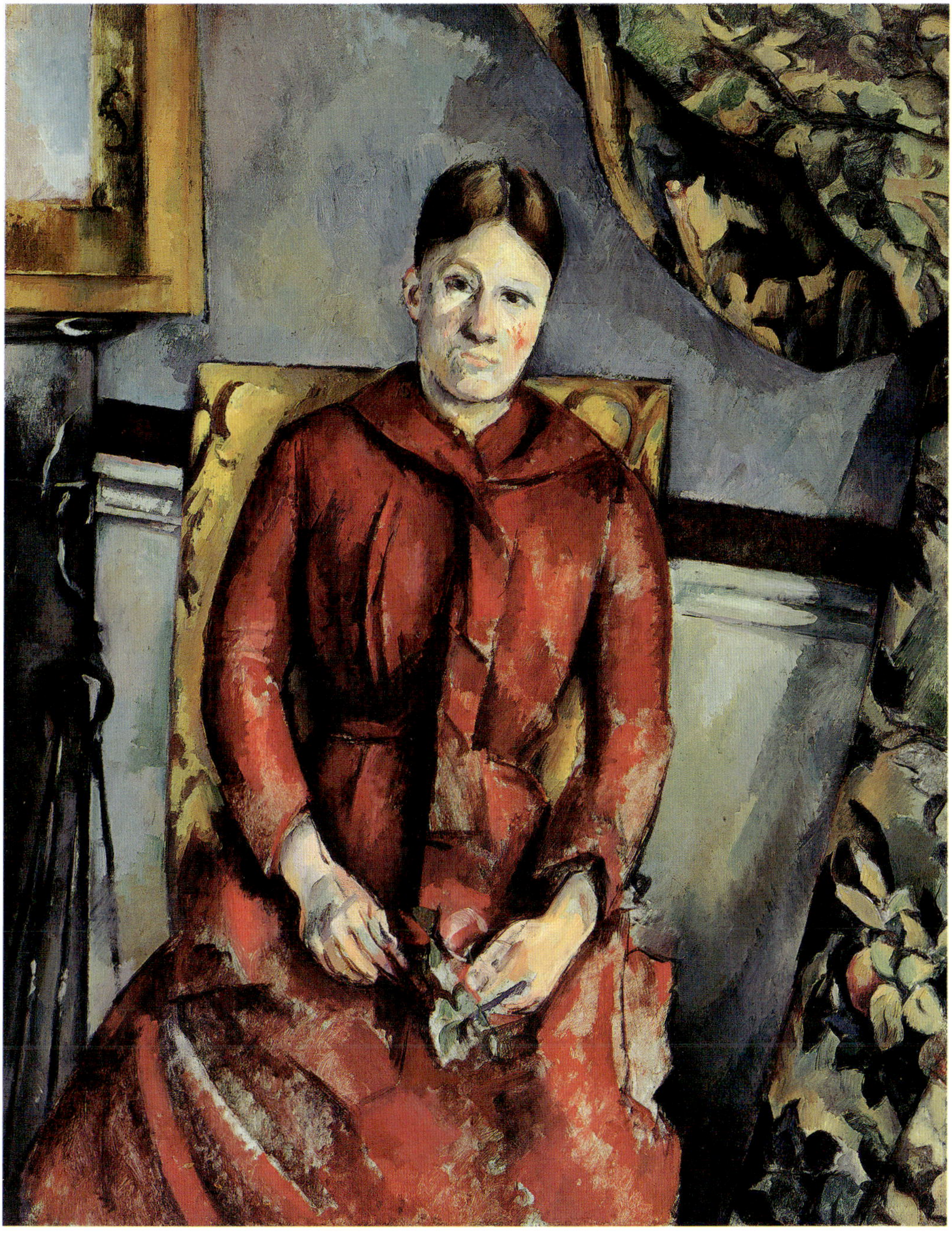

The Boy in the Red Waistcoat

1888–1890

Oil on canvas, 79.5 x 64 cm
Stiftung Sammlung E. G. Bührle, Zurich

This painting is a veritable homage to color and to the grand tradition of genre painting. This is due not least to the model's clothes, a traditional Italian folk costume consisting of a red waistcoat, a neck scarf, and a blue sash. Another element that refers to the traditions of the Old Masters is the curtain, which rounds off the composition on the left. The dark hair that frames the boy's face, the way he rests his head on his left hand, the over-long right arm, and the diagonal movement of the table covered with a green tablecloth—all of these elements are typical components of Cézanne's strict approach to composition. The diagonal line of the figure is complemented by the opposite slant of the table and by the horizontal lines of the wall in the background. This rigorous structure gives support to the strongly applied color, confines it to the surface, and largely robs the painting of its spatial depth. The portrait has been commended by critics for its balance and spontaneous painting style. Cézanne used this young professional model of Italian origin, named Michelangelo Rosa, for four oil paintings and one watercolor around 1890. These paintings were probably executed in Cézanne's apartment in the rue d'Anjou in Paris, which is also the setting for his portrait of his wife Hortense. His portraits are characterized by the sitter's pensive, meditative pose and demeanor, possibly inspired by works of art from the Renaissance, such as those of Bronzino and Michelangelo, but also by the interplay between such classical models and the everyday.

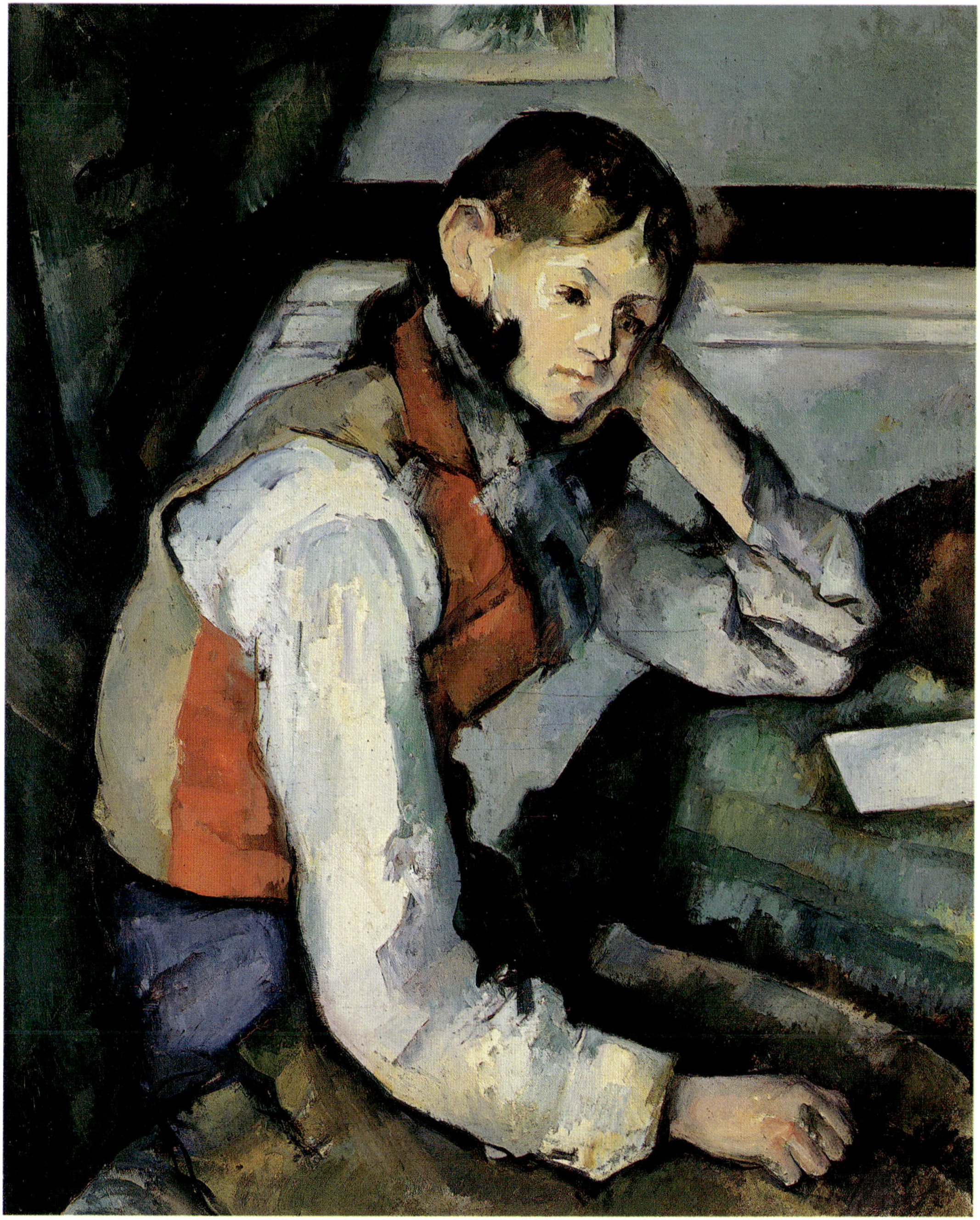

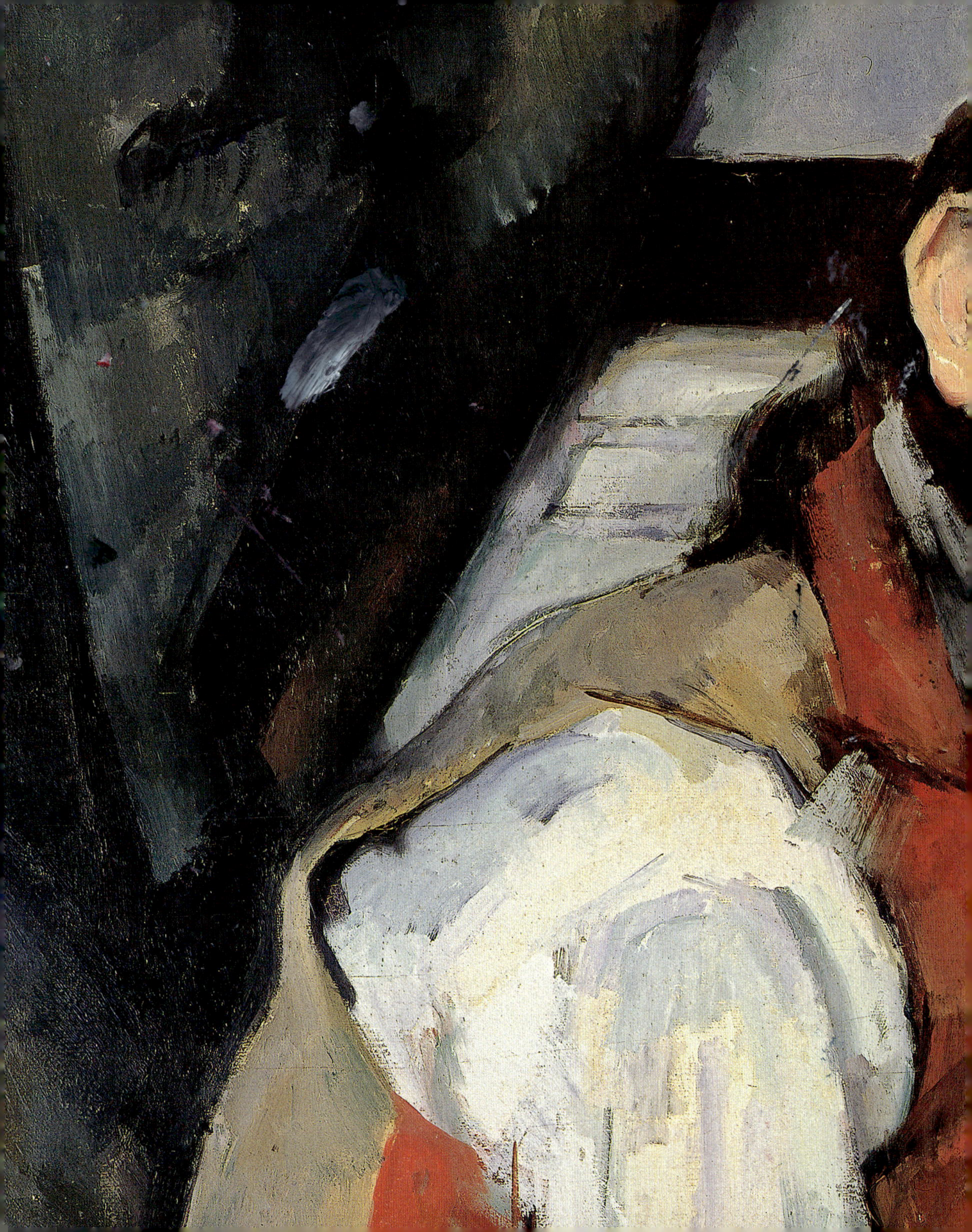

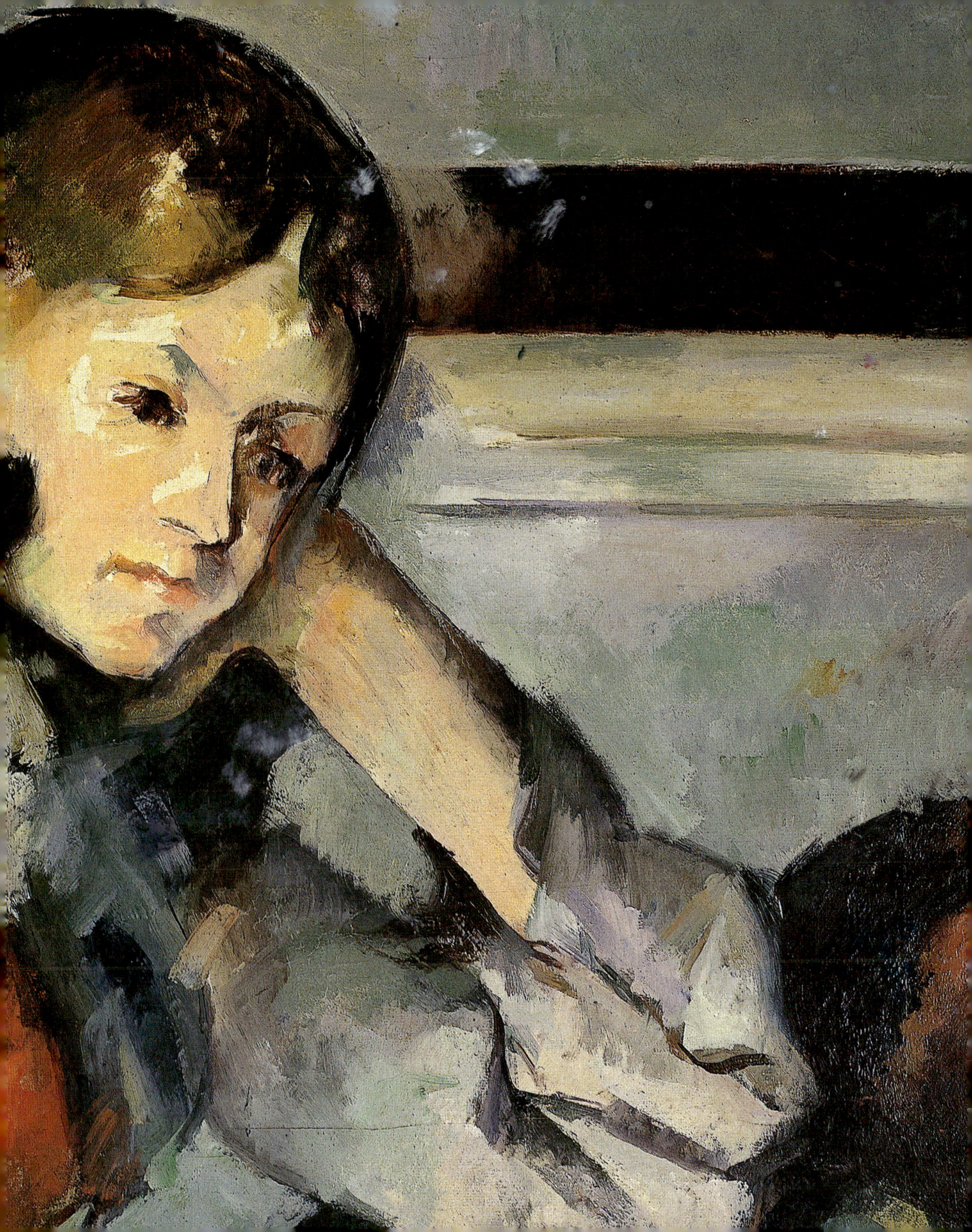

The Blue Vase

c. 1889

Oil on canvas, 61 x 50 cm
Musée d'Orsay, Paris

Referring to his still lifes from the late 1880s and early 1890s, Cézanne said that he had found "a nice formula." It is certainly true that these still lifes are very charming, depicting bright, elegant objects. The arrangement of these objects is considered to the last detail, creating a whole that is harmonious in form and color. The *Blue Vase* is among Cézanne's most famous works from this period. He created a perfectly balanced structure through the arrangement of objects on the table. A colorful bunch of flowers, arranged with a great awareness of form and proportions, has been placed in the blue vase, which, positioned slightly to the left of the centre, plays an important role in the composition. A few stems are outlined against the wall in the background, whose color mirrors that of the vase. Further down, red and white carnations stand out against the mass of green leaves. Two oranges and a lemon lie in the foreground, their contours less clearly defined. A little further back on the table stands a small bottle, probably for ink. Behind the vase is a white plate. The clarity and legibility of the center is lost in the only partially rendered elements on the right and left edges of the painting, allowing the viewer's imagination free rein—the brown silhouette on the left may be a bottle, and the outline of a window is visible on the right, though this might also represent the wallpaper.

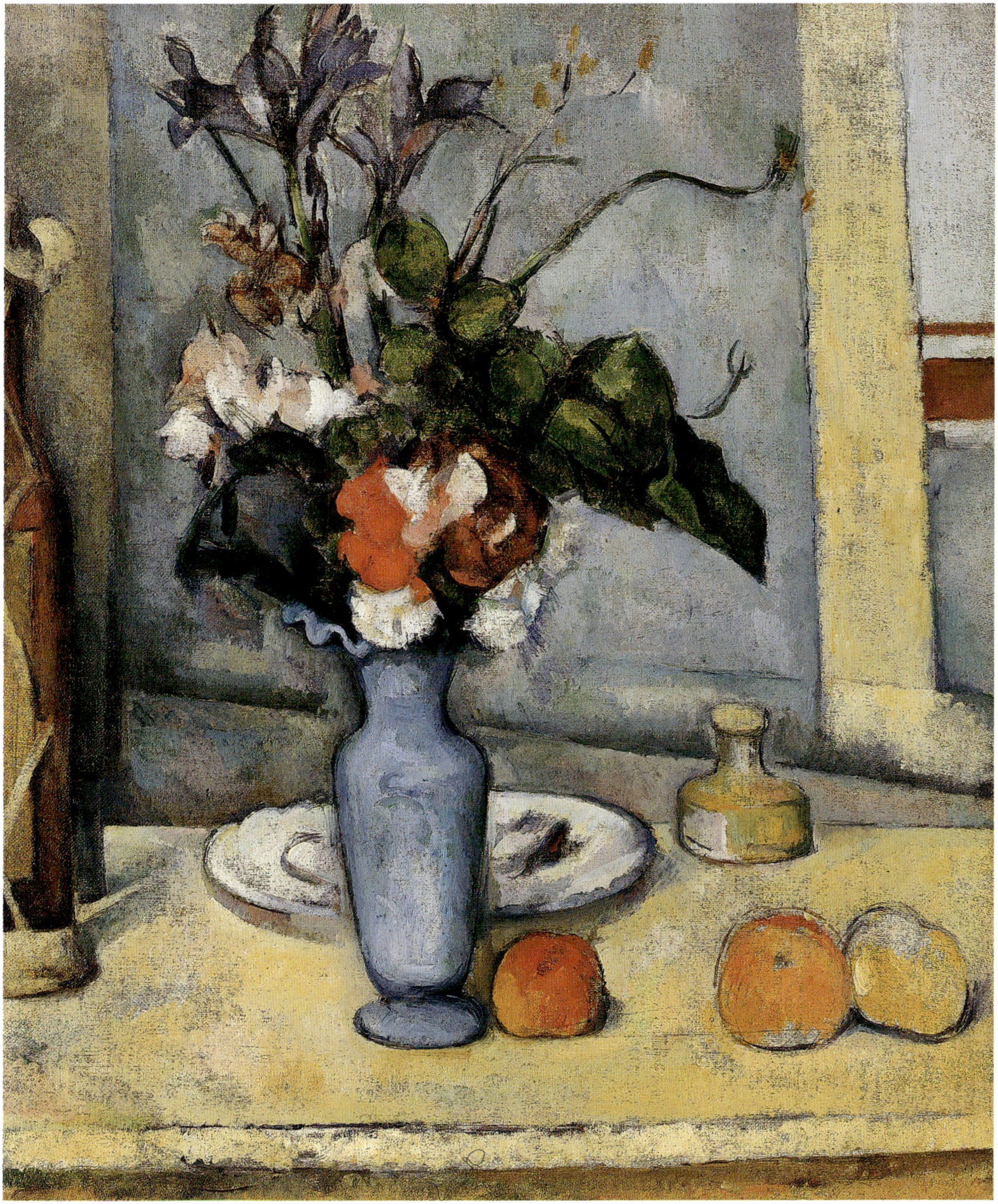

Madame Cézanne in the Conservatory

1891

Oil on canvas, 92 x 73 cm
The Metropolitan Museum of Art, New York

During the 1890s Cézanne paint a number of portraits of his wife, Hortense Fiquet. These paintings are often characterized by a serious, contemplative expression on the sitter's face. Her gentleness and apparently limitless patience made it possible for Hortense to bear the long sessions during which Cézanne's sought to capture every structural and formal detail of his subject. He painted this portrait in the conservatory at the Jas de Bouffan estate, the family's country residence near Aix-en-Provence. The tone is set by the powerful contrasts in color between the young woman's black dress and the warm tones of the background. Hortense sits with her body turned slightly away from the picture plane; her hands rest on her lap, and her gaze meets that of the viewer. The slightly tilted head gives an impression of meekness and submission. The eyebrows, nose, and cheekbones accentuate the face, which has the shape of a perfect oval. The chin is precisely on the line that divides the background into two halves. The painterly treatment of the tree and of the arm conjures up analogies that connect the foreground and the background. Cézanne's difficulties and his technical consistency are visible in this not entirely finished work. After he had laid out the basic compositional structure, he built up a sense of volume by using short, tentative brushstrokes.

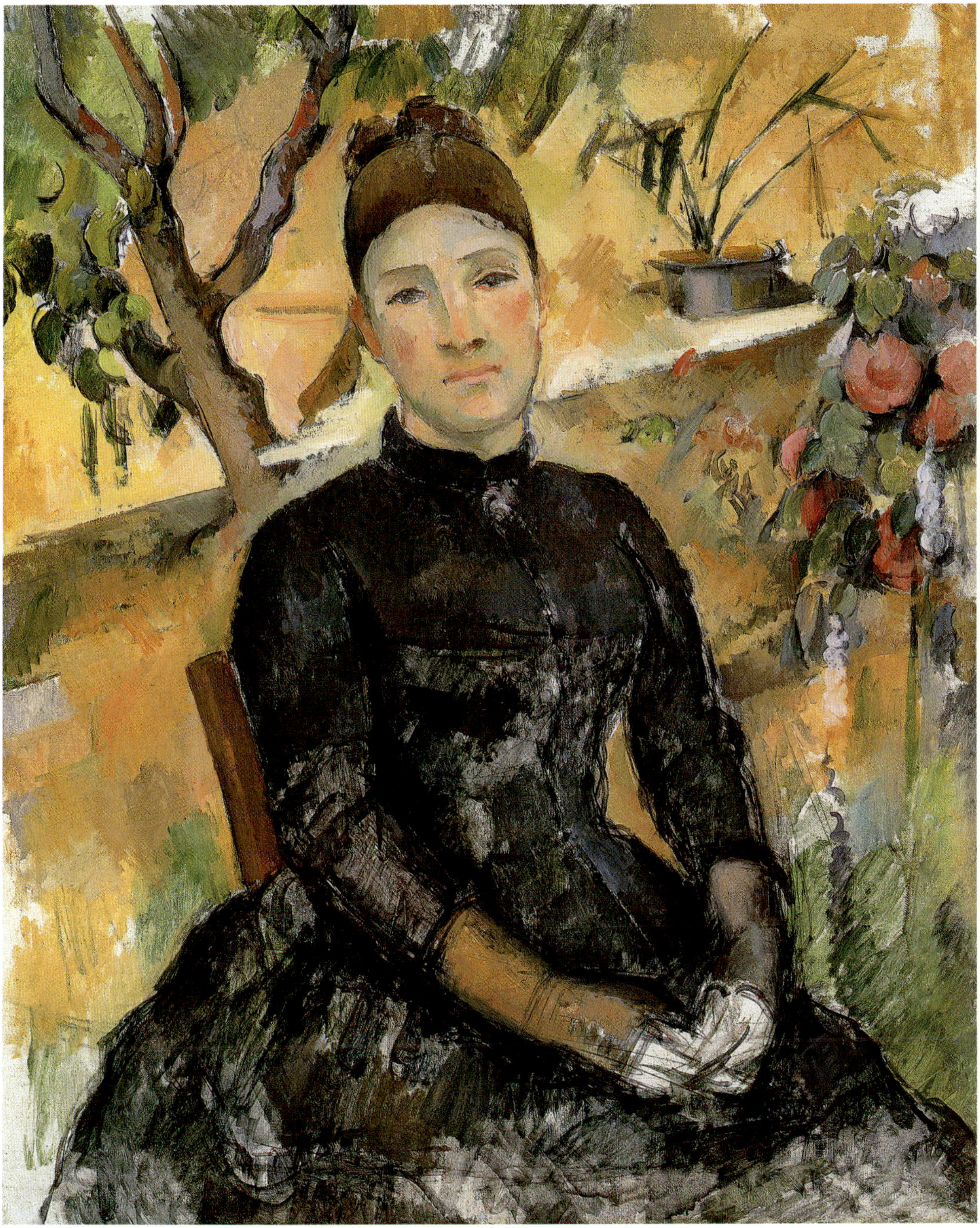

Bathers

c. 1890

Oil on canvas, 60 x 82 cm
Musée d'Orsay, Paris

Having spent a considerable amount of time on the subject of bathers, Cézanne began in the 1890s to tackle the subject of the male nude in a landscape. This resulted in paintings that were so experimental that they drew the attention of artists such as Monet, Denis, Matisse, Picasso, and Henry Moore, all of whom wanted to own a version. Most of them are preparatory studies that provide insights into the artist's long and complicated journey in search of a satisfactory composition. The figures, entirely free of any sort of mythological aura or anecdotal narrative, abandon themselves entirely to the natural landscape that surrounds them, all but melting into it. At this point, Cézanne had completely abandoned the aggressive nature of the nudes he had painted in the past. A cheerful, light atmosphere takes its place. In this painting, the bathers in their elegant, balanced poses embody a harmonious relationship to nature, which clearly features idyllic traits. The center of the composition is marked by a tall, slender tree, framed by two tall nudes shown from the back that are reminiscent of famous classical artworks, such as Michelangelo's cartoons for the *Battle of Cascina*, and the works of Luca Signorelli and El Greco. The nudes shown from the back have their counterparts in the figures in the middle ground, some of whom are half submerged in a stream. The two groups of figures describe an elegant, semi-circular movement that leads up to the tree at the center of the composition. The ocher of the strip of ground is subtly mirrored in the reddish shades of the clouds.

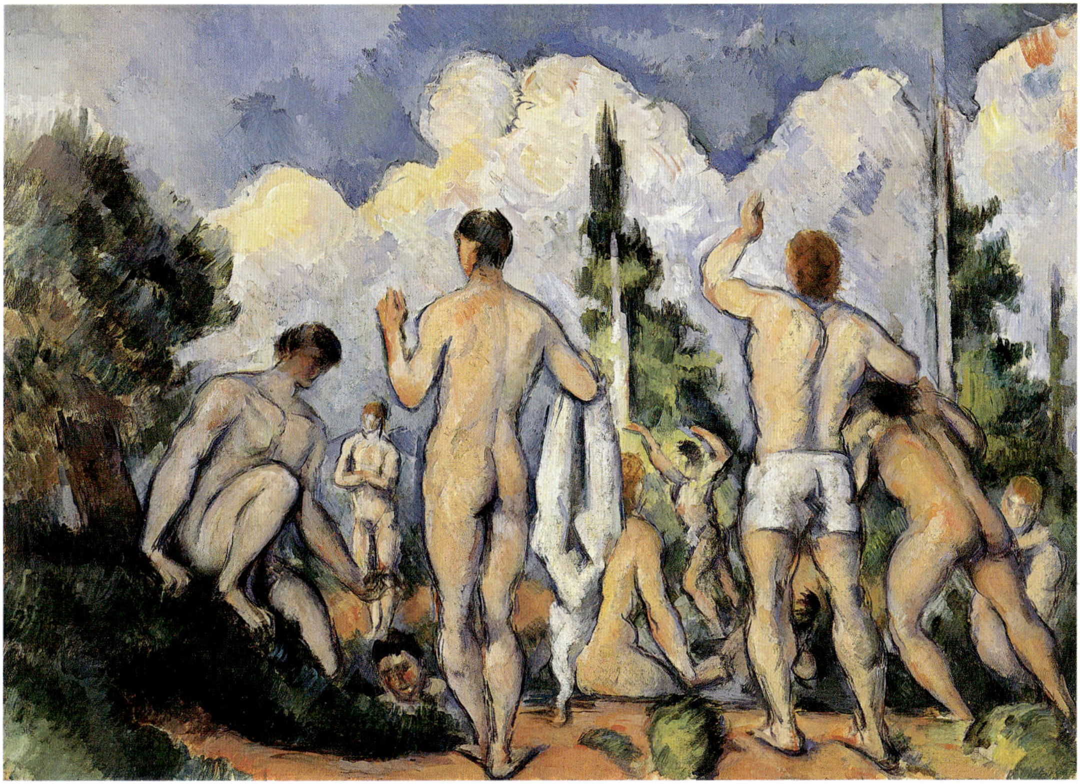

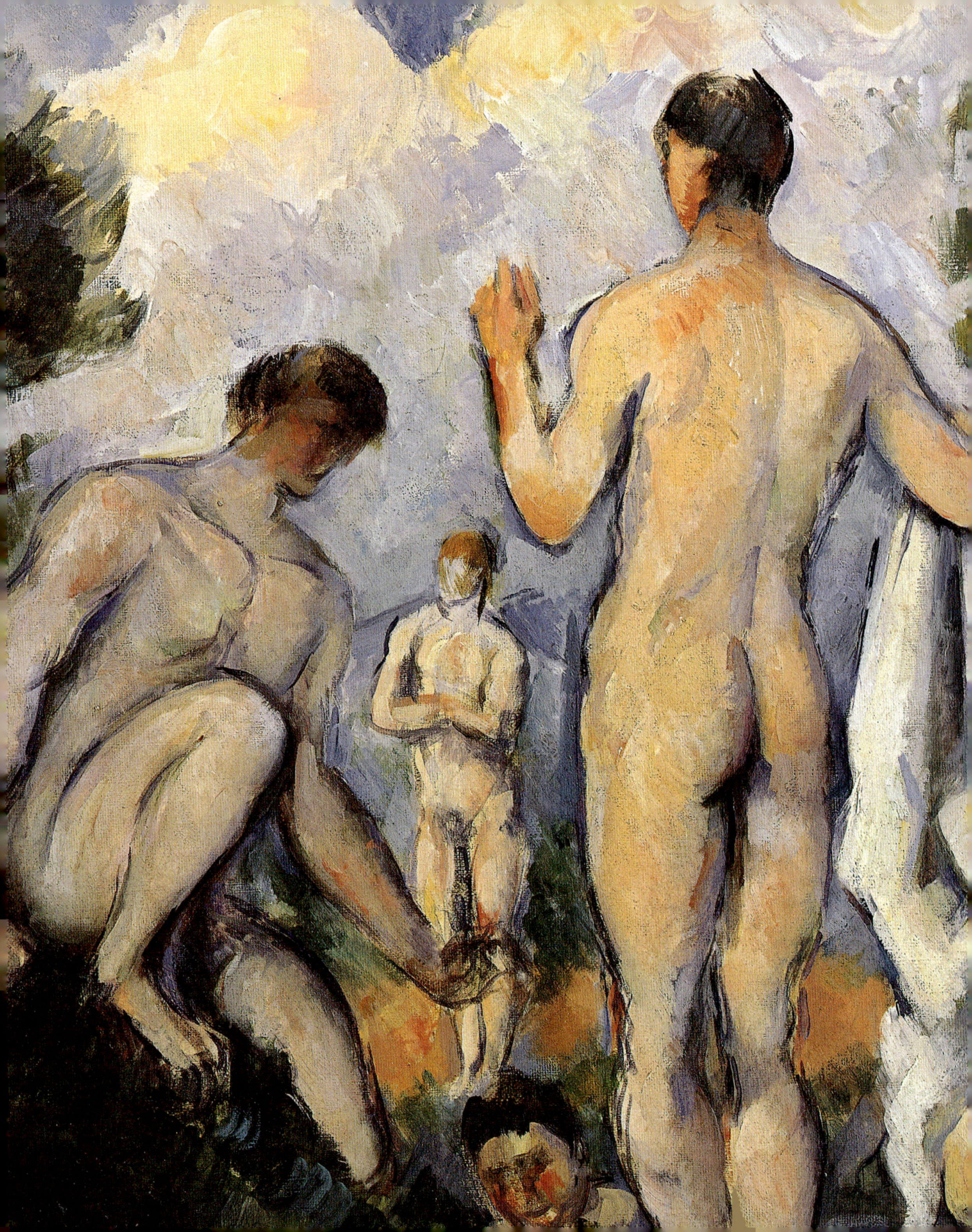

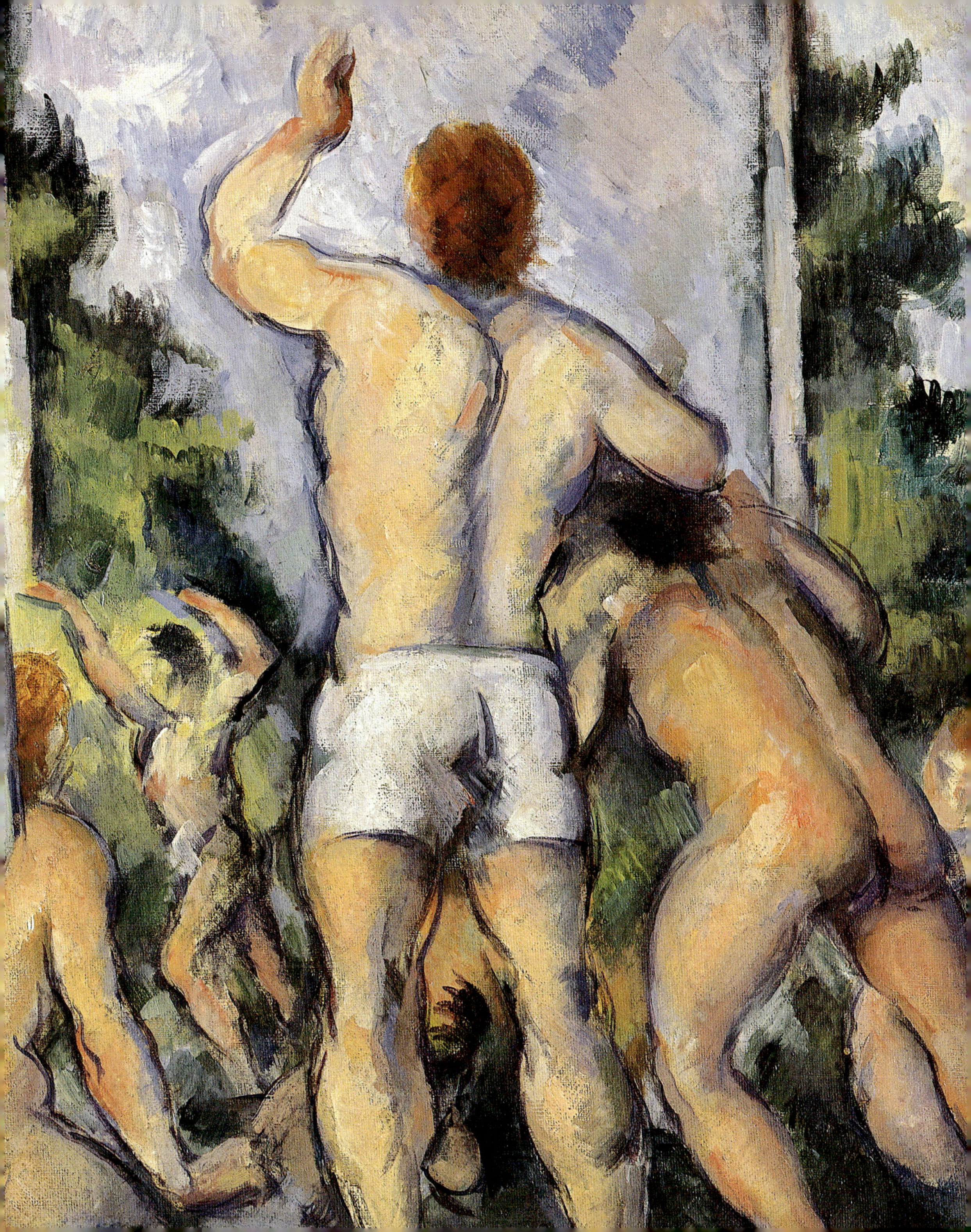

Still Life with Peaches and Pears

1890–1894

Oil on canvas, 61 x 90 cm
Pushkin Museum, Moscow

Cézanne, who explained to his friends that objects—like nature itself—change from day to day, often made use of the roundness and precarious balance of apples to analyze the relationship between objects and space. And so a series of highly sophisticated still lifes came into being during this phase of his artistic development, in all of which a cloth, crockery, and fruit are arranged on a table. Cézanne uses a double perspective here. The drawer at the front of the table contrasts with the representation of the tabletop, which appears to be slightly tilted in order to show the objects that make up the still life without causing them to be partially obscured. This painting constitutes a high point of Cézanne's "constructive" phase, in which he practiced the simplification of reality to the point where he created pure forms that are almost abstract in their elementary geometric shapes. The constant alternation between vanishing points undermines and destroys the rules passed down for many centuries in the academic tradition regarding central perspective. The brown of the table and of the indefinable object top right which, as is common in Cézanne's oeuvre, leaves the structure of the composition open and incomplete, contrasts with the bright white of the tablecloth, which is decorated by just a narrow red line. A sugar jar, a plate, and a jug stand on the table, and they, too, are reproduced primarily in white tones. With the repeated interplay of shades of yellow, red, and green, the gently luminescent hues of the peaches and pears soften the coloring and lend the composition a sense of movement.

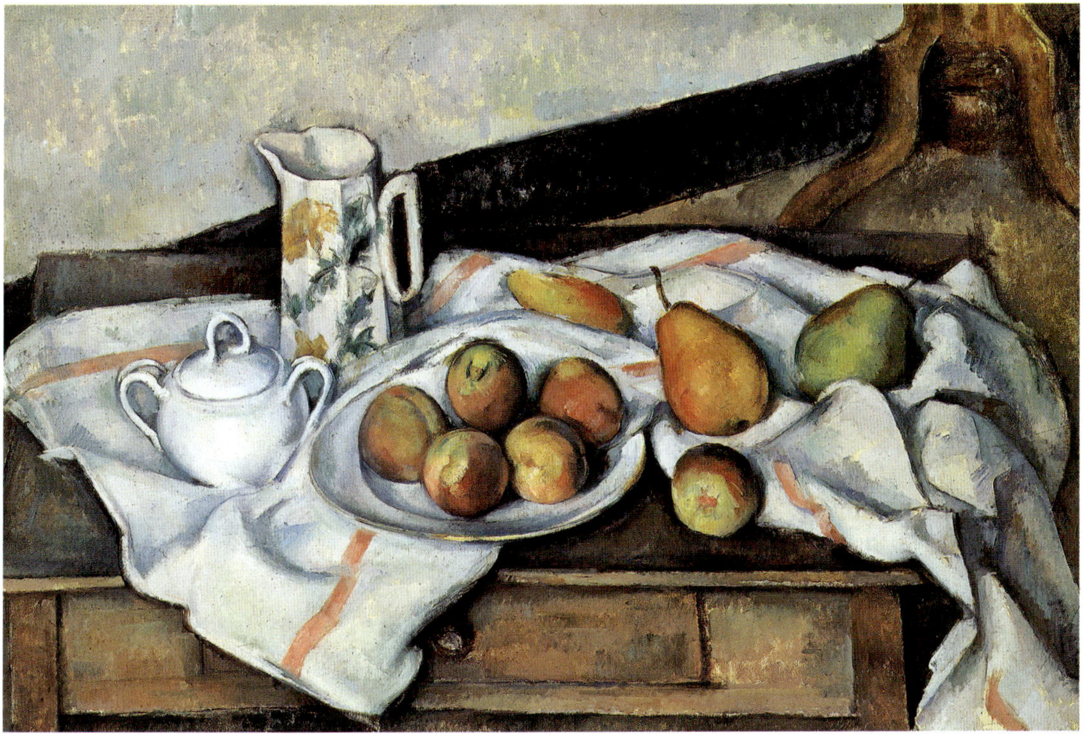

Large Pine and Red Earth

1890–1895

Oil on canvas, 72 x 91 cm
The State Hermitage Museum, St. Petersburg

In a letter to Joachim Gasquet, Cézanne describes the technique that he employed for painting landscapes *en plein air* when he worked on the same canvas day after day: "In order to paint a landscape properly, I first have to recognize the geological layering. I feel colorful, from all these gradations of color of the eternal. In this moment, I am absolutely one with my painting. We are a dazzling chaos. I stand before my motif, I lose myself in it ... One beautiful morning, the following day, the geological foundations slowly reveal themselves to me, the layers establish themselves, the great planes of my canvas, in my mind I draw the stony skeleton. I see the rocks glisten beneath the water, and the weight of the sky. Everything is as it should be. The linear elements are obscured by a gentle movement backwards and forwards. The red earths rise from an abyss. I begin to separate from the landscape, and to see it. I disengage myself from it with this first sketch, these geological lines. Geometry, the measure of the earth."
In the same way, the pine tree in this painting rises above the landscape and stretches its mighty branches until they fill the entire surface of the canvas. Cézanne constructs the space, the foreground and middle ground, around the mighty, structuring lines of the tree trunk using small brushstrokes in ocher and green, colors that communicate a sense of the heat and brightness of a summer's day. As is frequently the case with Cézanne, the central element of the painting—in this case, a tree trunk—is positioned slightly to the left of the center, so that the branches can reach far towards the right.

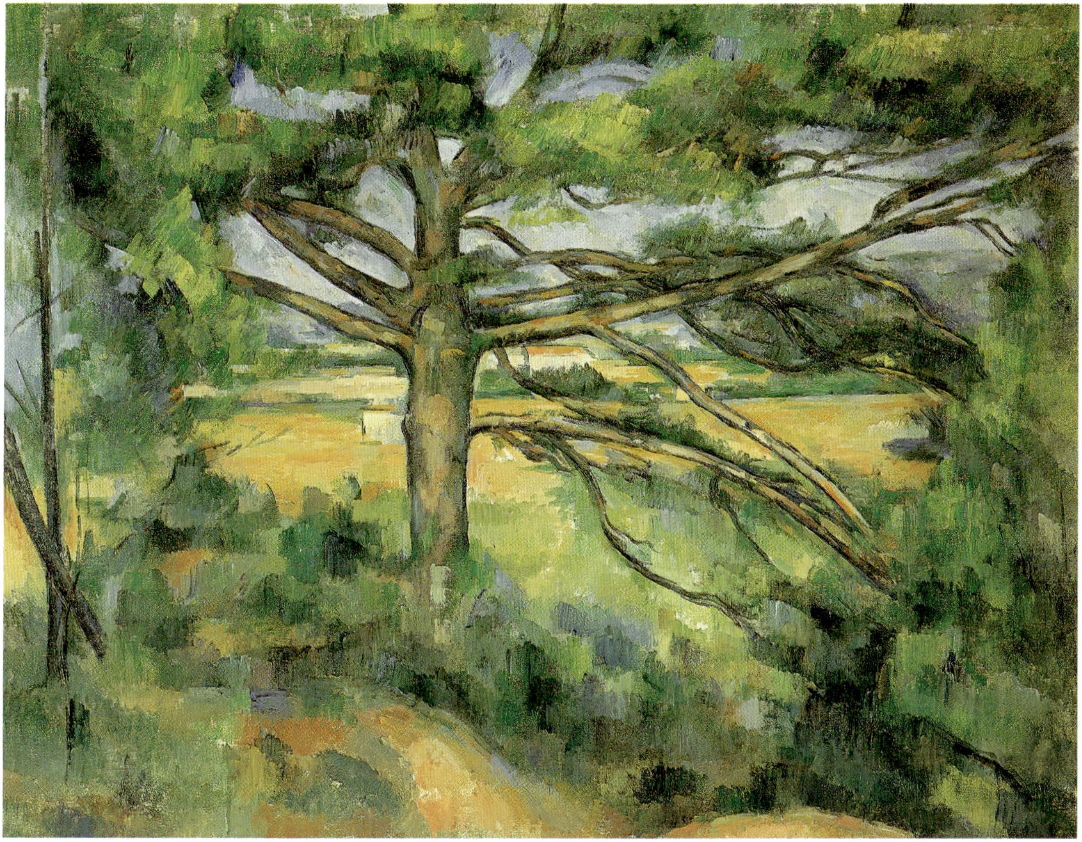

Man Smoking a Pipe

c. 1891–1897

Oil on canvas, 91 x 72 cm
The State Hermitage Museum, St. Petersburg

Following his retreat to Jas de Bouffan, the family estate, Cézanne created numerous paintings of figures for which the farmers and villagers acted as models. Cézanne was fascinated by their simplicity and rustic candor. At least three paintings from this period are dedicated to a young peasant who worked on the family's estate. The young man with the suntanned face sits in the studio that Cézanne had set up in his house. He radiates a serenity that is seldom seen in the Parisians from whom Cézanne occasionally felt the need to escape. A few paintings hang in the background, only some of which can be identified, including a still life with apples and bottles. The sitter, who has grasped the opportunity to earn some money without resorting to fieldwork, rests his head on his hand as though he were sitting in an inn. In order to make a good impression, the young man has put on his best suit, which stands in stark contrast to the slightly dented hat and white clay pipe, typical of the farmers and peasants of Provence. Cézanne worked as slowly as usual on this painting. First, he sketched out the basic features of the heavy body and the face, and then located the scene in the rich environment of his studio. The figure is propelled slightly forward by the curtain on the right. The structure of this painting is determined by the interplay of shades of green, pale violet, ocher, red and blue. The relatively rough left hand in the foreground is depicted with admiring attention of an artist who valued the rural honesty over the urban sophistication.

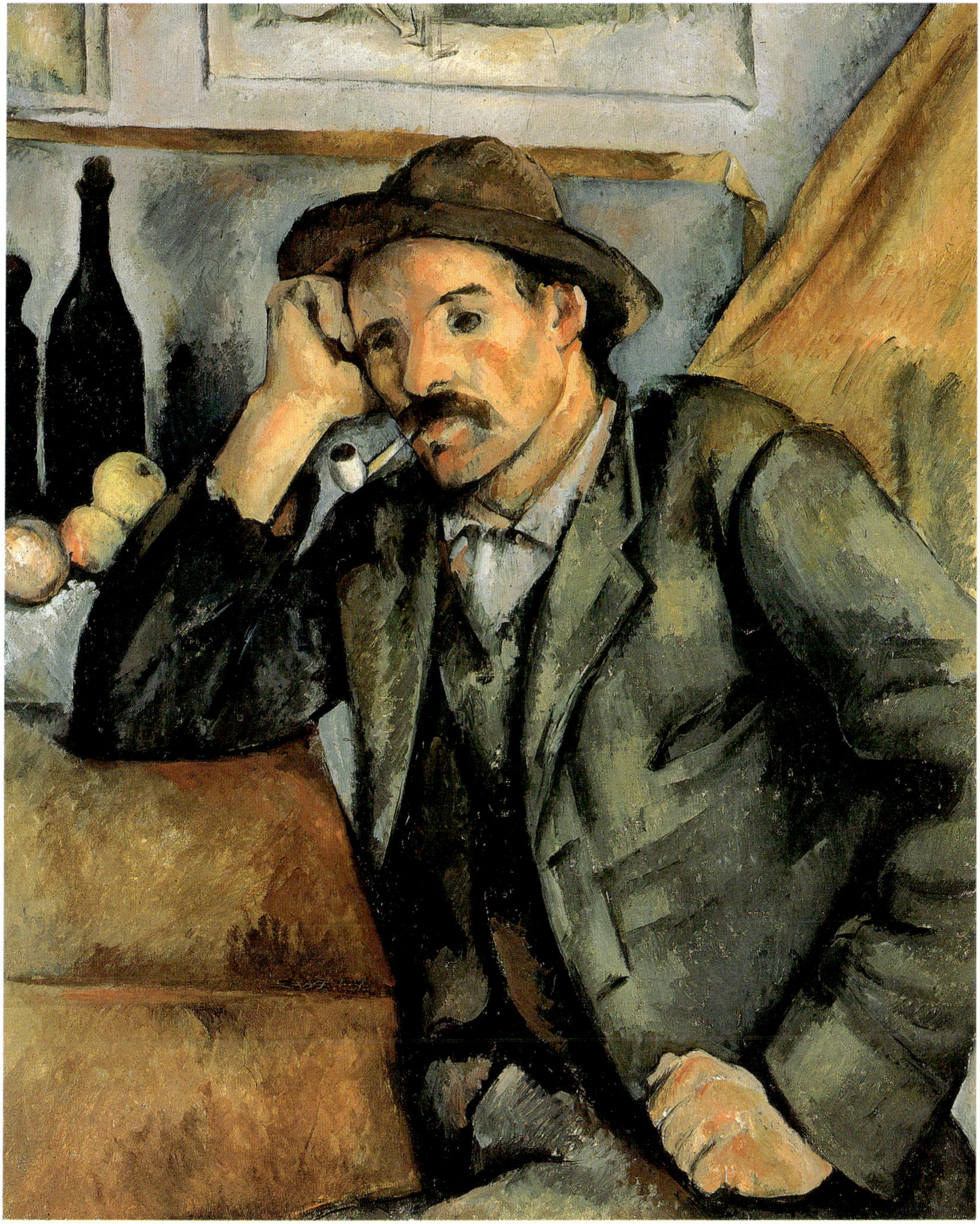

The Cardplayers

c. 1890–1895

Oil on canvas, 47 x 56 cm
Musée d'Orsay, Paris

A painting entitled *The Cardplayers* (1635–1640) by Louis Le Nain is in the collection of the museum of Aix-en-Provence; it is possible that it served as inspiration for Cézanne. In any case, he was a regular customer at brasseries, and five paintings depict their interiors. Two to five people populate the various versions. He made numerous studies in preparation for these paintings, and they reveal considerable interest in this subject. It is not clear whether the artist first created a version featuring five figures, before increasingly simplifying the composition, or whether he worked on all of the versions at the same time. The two card players sit opposite one another, silently concentrating on their cards. One of them holds a white clay pipe between his lips and the other wears on his head one of up-turned hats typical of rural workers in the region. Their postures and gestures are mirror images of one another, whereby Cézanne has shifted the axis of symmetry slightly to the right of the center, as is typical of his work. The narrow room is suggested only by a few essential brushstrokes and pushes the figures into the foreground. Cézanne was clearly not interested in psychology, here; instead, he concentrates entirely on shapes created by the figures' bodies, gestures, and movements. The man waiting for his turn exhibits a certain stiffness, whereas the player who is about to make his move leans forward slightly and is depicted in lighter, brighter colors. These figures are not merely tools for spatial construction, however; they are also, at least to some degree, elements of pictorial narrative.

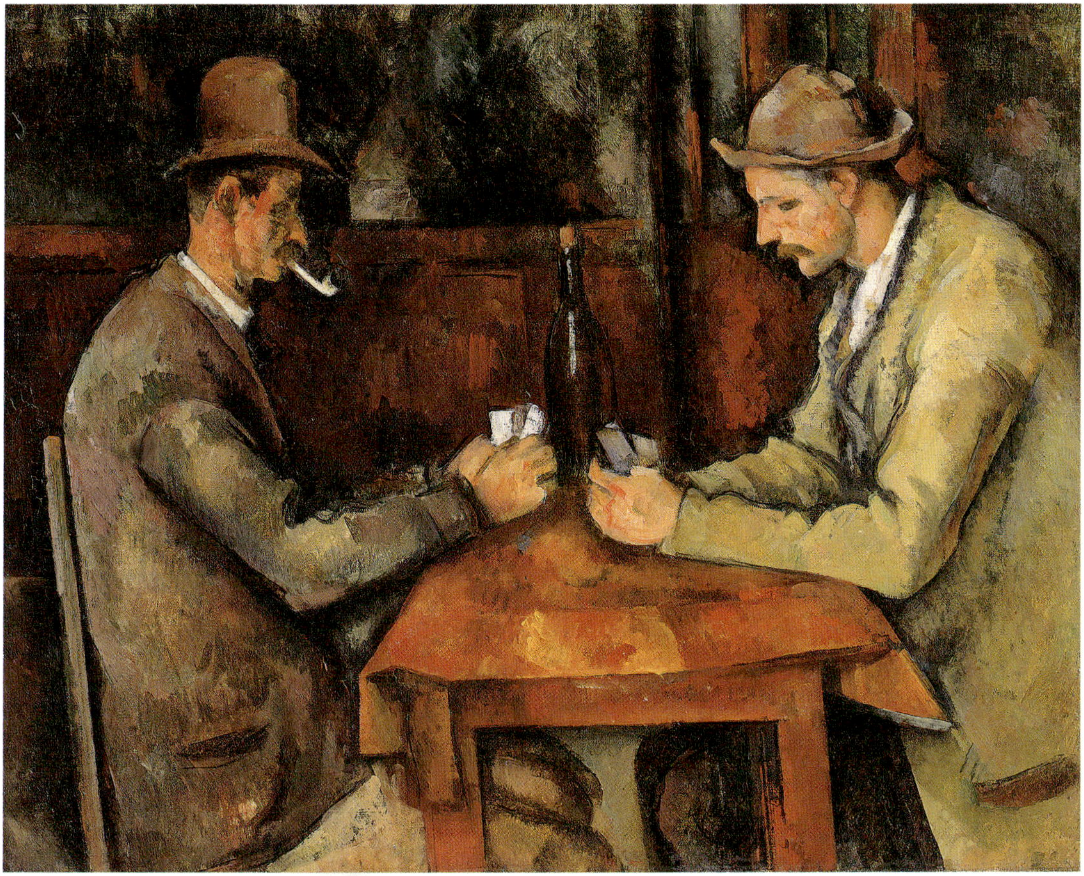

Still Life with Plaster Cupid

1894–1895

Oil on canvas, 63 x 81 cm
Nationalmuseum, Stockholm

Joachim Gasquet, the son of a long-time friend of Cézanne's, described this painting, which he had the opportunity to admire in the artist's studio, as follows: "He goes to the pile of canvases, and searches ... He pulls out three still lifes, and lines them up against the wall, on the floor. They radiate warmth, depth, liveliness, like a supernatural piece of wall, and yet they are entirely rooted in the most everyday reality ... And the third is elegant, delightful, bright, entirely French, decorative and yet haunting: on one side, a plaster Cupid, his arms missing, stands in front of a cloth with a complex pattern of tight folds. To the statue's right is a plate with pears, and to its left a heap of plums. In the background, unexpected and rather bourgeois, but broadly painted, convincingly executed, is a so-called Prussian fireplace of the kind still used in the country houses of Provence."

This painting certainly stands out from the long series of Cézanne's still lifes through the unusual inclusion of a porcelain statuette (or plaster replica). It represents Cupid, and indicates the interest Cézanne had in the key motifs of the Western art-historical tradition. The top part of the elegant painting, which is painted almost entirely in shades of white and blue, contrasts with the warm colorfulness of the objects and fruits on the table. The space is thus clearly divided into two halves, which draws all the more attention to the statue in the foreground.

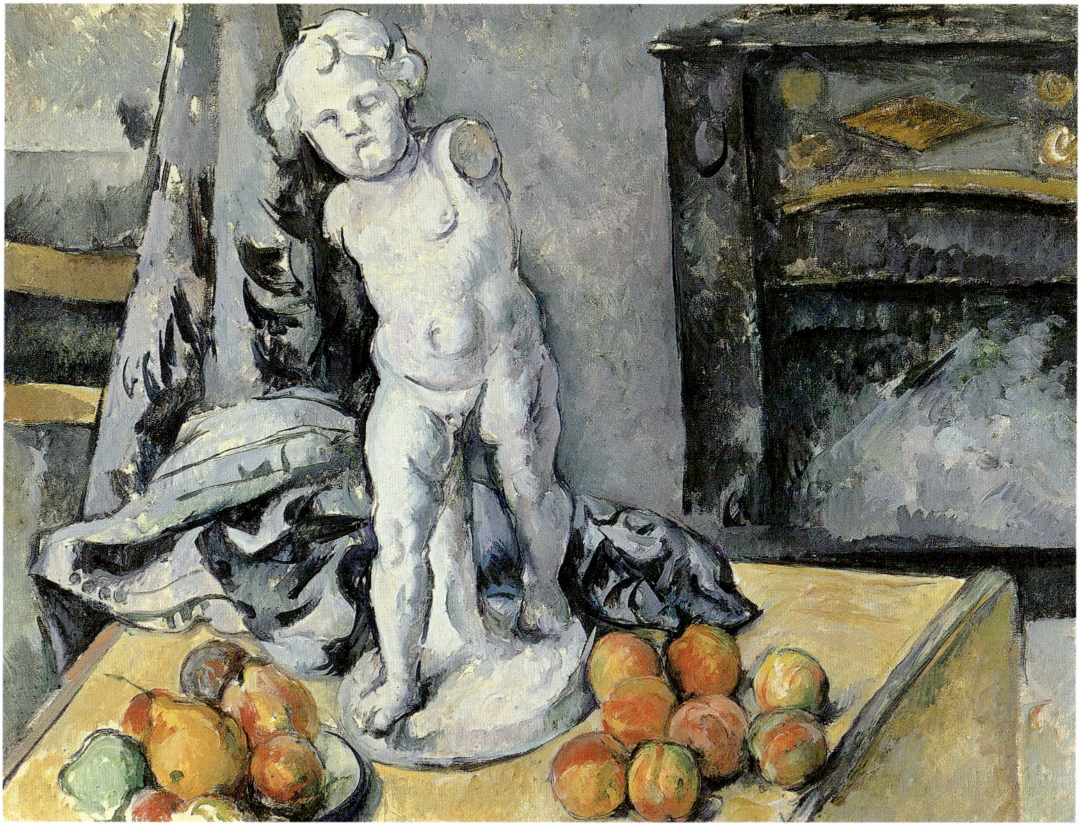

Woman with a Coffee Pot

c. 1895

Oil on canvas, 130 x 97 cm
Musée d'Orsay, Paris

Portrait painting always presented a particular challenge to Cézanne. He constantly searched for the inner structures of things, for their deeper and more permanent values. He attempted to imbue even the human form, whose nature it is to be constantly subjected to the tiniest of movements and changes, with this permanence. During the years he spent in seclusion at the family home of Jas de Bouffan, Cézanne worked with occasional models, whom he selected from among the people in the village, and who patiently subjected themselves to the extended sittings required of them. In this case, he painted the portrait of his domestic servant. She sits facing the viewer, in a pose that we are familiar with from various representations of his wife, Hortense. Sitting on a chair that she covers entirely, the sitter dominates the space around her. Her face, whose features reveal the traits typical of Mediterranean women, and the slightly heavy body, are the objects of a thoughtful and painstaking painterly investigation. The compositional structure is based on a system of parallel lines, which lead from the wallpaper on the left to the coffee pot on the right. These emphasize the verticality of the figure, the vertical lines of the door, and the spoon that stands unnaturally erect. The body is composed of two halves separated by the horizontal line in the middle. The light that enters from the left illuminates the lower half of her dress, the side of her face, and the coffee pot and cup. Her heavy hands and impenetrable face deepen the impression of stolidity. The geometrical forms of the cup and coffee pot are remarkable starting points for later experiments by the Cubists.

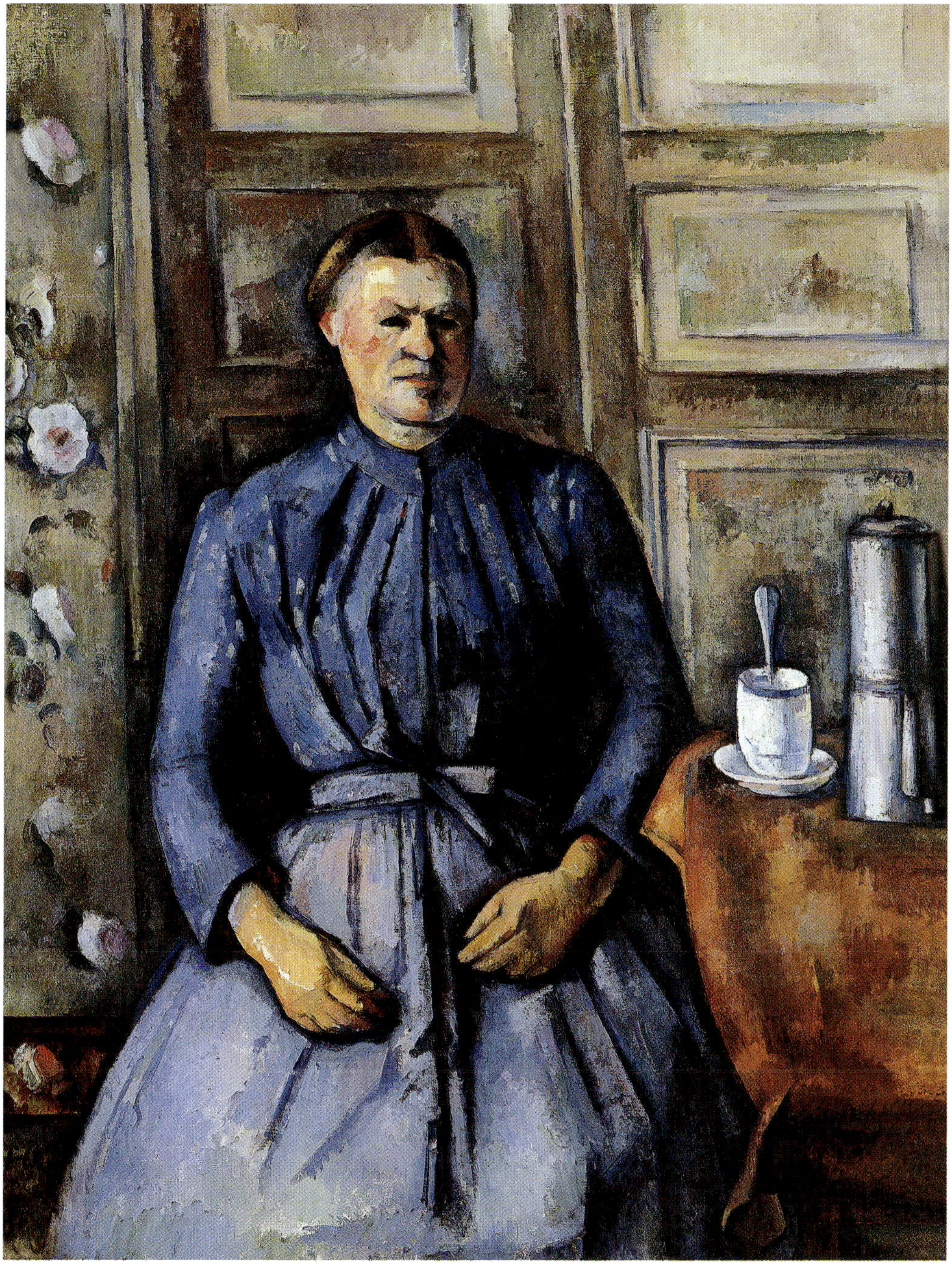

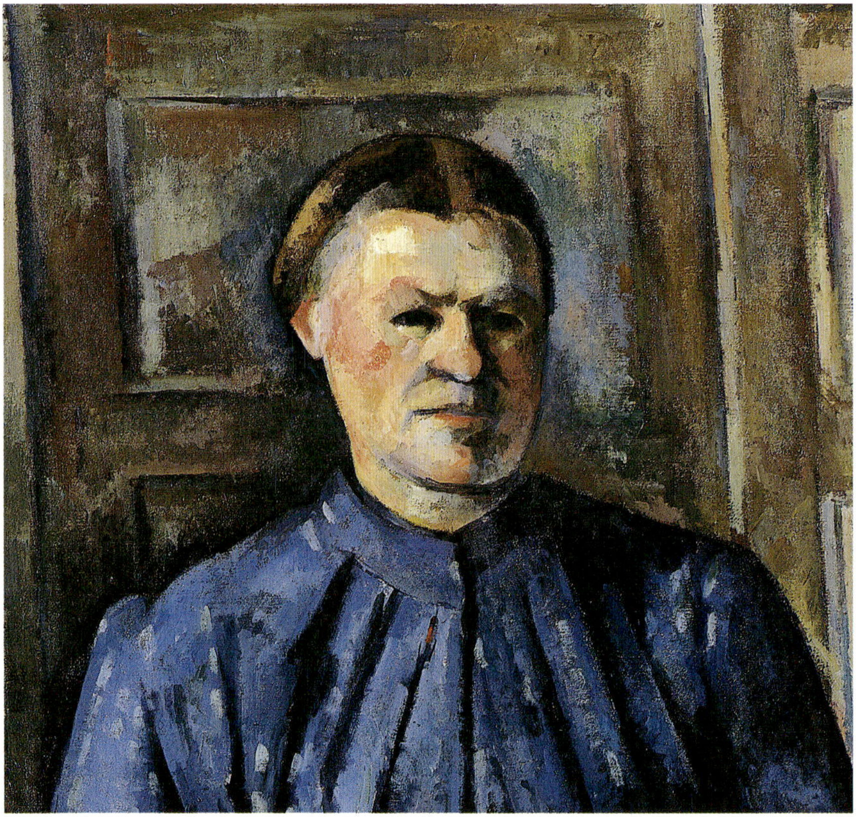

Woman with a Coffee Pot (details)

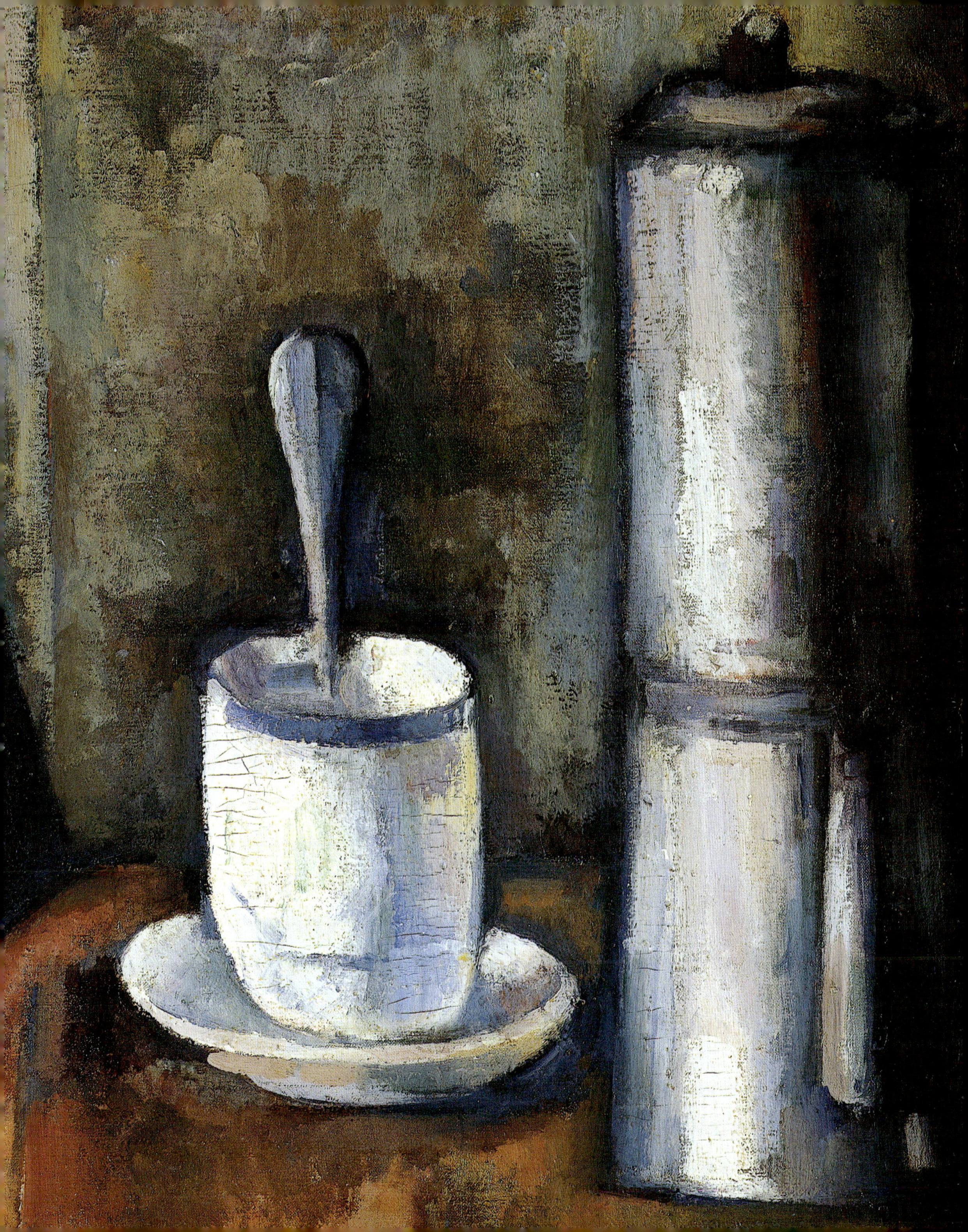

Portrait of Joachim Gasquet

c. 1896

Oil on canvas, 65 x 54 cm
Národní Galerie, Prague

Joachim Gasquet was the son of Henri Gasquet, an old friend of Cézanne's. He was also the author of an important book on the artist (1921). A poet and philosopher, he was drawn by Cézanne's return to nature and to the classical tradition of painting; he particularly admired his series depicting the Mont Sainte-Victoire. A close friendship developed between the young man and the elderly painter, as is reflected in their voluminous correspondence.
In this portrait, Gasquet appears with his upper body turned slightly towards his left; he has turned his head marginally to the right to gaze at the viewer. The spatial construction is created by the use of contrasting color values, and only to a lesser extent through the chiaroscuro and modeling found in traditional painting. The highlights on the dark suit are produced by patches of canvas that have not been painted. They are balanced by the small but conspicuous white collar, which lightens the face, a technique used by Old Masters. Cézanne has also made use of areas of unpainted canvas in the structure of the face and hair. One might even imagine that the work is unfinished. In fact, this approach is an expression of the increasing abstraction that can be discerned in Cézanne's pictures. As the artist himself points out in a letter to Émile Bernard dated 23 October 1905, it is the "color impressions that convey the light that are the cause of the abstractions in my work. They do not permit me to cover my canvas entirely, nor do they allow me to follow the contours of the objects when the points of contact are very fine and delicate."

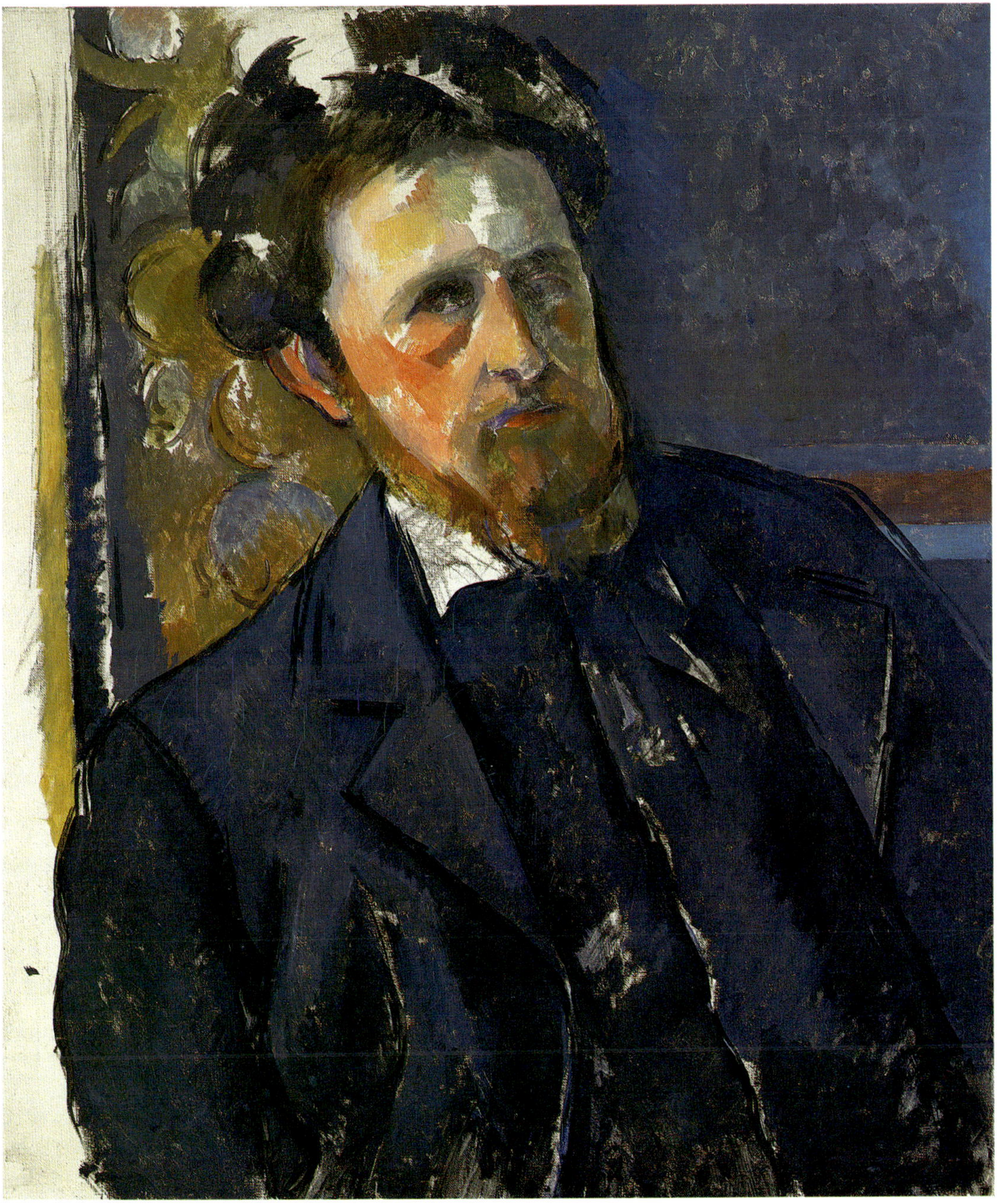

Road Before the Mountains, Mont Sainte-Victoire

c. 1896–1898

Oil on canvas, 78 x 99 cm
The State Hermitage Museum, St. Petersburg

At the end of the 1890s Cézanne began increasingly to concentrate on a the specific elements of landscape. His works, which until that point had mostly featured a distant horizon, were now dominated by large features. In this case it is Mont Sainte-Victoire, which blends wonderfully into the surrounding countryside. Here there is no line marking the boundary to the hills and their vegetation in the foreground. The color palette has been considerably reduced, but still corresponds to the requirements of a naturalistic representation of a landscape. The hills, between which a house can be discerned, are depicted by means of powerful brushstrokes in green and brown; the mountain in the background appears in bluish tones and soft shades of violet beneath a blue sky. The transitions from one area of color to the next skillfully allow the spatial elements of the landscape to appear, so that they are shown in detail. In order to convey highlights, the canvas remains unpainted in some places. Joachim Gasquet described how the artist attempted to record Mont Sainte-Victoire in his paintings: "The picture he saw in his mind's eye perfectly thought through in its arrangement and which he must have sketched out as he always did with rapid strokes of charcoal, emerged from these colored patches, which determined it from all angles. The landscape appears to oscillate, because Cézanne has carefully outlined each object; he tried out each color before adding it, so to speak, and from day to day he imperceptibly balanced out all these values in confident harmony, linking them with each other in a muted brightness."

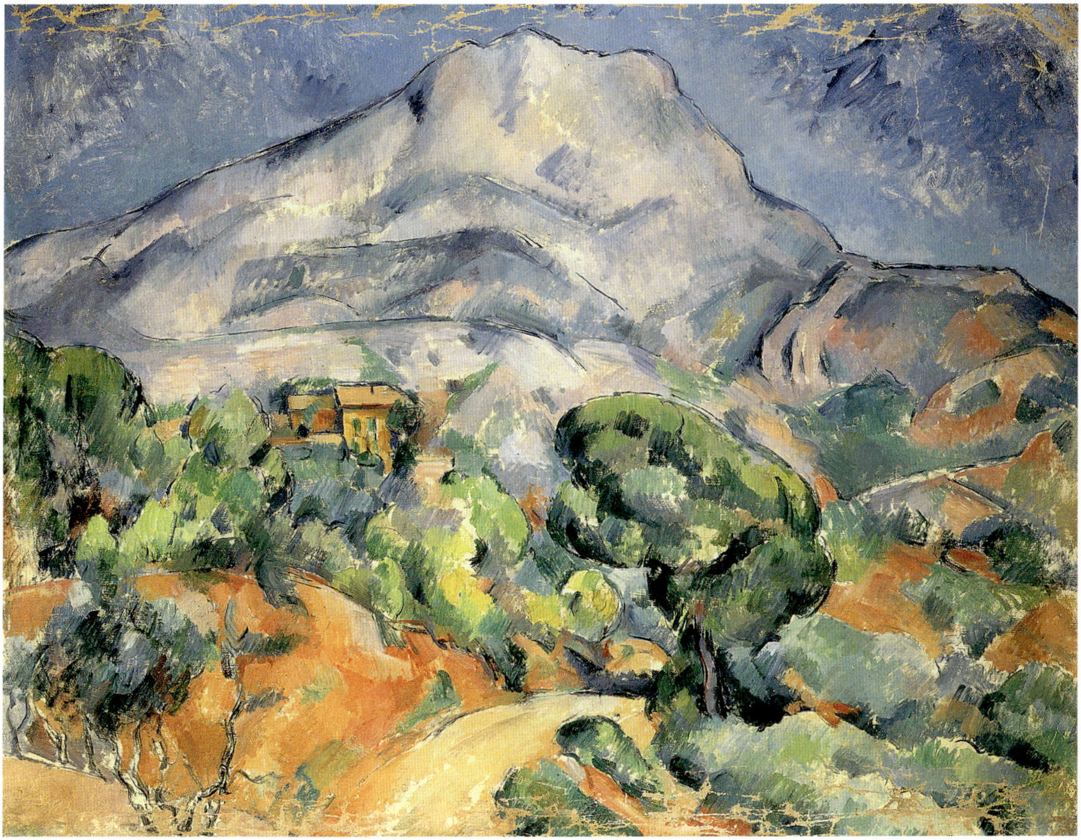

Still Life with Skull

c. 1896–1898

Oil on canvas, 54 x 65 cm
Barnes Foundation, Merion

The still lifes Cézanne produced during this period are characterized by a return to the darker color tones of his early years. The artist, by now a supreme master of his technique, worked on rich, complex compositions on large-format canvases. Already an old man himself, he here included a skull, which, with its strong chiaroscuro, contrasts with the delicate shades of the tablecloth and the lively freshness of the apples, pears, and lemons. They are symbols of life and at the same time the only strongly colored elements in a composition, which is otherwise composed of muted colors. Using a method that by this time was tried and tested, Cézanne here incorporated a number of different angles. Thus the surface of the table, on which the fruit lies in delicate equilibrium, is shown slightly from above.

By this time Cézanne had become aware of the extent to which he was beginning to feel his age. He wrote to his friend Joachim Gasquet from Aix-en-Provence in 1896: "During my whole life I have worked to arrive at the point when I can earn my living; but I thought that it would be possible to produce good painting without attracting attention to one's private life. Of course an artist wants to reach as high an intellectual level as possible, but the individual should remain in the dark. The pleasure should arise from study. If it had been given to me to realize, I would have remained in my corner with those few studio colleagues with whom we used to go drinking together ... Incidentally, it is as if I were dead. You are young and I understand that you want to be successful. But as for me, what is there left for me to do in my position but to capitulate; and if it were not for the fact that I loved the landscape of my native region so much, I would not be here."

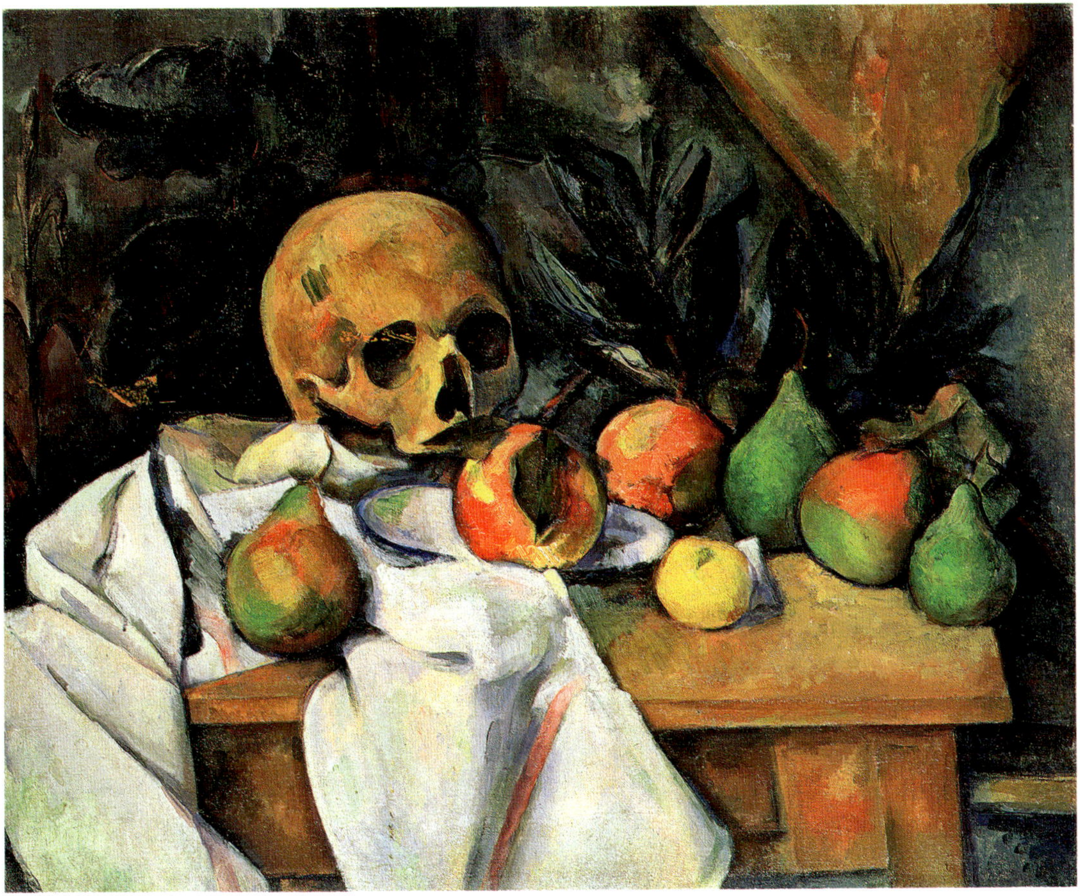

Bridge on a Pond

c. 1898

Oil on canvas, 64 x 79 cm
Pushkin Museum, Moscow

Towards the end of the nineteenth century, Cézanne's search for a new form of artistic expression came to a head. He selected aspects of nature and subjected them to complex processes in which he dismantled them and then put them back together in a new way. This so-called synthetic phase in his career is characterized by the extreme merging of light and shade, and by subjects that he had already treated in previous years, including Mont Sainte-Victoire as well as river and marshland scenes. Cézanne emphasized the "modular" aspect of his compositions through the color scheme, which he orchestrated like a piece of music by means of the interplay of themes and counterpoint, while omitting modeling using light and shade. The philosophical analysis of the relationship of art to reality now played an increasingly important role in the continued development of his painting style. Accordingly, the aim of his painting was to make visible on the canvas the original structure of the natural environment, even if subject to constant change. The little bridge that appears in the center of the picture shown here is almost obscured at first sight by the dense vegetation. The trees form a visual unity with their own reflections on the surface of the water of the pond. By using a rich palette of greens, Cézanne constructs the picture space by creating large areas that are rendered by countless brushstrokes applied in differing directions. He thus gives nature a formal order, creating an "effective architecture of levels, supports, arches, intersections and refractions" (Renato Barilli, *Da Cezanne alle ultime tendenze*, 1988). The variety of shades of green that the viewer encounters here, framed by ocher, yellow and blue, is remarkable.

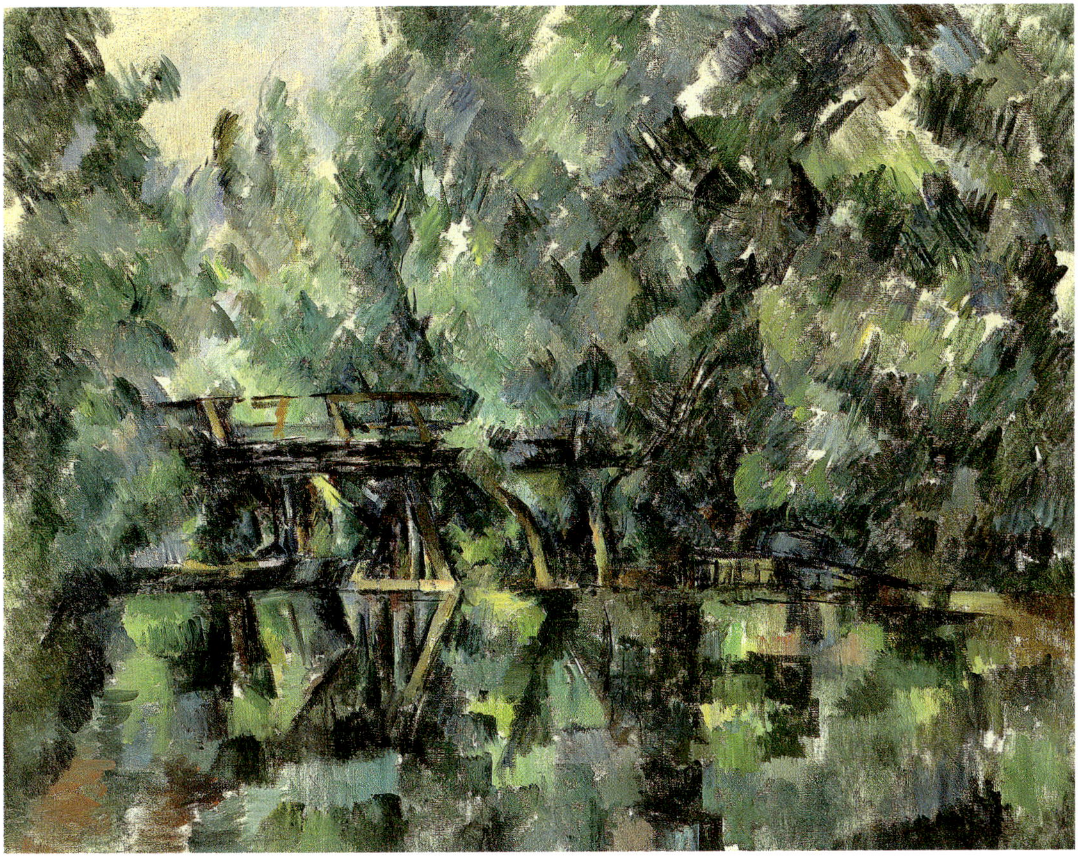

Bibémus Quarry

c. 1898

Oil on canvas, 92 x 73 cm
Barnes Foundation, Merion

At the end of the 1890s Cézanne's artistic concerns became increasingly philosophical and rational. His aim was to capture on canvas the innermost essence of things, regardless of the perpetual change to which the natural world is subject. During this time he liked to paint in the area around Bibémus, an abandoned quarry near Mont Sainte-Victoire. The ocher-colored rocks, which had once been formed during a long process of sedimentation from a sea that has long since disappeared, appear compact, solid, and bright. Cézanne was fascinated by this lonely, untamed place. He built a little hut there in which to store his canvases and where, if necessary, he could spend the night. Within a short space of time he produced some 60 landscapes there; among his most famous paintings, they already point forward to the Cubist experiments of Picasso. Émile Bernard describes how Cézanne painted near Bibémus: "He began with the shadowy parts and with a patch, on which he set a second, larger one, and then a third one, until all these shades of color, one on top of the other, modeled the object with their atmosphere. It was then that I realized that a law of harmony governs his work and that these modulations had a direction that had been determined beforehand in his mind ... In order to follow nature with the naiveté of a child, one sometimes starts working without preparation, completely impartial; one then observes with the greatest immediacy. But he did not use this method. He generalized to arrive at regularities and he used them to deduce principles that he employed with such conviction that he was able to arrive at an interpretation without copying."

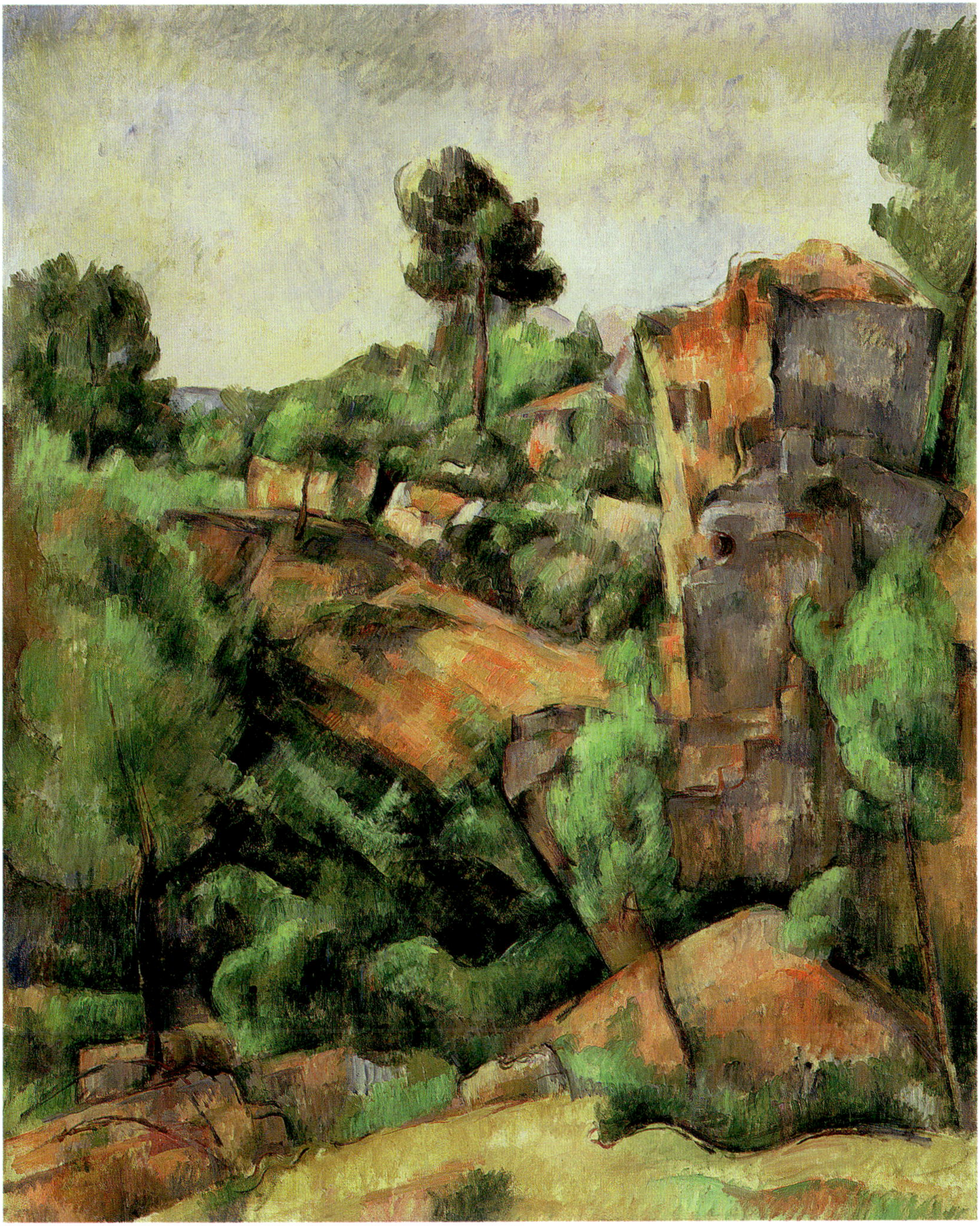

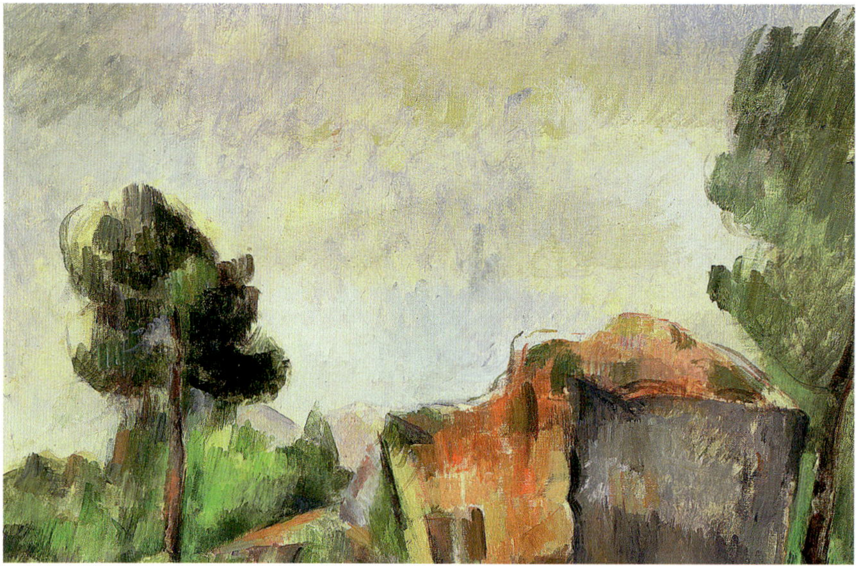

Bibémus Quarry
(details)

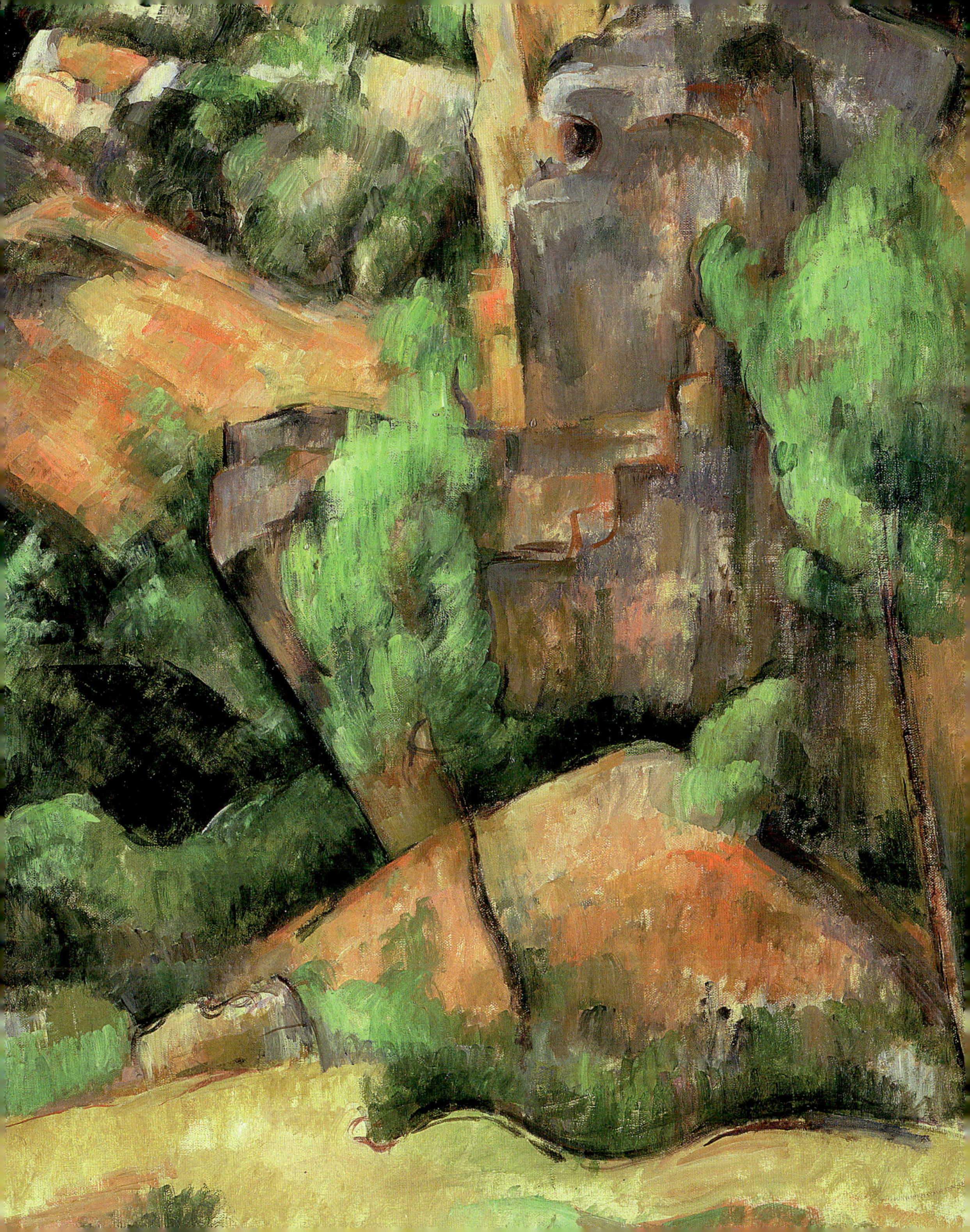

Still Life with a Curtain

c. 1899

Oil on canvas, 54.7 x 74 cm
The State Hermitage Museum, St. Petersburg

Cézanne consciously broke with the tradition of academic painting, which placed history painting at the top of the genre hierarchy. The task of history painting was to translate events that had been handed down in written form (history, mythology, literature) into visual form through the creative imagination of the artist. At the same time he also abandoned the route chosen by the Impressionists, since he put the construction of a clearly structured pictorial space in place of the recording of direct sensory perception. Painting thus becomes primarily an intellectual, even a philosophical, exercise performed through the genres of landscape, portrait, and still life. Still life above all is a genre that permits the artist to take full control of the objects he is painting, since he can arrange them in his studio according to the principles of art. The artist circles round objects, observing them from every possible angle in order to grasp their basic geometric structure.

This still life is one of the must extraordinary examples of painting at the end of the nineteenth century. The various pictorial elements—fruit, dishes, cloths, curtains—are arranged with rare artistry, the colors elegantly coordinated. The yellow and red shades of the fruits recur in the pattern on the plates and jug, the white of the cloths in the dishes, and the curtain unites all the browns and grays as well as the black of the table and the background. The picture space is so constructed that the various perspectives are interleaved into each other. The edge of the table is shown from the front, while the tabletop is seen slightly from above so that it conveys a precarious instability that contrasts with the solid three-dimensionality of the fruits.

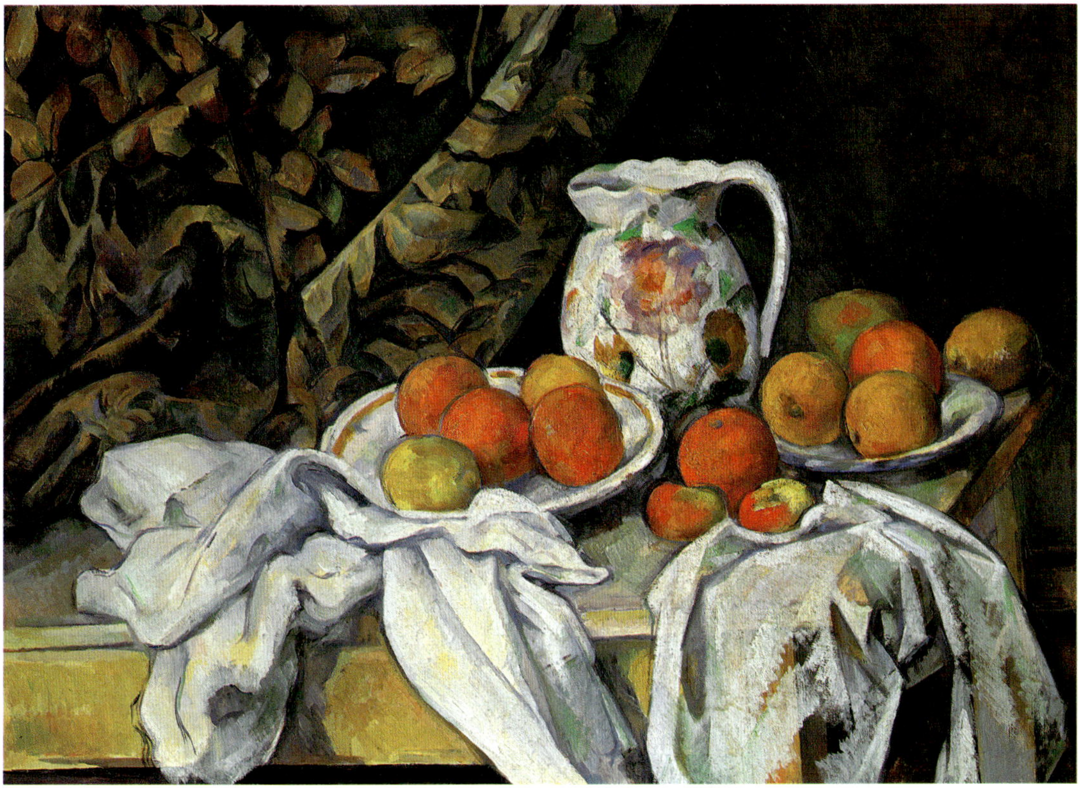

Portrait of Ambroise Vollard

1899

Oil on canvas, 100 x 82 cm
Musée du Petit Palais, Paris

The first exhibition of works by Cézanne was organized by Ambroise Vollard in 1898, a courageous young art dealer in Paris. After endless sittings for this portrait, Cézanne left Paris and returned to Aix-en-Provence. Vollard himself reported on the long and painful genesis of this picture: "Every afternoon Cézanne went to the Louvre or the Trocadéro, where he would draw after the Old Masters. He frequently spoke briefly to me at about five o'clock and reported radiantly: 'Monsieur Vollard, I've got good news for you. I am fairly pleased with the study I have just produced; if the weather is light gray tomorrow, I think we shall have a good sitting.' That was his main concern at the end of the day: what would the weather be like tomorrow? ... Very few people have been able to observe Cézanne working. He could not bear being watched when he was standing in front of the easel. Anyone who has not seen him painting can simply not imagine how slowly and laboriously his work took shape on some days. In my portrait there are two small places on the hand where the canvas has not been painted over. I pointed it out to Cézanne. 'If my session later on in the Louvre goes well,' he answered, 'maybe I shall find the right shade tomorrow to paint the bare patches. Can you understand just a little, Monsieur Vollard, if I were to just put any random color there I would be compelled to overpaint my entire picture from that spot.' It was a prospect that made me shudder!"

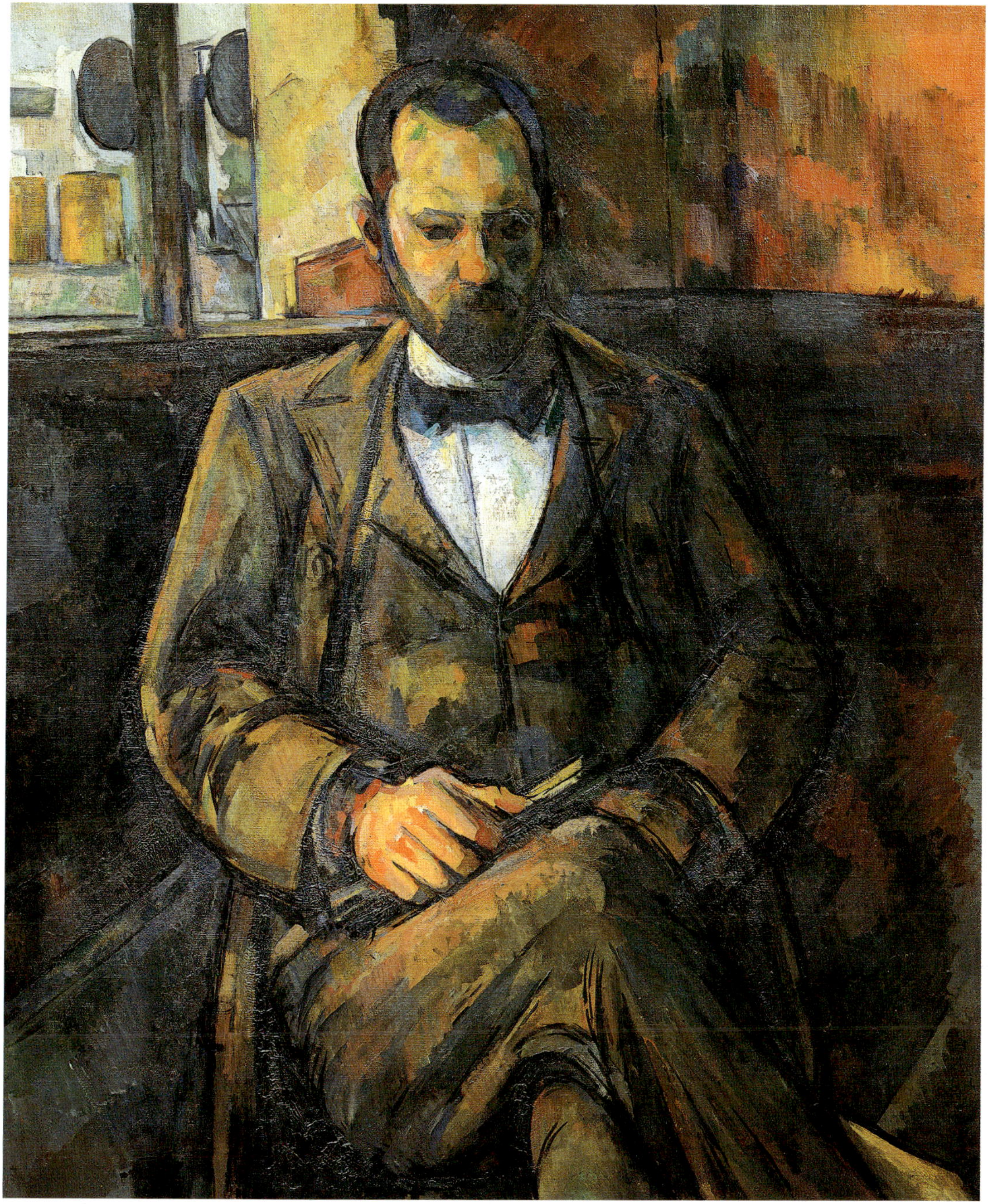

Apples and Oranges

c. 1899

Oil on canvas, 74 x 93 cm
Musée d'Orsay, Paris

Appearing for the first time in the 1860s, apples later became one of Cézanne's principal subject; he doubtless valued apples because of their spherical shape, which could easily be reduced to purely geometric forms. According to the art historian Meyer Schapiro, this still life is notable for "its luxuriance and profusion":

"The compotier grows out of the beautiful white cloth, and the decorated jug seems to be a fusion of that cloth with the apples and oranges and the ornamented drape behind it. The effect is dense, even crowded, like his landscapes with woods and rocks, and is enormously rich in unexpected shapes and chords of color, almost to the point of engorgement. It is not al all a 'natural' still life ... but a fantastic heaping up of things, in which we discern, however, a clear controlling taste."

Cézanne's still lifes with apples are marked by a very carefully developed compositions. In this example, the spherical fruit is placed on a tabletop that is depicted from a slightly raised position and that therefore looks as if it is tilted in a rather precarious equilibrium. The tablecloth and the white dishes, the red and yellow apples and the oranges, embedded in the complex folds of the cloth, stand out clearly against the dark background. The objects and the fruits lie along lines that intersect each other at different angles, thereby creating a complex perspectival diversity.

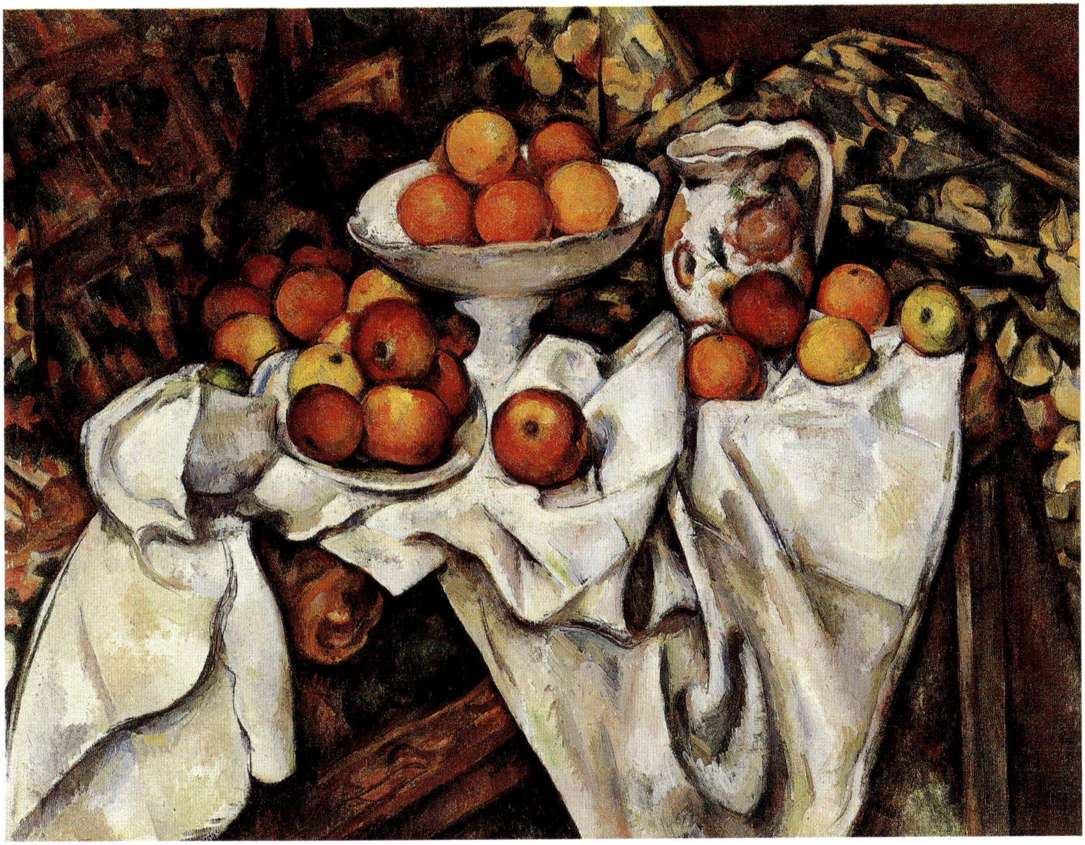

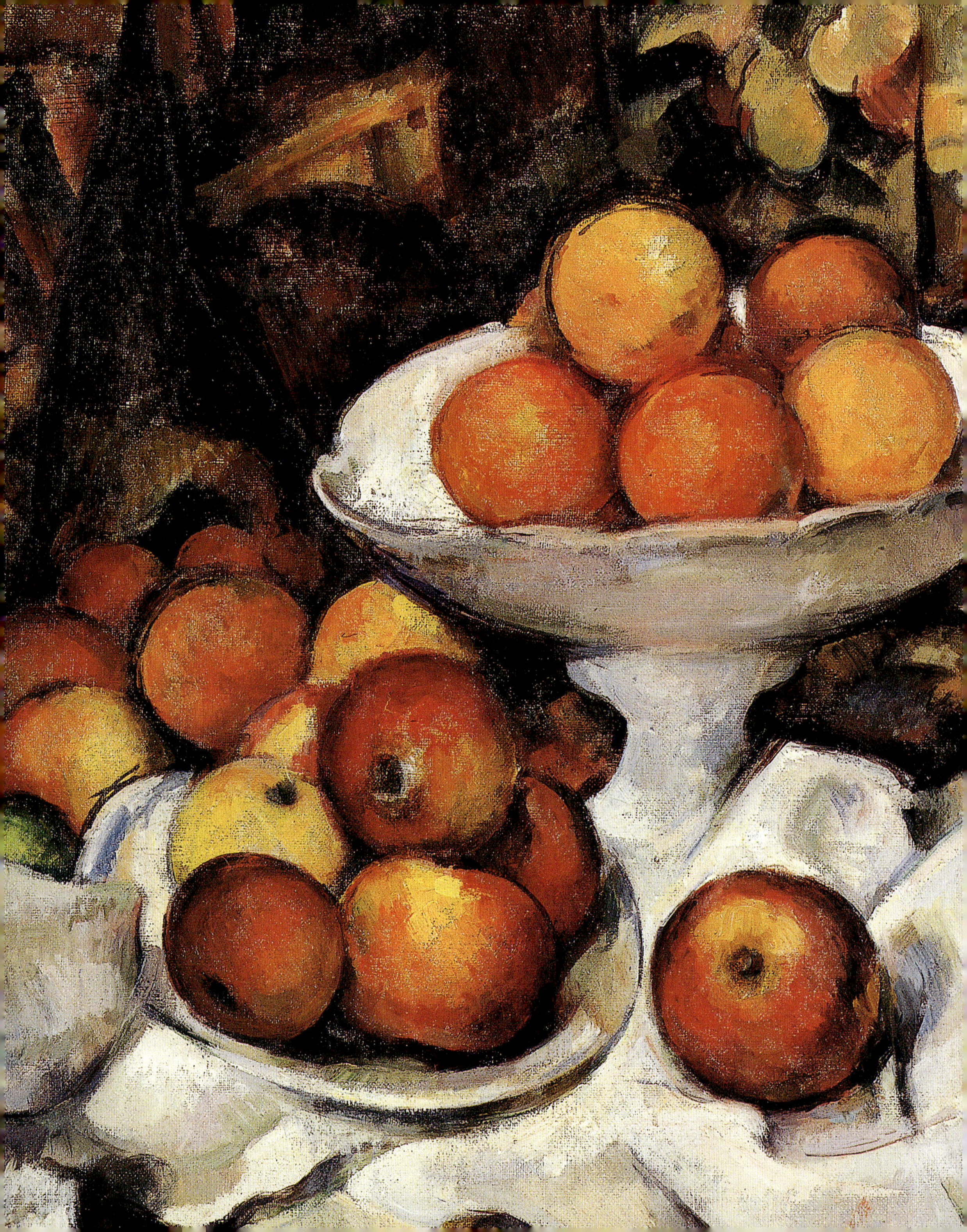

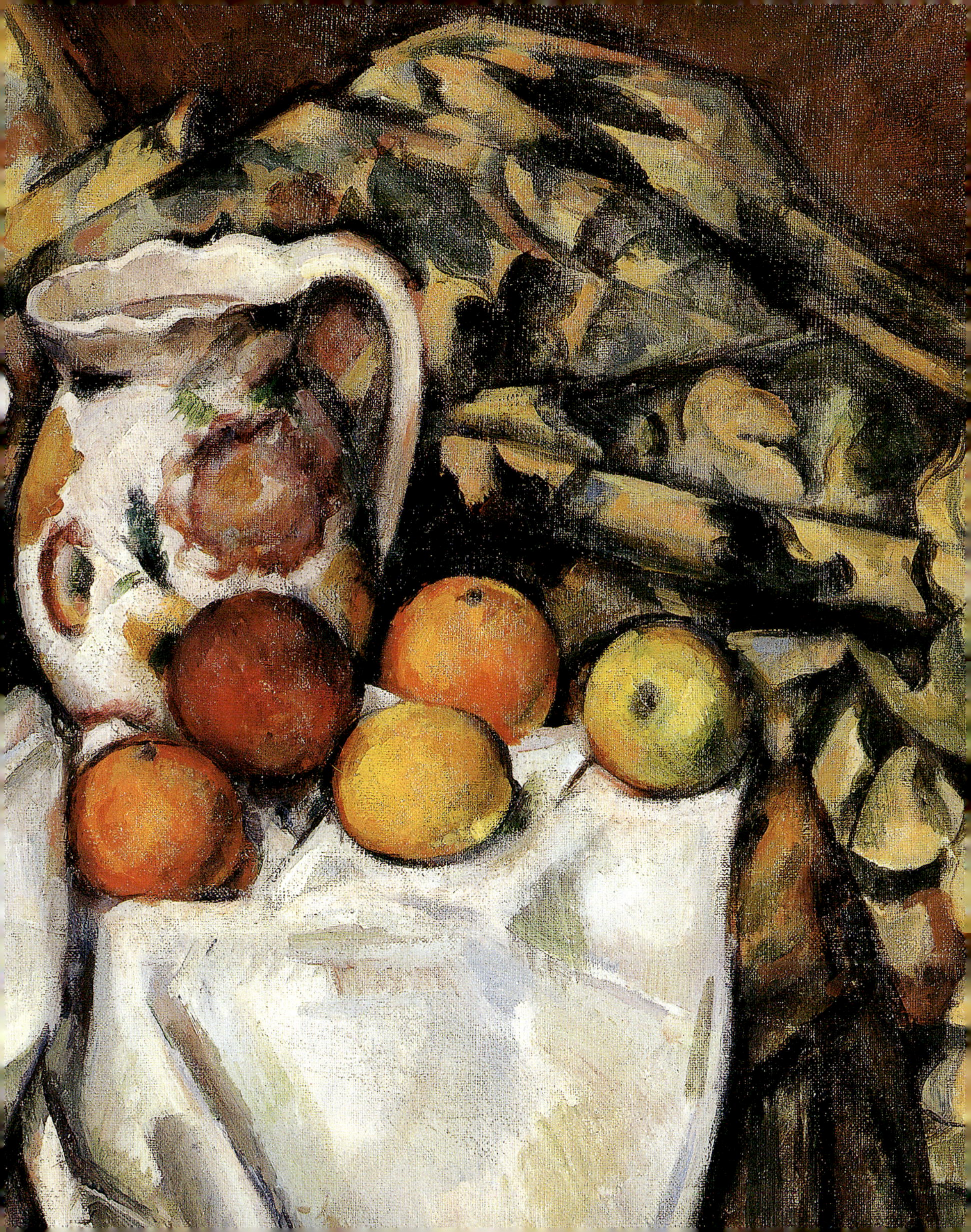

The Bathers

c. 1899–1900

Oil on canvas, 22 x 33 cm
Musée d'Orsay, Paris

During the last years of his life, Cézanne, who turned his attention on several occasions to female, and also male, nudes in a landscape setting, increasingly focused on the subject of bathers. The idyllic motif of men and women bathing represents part of his attempts during these years to achieve a classical monumentality in which every picture element contributes to the construction of the overall composition. In this relatively small oil sketch, the figures are presented in natural surroundings. Here Cézanne harks back to a work he had painted ten years previously, also preserved in the Musée d'Orsay today (see p. 87). What looks like a preparatory study is actually the profound examination of one of the artist's preferred subjects. He reduces the number of figures from nine to six, but largely retains their semicircular arrangement; some of the bathers are on the shore, while others are in the water. The figures, barely hinted at in remarkably summary brushstrokes, recall in their poses some of the masterpieces of ancient art. The man on the left extends his arm like the famous discus thrower, while the muscular form of the repoussoir figure in the left foreground is reminiscent of the figures of Luca Signorelli. The landscape, almost completely filled with dense vegetation, is painted in the same rich spectrum of greens, ochers, and blues as the bodies of the bathers. The figures are enveloped surrounded by the blue of the sky and the water. In the figure portrayed in the greatest detail, the repoussoir figure in the foreground, the ocher tones of the ground are echoed.

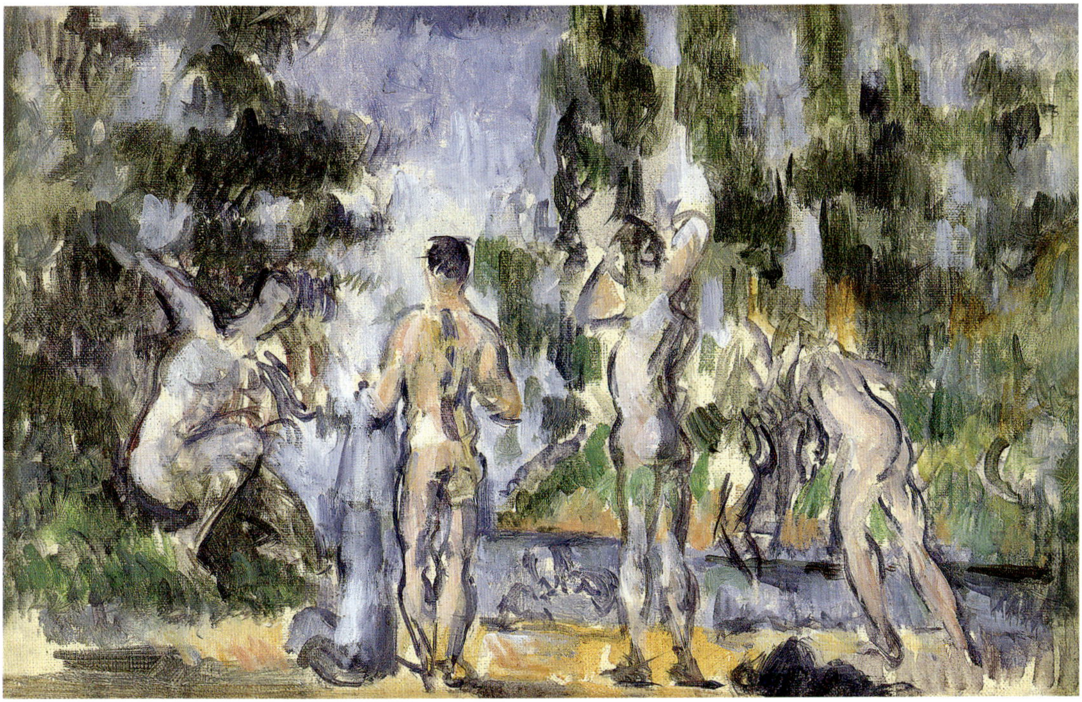

Bathers (Les Grandes Baigneuses)

1894–1905

Oil on canvas, 127 x 196cm
National Gallery, London

During the last years of his life, Cézanne worked in his studio in Aix-en-Provence on three remarkable large-format paintings that are generally known as the *Bathers*. This term, referring also to the numerous works he had hitherto produced showing bathing men and women, is actually not appropriate for these works, because they show neither the sea nor a lake or stream. The models are rather the antique-style female nude figures of art-historical tradition, for example in the works of Delacroix, Titian, or Rubens. The number and arrangement of the figures differ considerably in the various versions. The group of women shown here, quietly and peacefully gathered together, blend in harmoniously with nature—an idyllic-idealized scene that recalls the poetical pictorial works of Poussin. Cézanne repeatedly declared that he wanted to "redo Poussin," in other words not so much to imitate his paintings as to recapture the magical and fantastic atmosphere unique to his works. In the thick layers of paint we can deduce that Cézanne continued to rework this painting until immediately before his death. It was finally exhibited for the first time in 1907 in the memorial exhibition. Picasso, who was working on the *Demoiselles d'Avignon* at that same time, was doubtless impressed by these angular female figures, with which Cézanne distanced himself from every form of naturalistic faithfulness to nature. Against an indeterminate background, they appear in a wide range of poses, probably in a reference to the sensuous nude odalisques of Ingres.

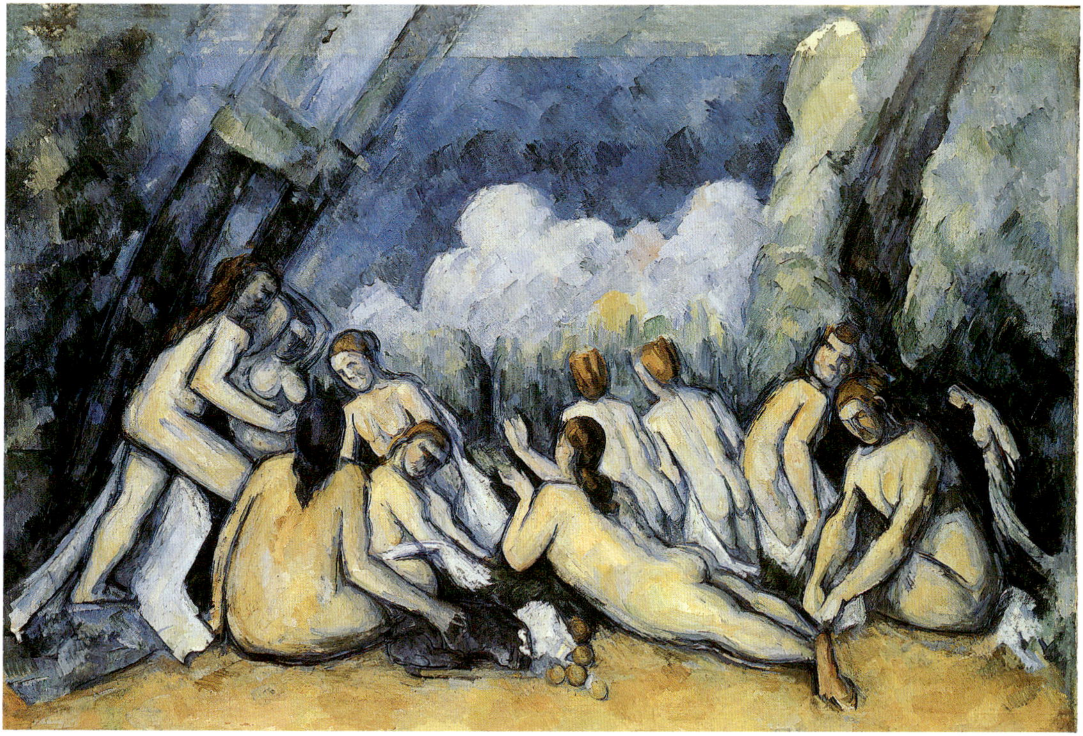

The Bathers

1898–1905

Oil on canvas, 210 x 250 cm
Philadelphia Museum of Art, Philadelphia

This version of the *Bathers* measures over two meters by two and a half meters and is thus the largest format of the three versions of this subject. It is without doubt the most impressive painting that Cézanne produced. He was even prepared to have one of the walls of his studio knocked down in order to get the painting out without having to roll it up. In this masterpiece he relies on an accentuated symmetry between the nude figures and the trees, which frame the river flowing peacefully in the background like a triangular stage setting. Here Cézanne varies three dominant color groups—green, blue, and brown—and thus creates an atmosphere of serene equilibrium. The artist Maurice Denis intuitively realized the revolutionary scope of this painting in 1907. He describes convincingly how the artist constantly attempted to create works characterized by their classicism: "Cézanne [has] given us the prospect of the possibility of a classical renaissance ... The most astonishing thing in Cézanne's work is without doubt the search for forms, or, to put it more accurately, for deformations: in this we can most clearly recognize the artist's hesitancy and his moral dilemma. The great painting *The Bathers* ... is typical in this respect. Although over a period of many years it was reworked on countless occasions, it changed little in appearance or color, and even the distribution of the patches of color remained more or less the same. The size of the figures, on the other hand, was changed several times. Sometimes they were life-size, and sometimes they shrank to only half life-size ... There is no line, there is no modeling, there are only contrasts. When color has its wealth, then form has its fullness."

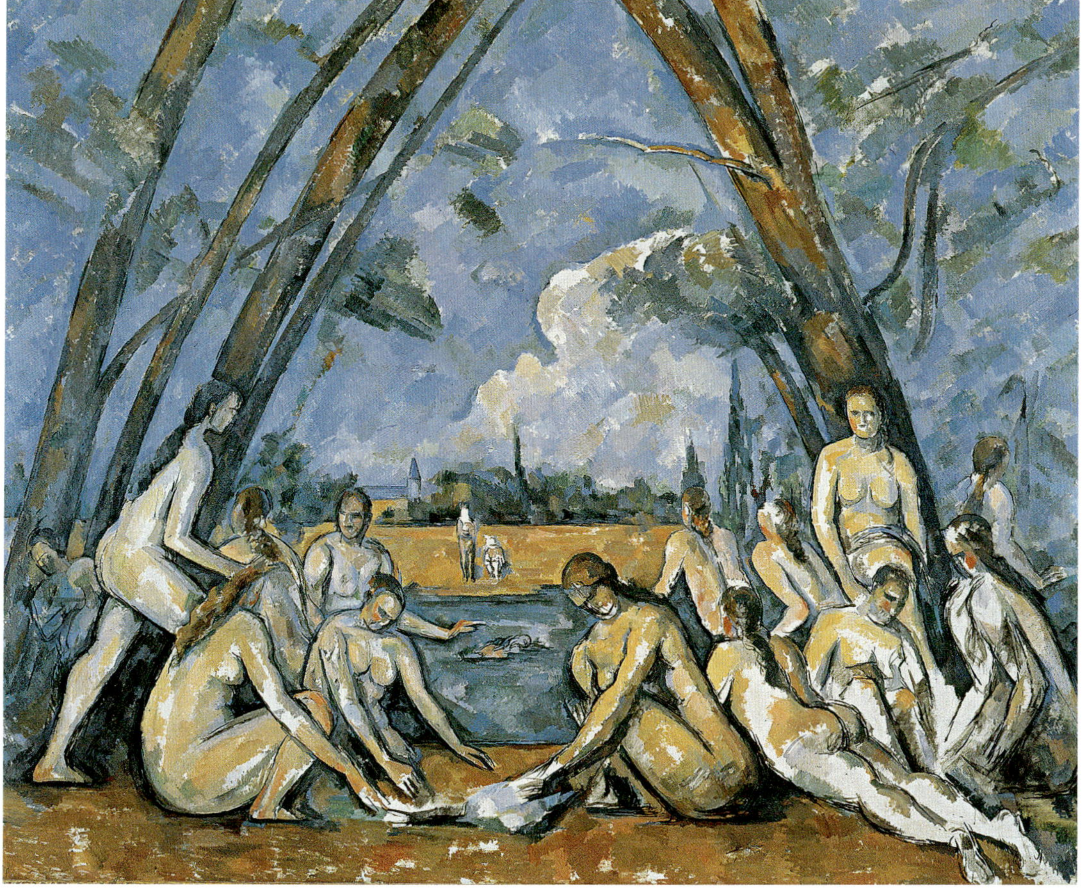

Mont Sainte-Victoire (Seen from Lauves)

1902–1906

Oil on canvas, 64 x 81.3 cm
Nelson-Atkins Museum of Art, Kansas City

During the last four years of his life, Cézanne worked in a studio he had set up in a house on Chemin des Lauves, a road that led from Aix-en-Provence to the village of Puyricard, past the limestone massif of Mont Sainte-Victoire. The views of the mountain produced during these years reveal a bold, intense, profound creativity. At the age of 60, Cézanne, always in search of a perfect harmony between man and nature, again took up subjects that had attracted his attention earlier: Mont Sainte-Victoire, bathers, and still lifes. While in the earlier works Mont Sainte-Victoire is embedded in the surrounding landscape, the artist now takes advantage of the opportunity to study the subject at close quarters from the terrace of his house. The problem of finding the right relationship between form and color became ever more pressing during this period. Cézanne dismantled nature into a mosaic of patches of color and built up the materiality of the picture elements piece by piece using tonal color relations. One color responds to another systematically. The green of the meadow in the foreground recurs on the mountain and continues in the sky, which in its somber autumnal mood is painted not only in blue but also in gray and violet. These in turn are reflected on the mountain and in the plain, which contains the richest array of colors in the picture. In his attempt to record all the secrets of the forms and structures of reality, Cézanne spent long hours in his studio and studied the mountain at all seasons and in all weathers.

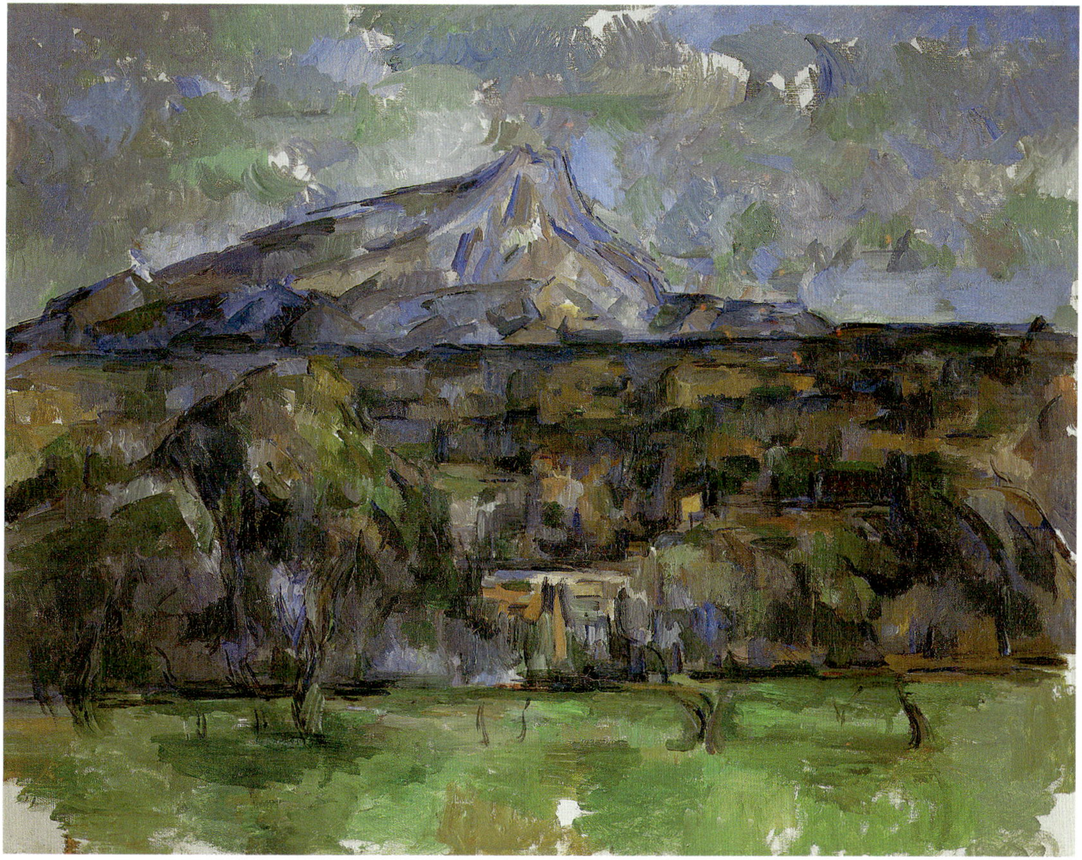

Rocks above Château Noir

c. 1904

Oil on canvas, 65 x 54 cm
Musée d'Orsay, Paris

It is to the art historian Meyer Schapiro that we owe the observation that during the last years of Cézanne's life his painting became exceptionally free. He finally had at his disposal the entire repertoire of painterly possibilities. His painting encompassed heaven and earth, which were always the poles of his *plein-air* painting. Translating them into a single colored structure, he produced not only airy overviews of landscapes and pictures of Mont Sainte-Victoire but also close-ups in the form of detailed views, as is the case with this painting. The colors produce a representation of nature on the canvas that is both concrete and abstract, the result of a bold synthesis that aims to record the essence of objects. Émile Bernard wrote in a letter to his mother on 5 February 1904: "He sees in finely gradated shades. His pictures consist of segments. He leaves white patches all over them. In short, he works like Ingres, by concentrating on the details and completing the components before he tackles the whole." In the detailed landscape studies of this period that were painted in the open air, the horizon is often hidden behind the vegetation. In this case, for example, the rocks and trees completely fill the canvas, so that only a small patch of sky shines through in the middle at the very top. Cézanne presents the random disorder of the natural landscape on the canvas in the rigorous order of a mosaic of colored patches that he has used to depict the stones and the trees. The result is a complex and elegant inter-play of color correspondences and contrasts. In this painting the palette is reduced to shades of brown, green, and blue. It is easy to see this as an anticipation of the coloristic reductions of Cubism.

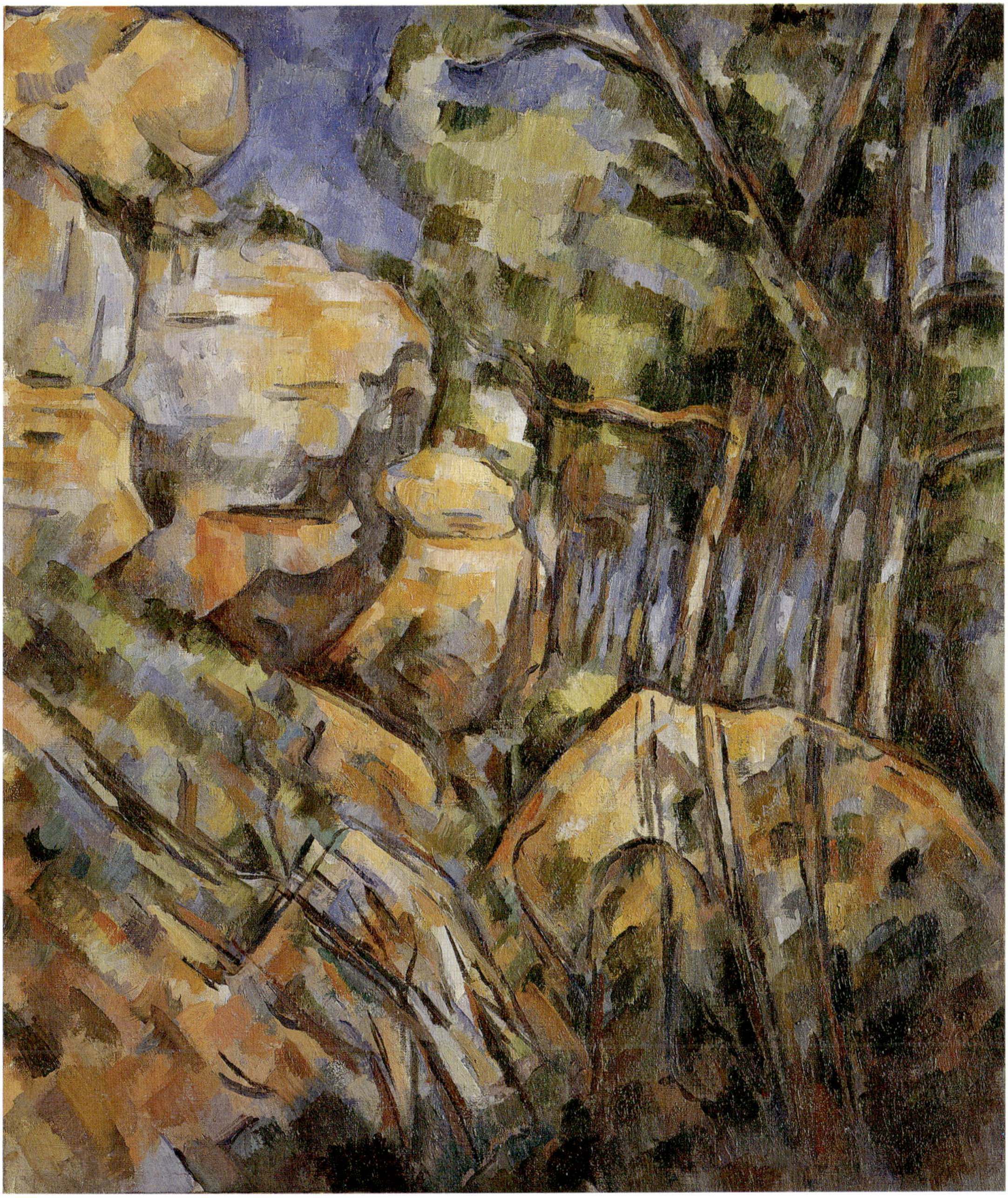

Mont Sainte-Victoire and Château Noir

1904–1906

Oil on canvas, 65.5 x 81 cm
Bridgestone Museum of Art, Tokyo

This painting belongs to the series of views of Mont Sainte-Victoire that Cézanne produced during the last years of his life in his studio on the Chemin des Lauves in Aix. The elderly artist was obsessed by the mountain. In this case the picture was produced in the open air. The Château Noir, a neo-Gothic building some distance away, has become a part of the composition. The palette of the painting, which was doubtless painted in autumn, is dominated by a range of dark shades. Above, the gray sky is darkened by heavy clouds painted in shades of gray, black, blue, and green—colors that reappear in the trees around the Château Noir. The forms of the building—a patch of yellow in an otherwise almost monochrome setting—are reduced to a few cubic elements. This reduction to essentials, this abstraction of forms, accorded with the artistic experiments of the avant-garde painters that were taking place at the same time. The mountain, the brightest element in the composition, rises in the background between the two dark masses of the vegetation on the left and the cloud on the right. During this final phase of his life, painting was Cézanne's sole occupation. On 21 September 1906 he wrote to Émile Bernard: "But I am old and sick and have sworn to myself that I would prefer to die painting."

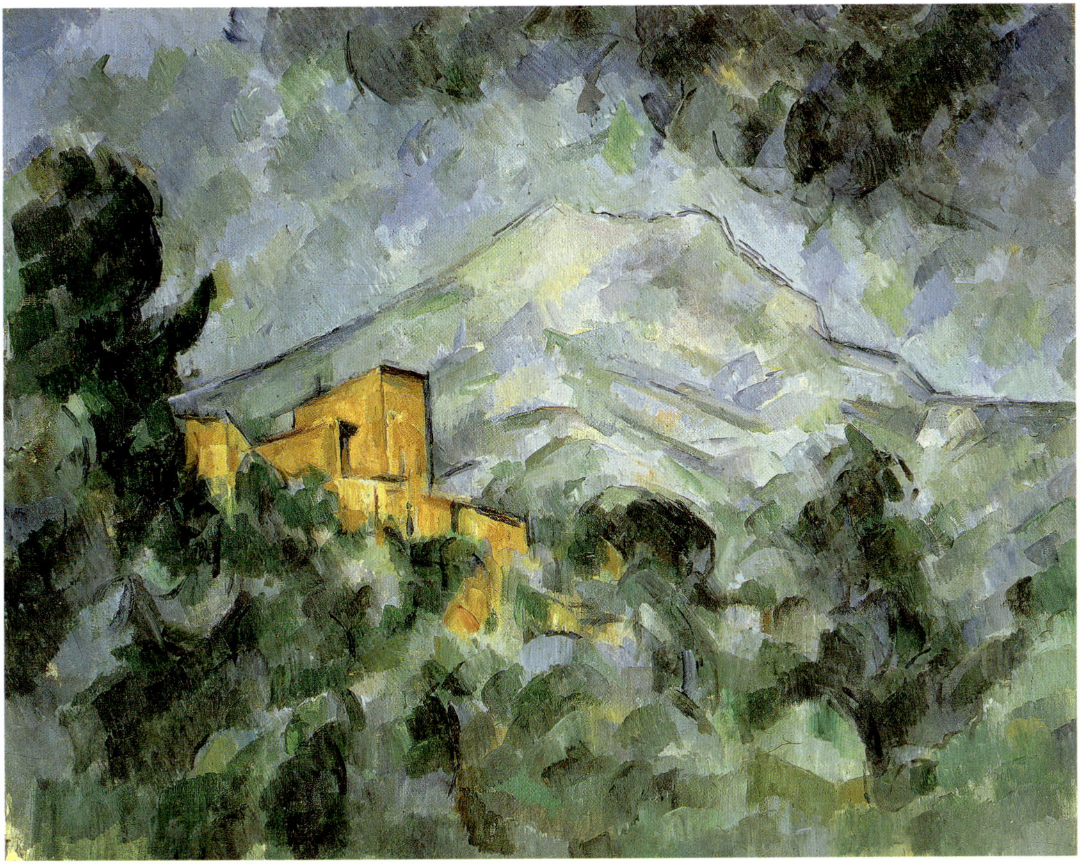

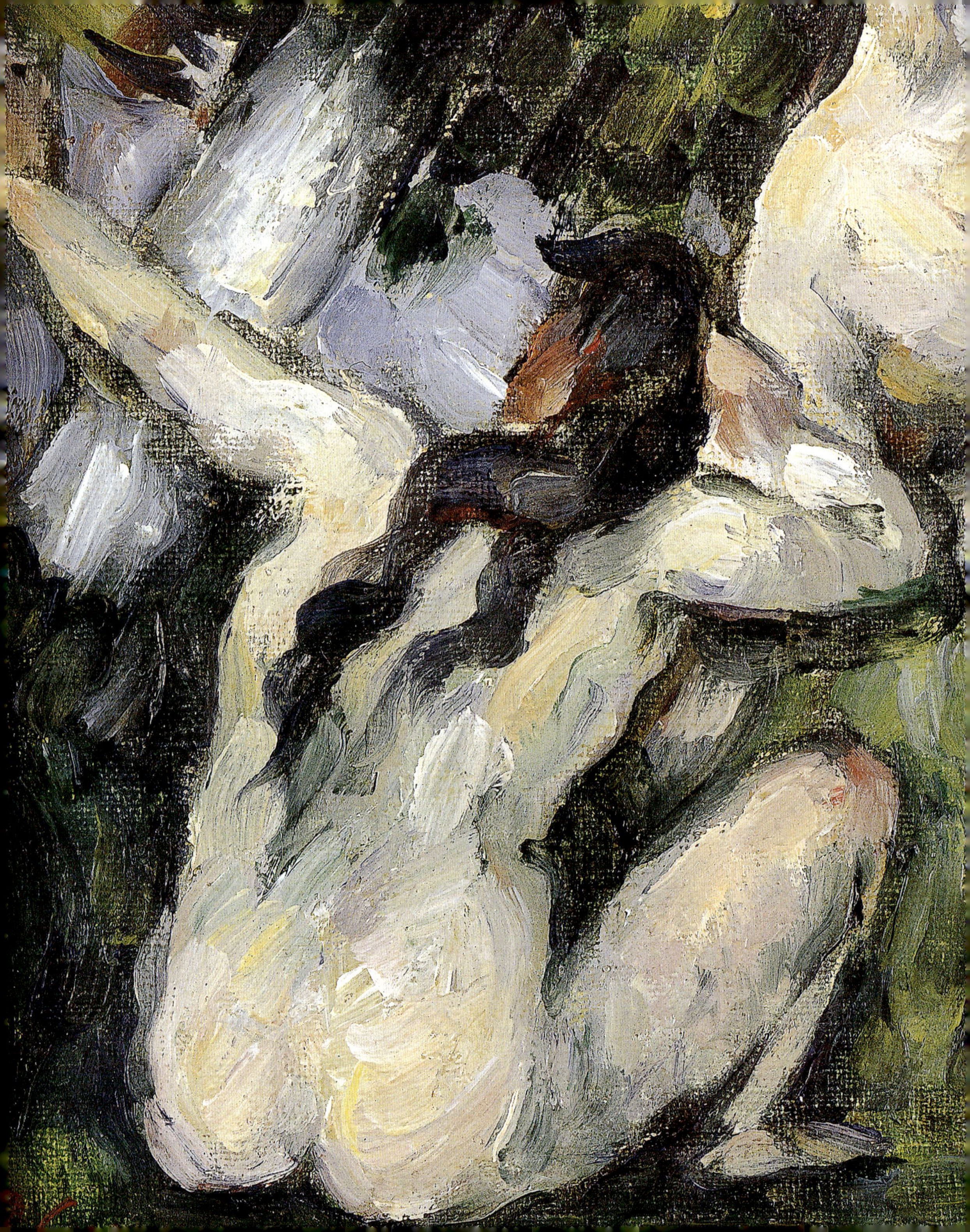

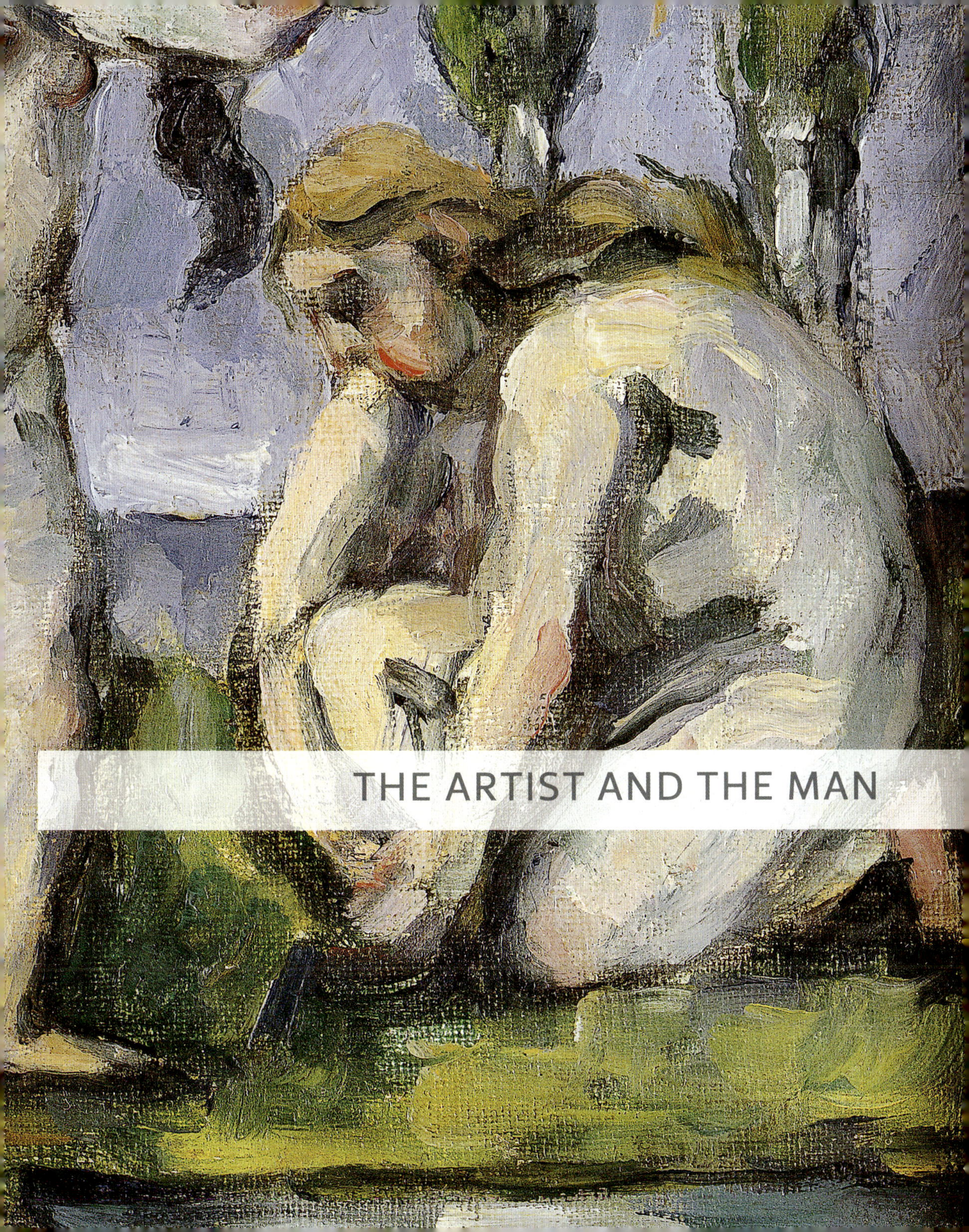
THE ARTIST AND THE MAN

Cézanne in Close-Up

A lonely, misunderstood genius

Throughout his life, Paul Cézanne, the "hermit of Aix-en-Provence," avoided compromises. He lived entirely for his art, and everything else, from his family to his friends, had to take second place. He said he "would prefer to die painting." Although he is considered one of the fathers of modern painting, and though his search for new artistic forms of expression formed an important basis for the avant-garde, Cézanne himself was painfully aware of the fact that he was misunderstood and despised. His life was one long struggle, a relentless search for ways to translate his ideas into forms and colors on canvas. In his hometown he lived a very retiring life and had little contact with others. But he knew that "an artist like me is only born once every 200 years."

In 1902 the poet Léo Larguier was doing his military service in Aix, where he eventually met Cézanne through Joachim Gasquet. Larguier had heard disparaging tales of the elderly artist, who was even described as "a sort of tramp suffering from hallucinations, with a blue nose and red eyes ... who was constantly cursing and angry." But when Larguier was invited to lunch one Sunday by the artist, he spent the entire day with him and had every reason to change his opinion: "I do not know if in the meantime Aix has become an elegant county town, but around 1900 in my opinion Cézanne was better and more comfortably dressed than most of the citizens of Aix ... He owned only those things that an elderly man who lives alone truly needs. He eats simple meals and does not waste his time smoking oriental cigarettes and drinking coffee after lunch ... As Cézanne had informed me, it was Madame Brémond who opened the door that Sunday on which the master had invited me to lunch ... Cézanne greeted me with open arms and recited amusing poems from about 1880, which were no doubt written by a long-forgotten rhymester whose muse frequented the café-concerts.. Unfortunately, I can't remember the lyrics. He shook my hand with great ceremony, like a farmer on the market square who has finally reached a decision and wants to confirm an agreement ... Cézanne told all sorts of harmless stories, but when he had finished he dropped his arms dispiritedly and said: 'Life is dreadful!' ... Cézanne poured me a glass and recited entire passages of Horace, his eyes twinkling ... His memory amazed me, and he was familiar with Latin ... Many people claimed—with stories to prove it—that the old man of Aix was not very sociable and that he was a difficult person to be with, but I always found him even-tempered, and during my visit he was delightful."

Cézanne according to Jules Borély

During the early years of the twentieth century, there were a number of artists and friends of Cézanne who were aware of the significance of his new pictorial language; they saw that he had succeeded in providing decisive answers to the basic problem of the modern age, namely the question of the autonomy of art. The archaeologist Jules Borély recorded his impressions of a visit to the artist in an article published in the magazine *Vers et Prose* in 1911:

"Last July I traveled to Aix in order to visit the artist Cézanne. I arrived without introduction and enquired of a bookseller in the town where he lived. At about two o'clock, I started to walk uphill along a path to his house, which lay surrounded by fields. Since I found the door locked I continued along beneath blue skies between two drystone walls; and then, at a bend in the road, I came across the man I was looking for. That is, Cézanne. Like a tradesman returning from a villa with his tools, he was wearing a glazier's shirt and a pointed cap, and shouldering a hunting bag from which the green neck of a bottle emerged. He was carrying his capacious box of paints, his canvas, and his easel. 'Monsieur Cézanne?' 'Monsieur? ...' And that was how I surprised this man, who was completely lost in thought as he came down the path. I saw him wince, and observed the way a nearby treetop cast its shadow across his sunburnt potter's face: a small, bony face with rosy skin, lively eyes, and a white mustache that he had absent-mindedly rubbed with Prussian blue. I went up to him. 'Monsieur Cézanne, I have been looking for you because I am longing to see your paintings again.' I was touched by the obvious humility that this trivial sentence provoked in this dear man. It immediately sparked a kind of sympathy that I could no longer explain today. 'Monsieur,' he said to me, 'You are too kind, you know! ... Show you some of my attempts? You know, even though I am old, I am still only at the beginning. But I am beginning to understand, if I may say so, I think I understand. So! You love painting. I wish I could show you some Monets. I don't own any; they are very expensive these days ... In my opinion, Monet is one of the most talented painters of our time.'

We went on up to his studio, because I had asked him if I could see it. I saw a high-ceilinged room with bare walls, and an open glass door overlooking an olive grove ... We went out. Cézanne had removed his smock; he carried his rustic bag over an old coat. As he locked the door he started to laugh again and said: 'I am the unhappiest of men.'"

Leaving the studio, they set off towards the town. As they arrived, Borély asked Cézanne: "Do you love Aix?," and Cézanne replied: "I was born here, and I shall die here. I left the town after I had finished school, in order to go to Paris, and twenty-one years later I no longer recognized it; the faces of the young girls I had observed before leaving had changed so greatly. Today everything changes in reality, but not for me; I live in the town of my childhood, and it is in the gaze of the people of my age that I see the past. I love more than anything the sight of people who have grown old, without violating the customs of old by adopting the laws of time."

The visitor thanked Cézanne for spending the afternoon with him. "My train leaves this evening. I shall be leaving this man whom I so love to watch and listen to. It is sufficient to be captivated by the charm of his fickle soul, his soul that is so simple and yet so complex. I have breathed in the incense of a heart that is being consumed."

Émile Bernard on Cézanne

The year 1904 was an important one in Cézanne's life, for an entire room of the exhibition at the Salon d'Automne was reserved for his works. During these years, his artistic forms of expression had reached unforeseen heights through a perfect equilibrium of rhythm and composition. He was now in a position to create life through static pigment, to apprehend the secrets that lie at the bottom of the "silent life of things."

At the age of 52 Cézanne had retired to Aix in order to be able to live and paint there in total seclusion, far from the bustle and distractions of Paris. Here, too, he hoped to find the familiar places of his childhood. In 1904 many artists and friends visited Cézanne in order to share the secret of his perfection or simply to see again the man who expressed his life and experience so vividly in his art. In early February the painter, illustrator, art critic, and poet Émile Bernard called in on Cézanne in Aix on his way back from a trip to Egypt. In 1891 he had published a short essay on the artist but had not seen him since. On 5 February 1904, the day after their meeting, he wrote to his mother and gave her an impromptu account in which he was still clearly moved by his visit to the great artist:

"Yesterday I went to Aix to see Cézanne ... He is an old man, simple, slightly suspicious, and strange. As he was just on his way to work, I went with him. He spoke to me in a friendly manner and repeated a hundred times: 'Life is terrible.' I don't know what he had to complain about. He seemed to me quiet enough; he works at his art as he likes, and he lives like someone retired ... In his art he speaks only of painting nature according to his personality and not according to art. I saw some of his pictures, including a large painting with nude women that is quite magnificent, because of its form and because of the power of the whole. It seems he has been working on it for ten years. What is remarkable about him is that he is a great original. But what should one think of such originality? I have seen how Cézanne speaks of the Great Masters (Michelangelo,

Raphael) as many writers speak of Homer, Dante or Milton—as if they had known them personally. Cézanne never went to Italy, though he was born on the doorstep; he admires ... what he has seen in the Louvre and in engravings ... My conversation greatly confused him, because he senses that I have pursued art from the same standpoint as he himself has done, and that we are both interested in the soul of things, because we already know the material side of painting."

A living legend

Two other artist friends also came to Aix in 1904: Charles Camoin and Francis Jourdain, the son of the architect and writer Frantz Jourdain, who was friendly with several important painters. An account of his meeting was not published until 1950, many years later, in Jourdain's book on Cézanne.

"I myself belong to the generation that first had to discover Cézanne; of course I do not wish to imply that his fame owed anything to our foresight; I should simply like to say that around 1894 Cézanne's work was to all intents and purposes invisible. Our frequent visits to the Galerie Durand-Ruel had made us familiar with the work of Renoir, Monet, Degas, Pissarro, and Sisley; we were already following with great zeal the first steps of Bonnard, Toulouse-Lautrec, and their friends at Le Barc de Boutteville; but at none of these places could one see even the smallest painting by Cézanne, who had long since abandoned the practice of exhibiting his works ... We knew little of Cézanne's 'ideas,' about which we were badly informed (though that did not prevent our ascribing a certain number of them to him), but in general we knew nothing about the painting that had resulted from them. Léon-Paul Fargue and I were very proud of the fact that at Le Père Tanguy's we had turned over a stack of paintings and had discovered a landscape, for whose seriousness we were, however, less receptive than for the frenetic and eccentric eloquence of dear van Gogh, that madman whose 'sunspots and sunsets' glowed in the tiny shop in Rue Clauzel. Émile Bernard ... had led us to Tanguy ... Bernard was also one of the few who were curious enough to seek out Cézanne. He had given a fascinating account of his visit to the brilliant eccentric, who was also a moody old artist ... Two years before Cézanne's death I had an opportunity to determine how truthful the portrait was that Bernard had drawn up over a few pages. Charles Camoin, whom I had met in Marseilles, suggested that I accompany him to Aix the following day ... I could never have dreamt that I would one day meet Cézanne, to whom legend ascribed all the qualities of a mythical creature. I excitedly accepted Camoin's offer.

My excitement grew when I heard the scrunching sound of an old man's slow footsteps on gravel behind the door at which my companion had just rung the bell. The door opened and I saw Cézanne! I saw his bald, shiny skull, on the back of which a few grey strands of hair hung down onto the worn collar of a stained coat ... He greeted us warmly. We entered the house that Cézanne entered only in order to work. An indescribable disorder reigned: the tube of an old enema pump wound its way up to a skull which, lying on a dubious-looking oriental carpet, represented the motif of a still life ... Cézanne apologized that he was not up to date with things because he lived with his memories of the youth he had spent with Zola ... He opened a dreadful album, which he had once bought in Paris at a boulevard kiosk. It contained some 15 ugly and inaccurate reproductions entitled *Le Nu au Musée du Louvre* [Nudes in the Louvre]. It required considerable imagination to be able to recognize even a trace of the beloved masterpieces in these crudely executed abominations. Cézanne was overcome with enthusiasm, gesticulating and waxing poetical. He was clearly delighted to break the silence to which his life had condemned him ... No doubt Cézanne was never fully aware of the moment at which he, though so concerned about objectivity, nonetheless slid off into arbitrariness; nor was he aware of the struggle that the naturalist and the fantasist fought out in his innermost soul; but he was without doubt one of those who attempted with painful exertion to retain that balance between instinct and logic whose realization is unique to genius."

Cézanne's studio

In 1905 Jacques Félix Simon Schnerb, a painter, graphic artist and art critic, and his friend R. P. Rivière, about whom very little is known, stopped over in Aix. The account of their visit was published on 25 December 1907 in the *Grande Revue*.

"When we rang Monsieur Cézanne's bell at number 23 in the tranquil Rue Boulegon in Aix, we were greeted without great ado in Provençal fashion, with a collegial handshake. Cézanne asked for news from the capital. He did not mind the fact that people called him 'Maître,' and when we enquired after his work he replied: 'I am an old man; I spend my time painting—what else should I do?' So he painted. He did not take care of his work, and in the corners canvases stood or lay around, some of them still on the stretchers and some of them rolled up. The rolls were just lying on chairs and had been crushed. Both his studios, the one on Rue Boulegon and the other on Chemin de l'Aubassanne in the countryside outside Aix, were extremely untidy and in a most unartistic disorder. The walls were bare, the light harsh. Half-empty paint tubes, paintbrushes with dried paint on the stiff bristles, remains of meals that become motifs for his still lifes, covered the tables. In one corner was an entire collection of sunshades for landscape painters; the coarse frame no doubt came from a shopkeeper in town and the coarse iron frame from a neighboring blacksmith. Beside them were hunting bags that he used to take snacks with him to the field. Because visitors were rare and Cézanne had few confidants in Aix with whom he could talk about art, he expressed himself in the roundabout and sometimes incomprehensible language of a lone wolf. Some of his tenets were answers to questions he had had to ask himself as a result of problems he had with his art, questions which he had thought about for a long time, and which perhaps had never occurred to the person with whom he was conversing ... The visit of which we give an account here took place in January 1905. At that time we saw in his studio in Chemin de l'Aubassanne a large picture of women bathing with eight figures, almost life-size, on which Cézanne was still working. He said: 'I hardly dare admit that I have been working on it since 1894. I wanted to paint it in pastose style, like Courbet.' He seemed to have abandoned his original admiration for the artist from Franche-Comté and referred to him as a 'handsome brute.' Cézanne also painted a portrait of a man in profile wearing a cap; incidentally, he said that he had been pursuing his study of nature and his practical work at the same time. He seemed to attach great important to this picture: 'If I succeed with this fellow,' he said, 'then the theory is also true.'"

Ambroise Vollard: the first monograph on Cézanne

Ambroise Vollard's intuition, business acumen, and courage earned him a reputation as one of the pioneers among the art dealers of the late nineteenth century. He played a decisive role in the development of modern art around the turn of the century. In November 1895 he staged the first solo exhibition of Cézanne's work. The latter sent him 150 paintings from Aix, far more than Vollard was able to show. The exhibition was a tremendous surprise, because at this time it was already almost 20 years since Cézanne had been represented at exhibitions in Paris. But the public was scornful, the critics disparaging; only artists, his old colleagues as well as the younger ones, recognized in him a great artist. After that, Vollard visited Cézanne in Aix once more, in 1896; he organized a second exhibition of Cézanne's works and became his dealer. In 1899 Cézanne painted a portrait of Vollard. They met for the last time in 1905.

In 1914, a few years after Cézanne's death, Vollard published the first monograph on Cézanne. If we ignore the fact that it places far too much emphasis on sensational and picturesque effects, and that it contains a series of inaccuracies, it is nonetheless a convincing and lively account of the artist, and it contributed in no small part to the creation of Cézanne the "character."

"Paul Cézanne was born on 19 January 1839 in Aix-en-Provence. At that time his father was still far removed from seeing the realization of his life's dream, that of pursuing the 'elegant business' of banking. But Cézanne the hatter was also doing well, and Monsieur Cézanne's most urgent wish was that his son, too, would also one day learn a decent trade, which would enable him to earn his living and be a credit to his family."

Paul, however, was irresistibly drawn to becoming an artist. At the grammar school in Aix he became friends with Émile Zola and Jean-Baptistin Baille. The three friends were inseparable and often roamed the fields and woods around the town after school. To please his father, who had no faith in his son's vocation, Cézanne initially began to study law at the university of Aix after completing his schooling. Although he experienced a "profound feeling of reluctance" in doing so, he nonetheless completed the first part of his state examination. He subsequently entered into an intensive correspondence with Zola, who had gone to Paris. The future writer exhorted his friend to dedicate himself to art "with strength and determination." At the insistence of Paul and Paul's mother, his father finally agreed to allow his son to go to Paris. His father, however, was still convinced that Paul would not be successful as a painter and that he would very soon return home.

"So Cézanne finally set off for the capital in 1861, accompanied by his father and his sister Maria." At last he was to be able to make his dream come true. "As soon as he arrived in Paris, Cézanne rushed off to see Zola. 'I have seen Paul,' the future author of *L'Œuvre* wrote to their friend Baille. 'I have seen Paul; do you realize it, do you realize the music there is in those few brief words?' The two friends embraced warmly. Zola was living in Rue Saint-Victor, not far from the Panthéon, at the time. In order to be near him, Cézanne took a room in a *hôtel meublé* in Rue des Feuillantines." However, Cézanne did not really feel at home in Paris, and after his attempts to gain entry to the École des Beaux-Arts failed, he returned to Aix, totally dispirited.

"Obedient as ever, Cézanne submitted himself to his father's wishes and attempted to take an interest in accounting." In the account books of the bank he wrote: "The banker Cézanne sees, not without alarm, a future artist appearing behind his counter." Eventually his father agreed to allow him to go back to Paris once more, where he took lodgings on Boulevard Saint-Michel. Once again he regularly attended the courses at the Académie Suisse.

"His first forays through the Musée du Louvre had left in the young artist with a tangled mass of impressions, a stunning vision of light and colors." Cézanne's first pictures display a "raw, unadorned reality, and the judgment of the critics who saw these first works was that he painted as if he were shooting at a white canvas with a pistol filled with a vast array different-colored paints."

In 1863 Cézanne met Auguste Renoir. At that time the Café Guerbois in Grande Rue des Batignolles was the rendezvous of a circle of artists Manet had gathered around him, and Cézanne also frequented the place. Vollard does not tell us anything about the artist's encounter with Hortense Fiquet, who later became his wife. The biography continues with the artist's return to Paris after the end of the Franco-Prussian War and his encounter with Dr. Gachet in 1872, an "ardent supporter of the new painting. The revolutionary tendencies, which that excellent man believed he could perceive in Cézanne's art, delighted him, and he urged the artist to come and work in Auvers, where he had his practice." The first Impressionist exhibition was held in 1874, at which Cézanne exhibited several works (as he did again in 1877 during the third exhibition). Both critics and public alike expressed negative opinions about his work. "Although he recognized the pure artistic intention of the artist, even Huysmans spoke of the 'unbelievable disturbance of equilibrium, houses which totter like drunkards and messy fruits in befuddled dish-like objects...'

"Although at that time painting was Cézanne's overriding passion, as it was to remain during virtually his entire life, he nonetheless retained a lively affection for the masterpieces of literature. He preferred Molière, Racine, and La Fontaine; among the contemporary authors he had a high opinion of the Goncourts brothers, Charles Baudelaire, Théophile Gautier, and Victor Hugo, in other words all those who painted colorful word pictures ... Cézanne, moreover, was one of the regular guests of Nina de Villars, who kept open house and always offered hospitality to the poets of the age. Everything there was very informal, and those who came after supper were offered warmed-up food; people moved their chairs closer together to make room for the new arrivals at the table. And there was, at least, always something to smoke. It was there that Cézanne met Ernest Cabaner, one of his earliest admirers. Cabaner was a terribly polite man, something of a poet, something of a musician, something of a philosopher...

"Cabaner was not the only person to encourage Cézanne. The latter had also found a good deal of 'moral support' in Victor Chocquet, a modest ministry official who collected art as a hobby. Fascinated by the art of Delacroix, Chocquet had recognized his favorite artist in Renoir. A relationship developed. Before long Renoir told M. Chocquet about Cézanne and even persuaded him to purchase a study of the *Baigneuses* ... When Madame Chocquet has been persuaded to put up with the *Baigneuses* in order to please her husband, Monsieur Chocquet asked Renoir to introduce him to Cézanne. The latter, as usual totally unconcerned about his appearance, turned up wearing an old cap he had borrowed from Guillaumin. The reception was no less warm despite that fact ... Chocquet's enthusiasm for Cézanne's pictures increased steadily, and in the same way his estimation of the man grew too, so that Cézanne was soon a regular visitor at his house. Monsieur Chocquet never lost an opportunity to sing Cézanne's praises. It was not possible to speak about painting in his presence without his enquiring immediately: 'And what about Cézanne?'... Cézanne painted several portraits of Monsieur Chocquet. One of them, dated 1877, in which his subject is portrayed sitting in an armchair, enjoyed considerably fame for quite some time due to the fact that it was thought to be a portrait of Henri Rochefort."

Vollard discovers the works of Cézanne

Vollard then reports how he first saw Cézanne's paintings in 1892, "at Tanguy's, a little paint shop in Rue Clauzel, whose owner had set himself up as the benefactor of misunderstood artists. Père Tanguy regarded himself as a sort of revolutionary because he had almost been shot dead by the guards during the Commune. In fact he was a good-hearted man who gave the artists credit and took a passionate interest in their work ... It rarely happened that people found their way to Rue Clauzel. But when a lover of Cézanne's work turned up, Tanguy would lead him to the artist's studio, for which he had a key, and there the purchaser could make his choice among the piles of pictures, for the fixed price of 40 Francs for the small pictures and 100 Francs for the large ones. Père Tanguy appeared armed with a pair of scissors and also peddled the small 'motifs,' if an impecunious patron offered him a Louis so that he could take home three apples by Cézanne."

Some time later, in November 1895, Vollard organized a solo exhibition in his art gallery with Cézanne's permission. The reaction of the critics was not so favorable. "The *Journal des Artistes* merely reflected the tone which the critics in general adopted in 1895, when it asked, full of concern, whether its dear lady readers would not suffer seizures 'when confronted with the nightmarish vision of these abominations in oil, which today surpass the degree of legally permitted foppery' ... For most of the curious viewers, at least, the scandal put an end to the matter..."

In 1896 Vollard finally decided to get to know Cézanne personally. So he traveled to Aix. "Stendhal found the road from Marseilles to Aix abominable, but I found the route delightful; it was as if the train ran through Cézanne's landscapes." The artist was in the company of his son Paul and received Vollard in the garden: "Cézanne loved everything that is art passionately, but he believed it should be in a museum. In his studio there were neither rare pictures nor precious items of furniture to be seen; nothing of all the bric-à-brac that artists normally love. On the floor lay a portfolio full to the brim with watercolors; on a plate were a couple of apples which were going moldy but which still had to serve as models. By the window hung a curtain which had served as a background for still lifes for goodness knows how long; on the walls were engravings or photographs which for better or worse, usually worse, provided reproductions of the *Shepherds of Arcady* by Nicolas Poussin, works by Luca Signorelli and Eugène Delacroix, Gustave Courbet's *Burial at Ornans*, the *Assumption* by Peter Paul Rubens, an *Amor* by Pierre Puget, Pierre-Paul Prudhon's *Psyche*, and even Thomas Couture's *Roman Orgy*. During supper, to which I was invited, Cézanne was in the best of moods. What I particularly noticed was his excessive courtesy and all the civilities with which he asked his neighbor at table for the slightest service."

The shock of Zola's *L'Œuvre*

After describing the first years after Cézanne's retreat to Aix, Vollard turns in his biography to the friendship between the artist and Émile Zola. The first Impressionist exhibition of 1874, at which Cézanne showed several works, created a mood of condemnation among the general public and art critics alike, which inevitably meant that many potential purchasers were deterred from acquiring works. Zola, too, who had been a friend of Cézanne's since youth, visited the exhibition, but instead of defending the group, which he could certainly have done, he merely contented himself with making notes for his planned novel *L'Œuvre* (The Masterpiece). Cézanne was supposedly the model for the main character, a failed artist. In the novel, Zola describes the reaction of the public to the exhibition by the Batignolles Group thus:

"The explosion continued, culminating in an ascending scale of insane laughter. ... Those who did not laugh flew into a rage: that bluish tinge, that novel rendering of light seemed an insult to them. Some old gentlemen shook their sticks. Was art to be outraged like this? One grave individual went away incensed, saying to his wife that he did not like practical jokes. The affair was becoming a scandal. The crowd still increased. People's faces grew red with congestion in the growing heat. Each had the stupidly gaping mouth of the ignoramus who judges painting, and between them they indulged in all the asinine ideas, all the preposterous reflections, all the stupid spiteful jeers that the sight of an original work can possibly elicit from bourgeois imbecility."

The publication of *L'Œuvre* in 1886 put an end to the friendship between Cézanne and Zola. Zola's novel was full of biographical details, and while the author could be recognized in the positive figure of the novelist and journalist Sandoz, the failed artist, Claude Lantier, was clearly based on Cézanne. The artist in the novel comes from Provence; he has failed to make his mark as a painter; he flees to a place far from Paris; he suffers a series of failures; and he is unbalanced, hovering between genius and madness, finally committing suicide because his ambitious dreams have failed painfully and tragically as a result of his own lack of creative ability. In his novel, Zola is unsparing in his unflattering judgments, and he wallows in grotesque descriptions of the weaknesses and negative character traits of his friend. While the public regarded the book a condemnation of Impressionism, Cézanne saw it as a personal betrayal. Zola ultimately lacked any understanding of the artistic aims of Cézanne and the Impressionists, and in the last analysis he also had no feeling for true loyalty.

The short, sad letter, in which Cézanne thanked him for sending him a copy of the book, is in fact a bitter letter of farewell; the two men would never meet again: "My dear Émile, I have just received the copy of *L'Œuvre*, which you were kind enough to send me. I should like to thank the author of the Rougon-Macquart for generously thinking of me and beg him to allow me to shake his hand in memory of the past years. Ever yours under the influence of past times, Paul Cézanne."

Of their artist friends, only Monet had the courage to express his disappointment at the publication of the book, in a letter dated 5 April 1886: "You were so kind as to send me *L'Œuvre*, for which I thank you. I always read your books with great pleasure, and this one interested me particularly because it discusses artistic questions with which we have been struggling for a long time. I have almost finished it, and to be honest it has perturbed and upset me. You have taken pains to ensure that none of your characters resembles any of us, but I nonetheless fear that our enemies in the press and among the public will raise the name of Manet or at least our own, in order to make us into failures, which, I assume, was not your intention ... I have been struggling for so long, and I am afraid that in the moment of our success our enemies will make use of your book to finish us off."

Like Cézanne, who terminated his friendship with Zola after 30 years, Monet, Pissarro, and Renoir all broke off contact with the writer.

Vollard's interview with Zola

In his description of Cézanne's life, Vollard devoted a chapter to the end of the friendship between the artist and the writer. First he wrote of his visit to Zola, where he wanted to look at some paintings by Cézanne that the writer had in his possession; and then he related a conversation he had had in Aix with Cézanne on the subject of his friend:

"Cézanne had told me about some works he had done in his youth, which he had given to Zola, and I was very anxious to see them. Monsieur Mirbeau, in whose presence I had once expressed this wish, was kind enough to give me a letter of recommendation to Zola in which, however, he made no mention of the Cézannes. 'Zola guards them so jealously that I dare not ask him to show you them.' ... When I arrived at Zola's I was led into an antechamber in which a vast composition by Édouard Debat-Ponsan imposed itself on us: *Truth Emerging from a Well* ... Then I entered a salon, which was full of all sorts of liturgical objects ... The place radiated a delightful tranquility, and I realized then the magnitude of the sacrifice which Zola made when he left his wonderful home in order to act as the defender of innocent people in the contaminated atmosphere of the people's assemblies. Before long the master himself appeared, clutching to his breast a grouchy, dreadfully ugly little pooch, his adored, sweet Pinpin. In his free hand he was holding a copy of *La Débâcle* ... In my anxiety not to arouse Zola's suspicion, I was very careful not to bring up the subject of the Cézannes myself. My plan was subtly to lead the master to mention them himself without his realizing it."

With great skill, Vollard managed to carry out his plan: "In Zola's features I could make out such a good mood that I finally dared to mention Cézanne. 'There is one question, master, that I have been longing to ask you. But I have already tried your patience for far too long,' ... Zola indulgently said: 'Speak, then!' I asked: 'The letters which you wrote to Monsieur Cézanne, and which would also be so valuable for us in order to learn how you felt and thought; do those letters still exist? I have not dared to speak to Monsieur Cézanne about them; if by chance he has not preserved these precious papers, he would be plagued by a guilty conscience for evermore, suddenly realizing what a responsibility he had towards future generations.'

"Zola: 'I, like you, have also been worried about these letters, in which I had given the best part of myself. But mercifully, in spite of his carelessness, Cézanne realized that he should carefully preserve every last note that I had written to him.' 'You had great confidence in Cézanne!'

"Zola: 'Our friends liked to believe that he was a 'failure,' but I never stopped proclaiming to them: 'Paul has the genius of a great artist.' Oh, why was I not a better prophet ... Dear, great Cézanne possessed the spark! But though he possessed the genius of a great painter, he lacked the willpower to become one. He succumbed too readily to his dreams, dreams that were never fulfilled. Or in his own words: his illusions were his wet nurse.' I asked him: 'Do you possess any pictures by Monsieur Cézanne?'

"Zola: 'I hid them out in the country. But Mirbeau wanted to see them, and at his insistence I had them brought back. But I shall never hang them on the wall. My house, as you are aware, is a house of artists. You know how fair they are, but also how strict they are with each other. I do not wish to submit the companion of my youth, my dearest friend, to the verdict of his fellow-artists. Cézanne's pictures are locked away in that cupboard over there, triple-locked and safe from unfriendly gazes. Do not demand of me that I get them out. It grieves me when I think what my friend might have become if he had had the willpower to give a direction to his imagination and to develop a form for it. One may be born a poet, but one must first of all learn to work.' I replied: 'And yet Cézanne was never short of your expert advice, Master?'

"Zola: 'I did all I could to goad my dear Cézanne into action. The letters I wrote him moved me so greatly that even the most trivial comment is engraved in my memory. It was he whom I meant when I wrote *L'Œuvre*. The general public was very excited about the book, but my friend remained indifferent. Nothing will ever be able to rouse him from his daydreams; he will gradually distance himself more and more from the real world.' ... I responded: 'But even if Cézanne was unable to complete his work, did he at least say something interesting about painting in his letters?'

"Zola, tenderly kissing his little dog: 'Everything that Cézanne wrote was surprising and original. But I did not keep his letters. For nothing in the world would I have wanted them to be read by other people: because of this rather careless form...' I interrupted him: 'There, too, your friendship...'

"After these words I took my leave of Cézanne's famous friend.

"Cézanne was deeply affected by Zola's death in 1902. He was just busy arranging his palette in his studio in Aix when Paulin, a former wrestler, whom he kept as both a servant and a model, came rushing in: 'Monsieur Paul, Monsieur Paul, Zola is dead.' Cézanne began to sob and indicated to his model that he should leave, whereupon he locked himself in ... The pictures by Cézanne that were found in Zola's house when the wall cupboards and wardrobes were emptied were taken to the Hôtel Drouot [auction house], together with all the antique bric-à-brac with which he had furnished his salon. The sale was held ... in 1903.

"One day, when Cézanne showed me a little study of Zola, which he had painted in his youth, around 1860, I asked him why he and Zola had quarreled. 'We never quarreled,' he said to me. 'I was the first to break off the contact with Zola. I no longer felt comfortable with him.'"

Then Vollard brought up the subject of the publication of Zola's book. "Cézanne was silent for a moment, caught up in thoughts of the past ... 'How could he dare to tell of a painter who kills himself because he has painted a bad picture? If a picture is a failure, you throw it on the stove and start again!' ... He looked at me with eyes that contained no anger, only a tremendous sadness. 'Listen a moment, Monsieur Vollard, I must tell you: I had stopped going to see Zola, but I couldn't get used to the idea that that would be the end of his friendship for me ... Later, when I was back in Aix, I learned that Zola had recently arrived. I imagined that he would surely not have the courage to come to see me. But there I am, thinking of the past again! Do you understand a little, Monsieur Vollard, my beloved Zola was in Aix! I forgot everything, *L'Œuvre* and various other things as well ... at that moment I was 'on the subject'; I had planned a study that was shaping up well. But now I could not care less about this study: Zola was in Aix. Without even taking the time to pack my things away, I rushed over to the hotel where he was staying; and there I met a friend who informed me that in his presence the evening before, someone asked Zola: 'So, will you dine with Cézanne?' Whereupon Zola replied: 'What's the point of seeing this 'failure' again?' So then I turned away and went back 'to my subject.' Cézanne's eyes were full of tears. He blew his nose in order to hide his emotions. Then he observed: 'You see, Monsieur Vollard, Zola was not a bad fellow, but he floated with the tide!'"

Vollard's visit to the artist in 1905 was his last: "This was my last conversation with the artist. I did not see him again. In spite of an illness which had tormented him for a long time, and which had cost him a great deal of energy, Cézanne continued to work with untiring determination."

His friends' posthumous homage

The summer of 1906 was unusually hot; Cézanne frequently went to paint on the banks of the River Arc. During the fall, the air finally cooled down somewhat and it rained frequently, though this did not deter Cézanne. With his usual tenacity, he continued to pursue his artistic interests day in, day out in the open air. On 15 October he was caught unawares by a sudden storm while painting outdoors. However, he ignored the wind and weather and remained outside for hours until he eventually lost consciousness; he was carried home in a passing cart. The next morning he was back in front of his easel and put the finishing touches to a portrait if his gardener, Vallier, after which, however, his condition deteriorated rapidly. He died in the early hours of 22 October 1906. During the September of the following year, an article about Cézanne was published in *L'Occident* by the artist Maurice Denis, who had visited his colleague almost 20 months previously.

"I have never heard an admirer of Cézanne who was able to explain to me clear and unequivocal reasons for his admiration; and that is a rare occurrence even among artists, in other words among those who had the most direct experience of Cézanne ... The mystery that surrounded the Master of Aix during his entire life contributed in no small part to increasing the incomprehensibility with which he was viewed, though it also contributed to his fame. Cézanne was shy, independent, a solitary person interested only in his art, always worried, and mostly dissatisfied with himself. Right up to the last years of his life he avoided the attention of the public. Even those who referred to his methods were largely unconcerned about him ... After his death the articles in the newspapers were unanimous as regards two points ... First, all these obituaries acknowledged Cézanne's influence on a large part of the younger generation; second, they noted that he strove to create a distinctive style. This implied that Cézanne was a sort of classicist and that young people considered him to be a representative of classicism...

"He is the Poussin of Impressionism. He has the delicacy of perception of a Parisian and is ornate and exuberant like an Italian decorator. He is as ordered as a Frenchman and as frenetic as a Spaniard. He is a Chardin of the decadence and sometimes he surpasses Chardin. In him there is something of El Greco, and sometimes he has the wholesome constitution of a Veronese. But everything that he is, he is naturally, and all scruples of his will, all the tenacity of his endeavors, were only there in order to serve his natural gifts and to exalt them.

"My intention here was to try to define the work of the artist: I have not attempted to express the poetry it contains. No amount of charmed words would suffice to convey the impression that a fine Cézanne makes to someone who has never seen one. Words cannot describe the charm of Cézanne, and even the nobility of his landscapes, the freshness of his shades of green, the purity and depth of his blues, the delicacy with which he paints the skin, the velvety sheen of his fruits, cannot be reproduced ... He liked to speak with apparent modesty of his small perception, of his small sensitivity. He complained that Gauguin had deprived him of them and that he had 'taken them away with him on all the ocean steamers.' In truth, his art is so natural and concrete, so lively and spontaneous, that it is difficult to adopt something from his technique and method without taking something of the best of oneself at the same time."

In a text published on 1 June 1915 in the *Mercure de France*, Émile Bernard summarized Cézanne's tenets in just a few lines: "Cézanne determinedly turns his back on Decadence, irrespective of whether it occurs in painting or in real life. He is a monk who is shut away in the monastery of painting; he lives, he thinks, he breathes only through painting and for painting. To be there only for art, to deny everything else, that is the valuable example that he gave us. Contempt for the expediency that restricts life; contempt for prejudice, contempt for official bodies, contempt for social conventions that govern public opinion, such as the dignity of office, of money, and of bourgeois appearances—Paul Cézanne embodied all of these things."

Cézanne's last letters

The artist's correspondence is a revealing document for understanding the artist and the man. Some of his comments read like explanatory picture captions to the individual pictures. His correspondence as a whole is a diary that is psychologically enlightening, a seismograph of his mood at the time, of the experiences, desires and frustrations of a man who had dedicated his entire life to painting. Written during 1906, the year of his death, his last comments are largely addressed to his son Paul. They are permeated by a nightmarish feeling of uncertainty.

On 8 September 1906, he wrote: "My dear Paul, Today (it is almost 11 o'clock) there was once again an amazing increase in the temperature. The air is unbearably hot, without a breath of air ... Finally, I want to tell you that I, as a painter of nature, have become more clear-sighted, but that for me the realization of my sensations is always very arduous. I cannot reach the intensity that develops before my senses; I do not possess that wonderful wealth of colors that enlivens nature. Here, on the banks of the river, the motifs multiply; the same subject, seen from another angle, offers an object of study of the greatest interest and of such diversity, that I believe I could occupy myself for several months without moving, merely by looking sometimes more to the right and sometimes more to the left."

In his last letter, dated 15 October 1906, Cézanne wrote: "Dear Paul, On Saturday and Sunday it rained and there was a thunderstorm; the weather has cooled down considerably. You are quite right to say that this is a rural backwater. I continue to work, with difficulty I admit, but something does finally come of it. That is the main thing, I believe. Since sensory impressions are the basis of my work, I think I am impenetrable ... Everything passes awfully quickly ... My dear Paul, to give you the satisfactory news you wish for I would need to be twenty years younger ... I think the young artists are much more intelligent than the others; the others can only see in me an ill-fated rival. Ever yours, your father, Paul Cézanne."

Anthology

Viewed from the present day, Cézanne could almost be an ancient Greek: his paintings exude the tranquility, the heroic composure of the paintings and terracotta sculptures of classical antiquity, and the ignoramuses who laugh at his *Bathers*, for example, look to me like barbarians mocking the Parthenon. Cézanne is a painter, a great painter. People who had never picked up a paintbrush or pencil thought he couldn't draw...

And yet I know very well that Cézanne will not enjoy the success of a fashionable painter ... but his painting has the indescribable fascination of biblical and Greek antiquity; the movements of the figures are simple and magnificent, as in classical sculpture; the landscapes are of an impressive sublimity; and his still lifes are so beautiful, so precise in the coordination of the shades of color, there is something solemn in them despite their faithfulness to nature. In all of his paintings, the painter is able to touch us, because he himself experiences powerful emotions in the face of nature, and is skilled at transferring them to the canvas.

Georges Rivière
in: L'Impressioniste, April 1877

Today I want to tell you a little about Cézanne. Where work is concerned, he claims to have lived the life of a bohemian until the age of forty. It was then, he says, that through his acquaintance with Pissarro he discovered the joys of work. So much so that he did nothing but work for the next thirty years of his life. But essentially without joy, it seems, in constant anger, feeling ambiguous about every one of his artworks, none of which seemed to him to achieve what he found to be most essential ... old, sick, sucked dry to the point of exhaustion every evening by his regular, everyday work (so much so that he often went to bed when the sun set at six, following an unconsciously consumed supper), irascible, suspicious, always laughed at, ridiculed, abused on his way to his atelier, but celebrating Sundays, listening to mass and vespers like a child, and very politely requesting a slightly better meal from his housekeeper, Madame Brémond. Perhaps he did live in hope from one day to the next that he would achieve the only success that he considered important.

Rainer Maria Rilke
Letter to Clara, 9 October 1907

Classical painters always painted the same painting again and again, and yet differently each time. At some point, Cézanne started to paint the same painting repeatedly: the *Bathers*. And yet although the Master from Aix painted the same painting tirelessly, one views every new Cézanne with great interest. In this respect, we are quite undiscerning; one might even ask whether the influence of the painter of *The House of the Hanged Man* and *The Cardplayers* is good or harmful. If only you knew how much moral strength, how much courage his wonderful example has given me throughout my life. In moments of doubt, while I was still searching, when at times I was shocked by my own discoveries, I thought to myself: "If Cézanne is right, then I am right, too." And I knew that Cézanne had not been wrong. You see, one finds in Cézanne's oeuvre certain principles that are very useful to a young painter. Among his greatest achievements was his attempt to make the shades of color in a painting powerful, which represented a supreme challenge to his claims as an artist. It should not surprise us that Cézanne hesitated for such a long time, and repeatedly. Where I am concerned, each time I step in front of a canvas, I feel as though I were painting for the first time. There were so many possibilities in Cézanne that it was necessary for him, more so than for others, to sort things out in his mind. You see, Cézanne is a sort of god of painting. Cézanne is the teacher of us all. Is his influence dangerous? And what if it were? Too bad for anybody who does not have the strength to endure him!

Henri Matisse
in: L'Art Vivant, September 1925

The landscapes of L'Estaque and the farm houses near Mont-Sainte-Victoire show, for the first time, one direction which Cézanne's mature style was to take—the direction which after his death was to lead to Cubism. The motives which led him to adopt this way of painting are quite simple, and are latent in all his early work. He wished to render the solidity of objects without degrading his colour or weakening his design by continuous modeling. The only means of doing this was to split up his planes into a number of small facets, each of which could, by its colour, make us aware of a new direction of the planes. This cubist, or perhaps we might say prismatic, approach to individual forms was also inherent in his compositions as a whole—in his strategy so to say, as well as his tactics. It is this which distinguishes him from the impressionists. For impressionism also offers a means of rendering continuous modeling by colour, which was developed by Seurat; but underlying all impressionism is the belief that the unity of a picture depends on the enveloping atmosphere rendered by a continuous weft of colours; whereas Cézanne wished forms to retain their identity and cohere in an architectural relationship. To achieve this, therefore, he began by choosing subjects in which the forms went some way to meet this kind of simplification.

Kenneth Clark
Landscape Into Art, 1949

To accomplish this fusion of nature and self, Cézanne had to create a new method of painting. The strokes of high-keyed color which in the Impressionist paintings dissolved objects into atmosphere and sunlight, forming a crust of twinkling points, Cézanne applied to the building of solid forms. He loosened the perspective system of traditional art and gave to the space of the image the aspect of a world created free-hand and put together piecemeal from successive perceptions, rather than offered complete to the eye in one coordinating glance as in the ready-made geometrical perspective of Renaissance art. The tilting of vertical objects, the discontinuities in the shifting levels of the segments of an interrupted horizontal edge ... contribute to the effect of a perpetual searching and balancing of forms. Freely and subtly Cézanne introduced besides these nice variations many parallel lines, connectives, contacts, and breaks which help to unite in a common pattern elements that represent things lying on the different planes in depth. A line of a wall is prolonged in the line of a tree which stands further back in space; the curve of a tree in the foreground parallels closely the outline of a distant mountain just below it on the surface of the canvas ... By such means the web of colored forms becomes more cohesive and palatable, without sacrifice of the depth and weight of objects. These devices are the starting point of later abstract art, which proceeds from the constructive function of Cézanne's stroke, more than from his color. But however severely abstracted his forms may seem, the strokes are never schematic, never an ornament or a formula. The painting is finally an image and one that gives a new splendor to the represented objects.

Cézanne's method was not a foreseen goal which, once reached, permitted him to create masterpieces easily. His art is a model of steadfast searching for growth. He struggled with himself as well as with his medium, and if in the most classical works we suspect that Cézanne's detachment is a heroically achieved ideal, an order arising from mastery over chaotic impulses, in other works the conflicts are admitted in the turbulence of lines and colors. In his first pictures, painted in the 1860s in his native Aix and in Paris, he is often moody and violent, crude but powerful, and always inventive—to such a degree that in his immaturity he anticipates Expressionist effects of the twentieth century. This early art is permeated by a great restlessness. Impressionism released the young Cézanne from troubling fancies by directing him to nature; it brought him a discipline of representation, together with the joys of light and color which replaced the gloomy tones of his vehement, rebellious phase. Yet the Impressionist pictures, compared to those of his friend, Pissarro, or to Monet's, are generally graver, more troweled, more charged with contrasts. Unlike these men, he was always deeply concerned with composition, for which he showed since his youth an extraordinary gift—he was a born composer, with an affinity to the great masters of the sixteenth and seventeenth centuries in the largeness of his forms, in his delight in balancing and varying the massive counterposed elements. The order he creates is cool, habitual calculation; it bears evident signs of spontaneity and the bias imposed by a dominant mood, whether directed towards tranquility or drama. Some of his last works are as passionate as the romantic pictures of his youth; only they are not images of sensuality or human violence, but of nature in a chaos or solitariness responding to his mood.

Meyer Schapiro
Paul Cézanne, 1952

The transformation of Cézanne's attitude towards loneliness must be understood as an event brought about by faith. It had to be thus because of the depth and violence of his nature, the tremendous vigour with which he experienced life and which shook his whole being. Here was a man who had suffered so greatly from solitude that he was driven to revolt against the world and was thus brought to the brink of self-destruction. The ultimate result of this experience was that he came to find security in the very emptiness of solitariness and was able to discover there a new meaning for the world. When this happens to a man, when he finds all values turned upside down, when he comes to the conclusion that to rebel is proof of weakness while to submit is humbly is a form of strength and a source of power; when he is able to recognize the outward appearance of things as the structure which sustains the world and to represent it thus; then this event can only be understood in all its awe-inspiring gravity as arising out of the experience of every degree of loneliness, down to the lowest depth, which is the modern malady analysed by Dostoevsky and Nietzsche, the state of being abandoned by God. In contrast to most of mankind, Cézanne successfully accomplished the transition from rage and dejection to resignation, to acceptance of suffering and so from the state of being abandoned by God to that of being protected by God.

...The invisible unity of the divine seemed to him to be visible here in the formal relationships of things to one another. This was their real nature, to represent which became the aim of his painting.

Kurt Badt
The Art of Cézanne, 1956

Cézanne may appear like an isolated artist, who attempts all by himself and with tremendous effort to return to classical greatness. In truth, he was well acquainted with the Old Masters, was a regular visitor to the Louvre; with great enthusiasm he studied the works of the Venetians—and Tintoretto in particular—and of French Neoclassicism, Baroque, Delacroix and, finally, also of Courbet and the Impressionists. He then withdrew, to work alone in the countryside near Aix. This education matured the spirit of an original artist, an observer who mistrusted all that was spontaneous. He did not lie in waiting, like his friends, for that which is momentary or that which changes. Even in the landscapes painted directly from nature, he constructed solid artworks, supported by a framework and based on a scheme, just like the masters who painted comfortably in their ateliers ... With Cézanne there was an important change: the novelty of the media he employed drew more attention to the components than to their synthesis. Painting essentially exploded: some of the painters of the twentieth century then saw themselves confronted with the problem of the third, and even the fourth dimension, some with the question of the harmonies of pure shades of color, and others with the geometric lines that subdivide the surface of a composition.

Charles Bouleau
Charpentes. La géométrie secrète des peintres, 1963

One morning, I was alone at the Musée Picasso. A wonderful day. Although not many people know it, the seventeenth-century *hôtel* has been entirely remodelled, and ennobled through the addition of paintings and sculptures by the painter of the *Demoiselles d'Avignon*. Paintings by Cézanne, too, are exhibited there, having been jealously guarded by Picasso. Deep, intimate, distant shades of blue, ocean blue, six shades of blue of a visionary calm in deep meditation. As reversible and interchangeable as the stately architecture of the exhibition space may seem to be, revolving entirely around the omnipresent artworks of Picasso, those by Cézanne seem to be exactly where they belong, as though they could not possibly be anywhere else. The Picassos draw attention to themselves through their dynamism, they project out of the wall, appear categorical, reveal a cocky, worldly demeanor. I appreciate many painters (and love Picasso very much), but not one of them moves me, inexplicably, as Cézanne does. I always try to explain to myself this detached, powerful feeling. It seems to me as though it were the same perception of a thought process beyond the representation of reality. The religious devotion that Picasso and Matisse felt for Cézanne feels absolutely appropriate to me. "Cézanne and God." Yes, but which one? Not a hidden god, that much is clear. "This god is close, and yet difficult to grasp," says Hölderlin. Very close. Infinitely close. And all the more difficult to grasp for that very reason. The Cézannes that Picasso owned are now there, in his museum; they are recognized as sources of inspiration for the master, an explained foundation and simultaneously a reproach. It is possible that Picasso wanted to express through this inclusion that something in the work of this "divine" reinventor of painting had been neglected, concealed, forgotten, when artists were already trying feverishly to succeed him.

Philippe Sollers
Le paradis de Cézanne, 1995

Locations

BRAZIL
São Paulo
Museu de Arte
Paul Alexis Reading Aloud to Émile Zola, 1869–1870

BRITAIN
London
The National Gallery
Bathers (Les Grandes Baigneuses), 1894–1905

CZECH REPUBLIC
Prague
Národní Galerie
Portrait of Joachim Gasquet, c. 1896

FRANCE
Aix-en-Provence
Musée Granet
Bathsheba, c. 1880–1890
Madame Cézanne, 1885–1887
Paris
Musée de l'Orangerie
Portrait of Paul Cézanne, the Artist's Son, c. 1882–1885
Musée d'Orsay
The House of the Hanged Man, Auvers-sur-Oise, 1872–1873
A Modern Olympia, 1872–1874
Three Bathers, 1874–1875
Still Life with Terrine, c. 1877
Self-Portrait, c. 1877
The Gulf of Marseilles from L'Estaque, 1878–1879
Maincy Bridge, 1879
Poplars, 1879–1880
The Kitchen Table (Still Life with Basket), c. 1888–1890
The Blue Vase, c. 1889
Mont Sainte-Victoire, c. 1890
Bathers, c. 1890
The Cardplayers, c. 1890–1895
Woman with a Coffee Pot, c. 1895
Apples and Oranges, c. 1899
Bathers, c. 1899–1900
Rocks above Château Noir, c. 1904
Musée du Petit Palais
Portrait of Ambroise Vollard, 1899
Musée National Picasso
L'Estaque, View Through the Trees, c. 1878

GERMANY
Berlin
Museum Berggruen
Heinz Berggruen Collection
Portrait of Madame Cézanne, c. 1885
Girl with Young Child, c. 1892–1896
Small Jug and Fruits, 1893–1895

JAPAN
Tokyo
Bridgestone Museum of Art
Mont Sainte-Victoire and Château Noir, 1904–1906

RUSSIA
Moscow
Pushkin Museum
Self-Portrait, c. 1882
Trees in a Park (The Jas de Bouffan), 1885–1887
Bridge Over the Marne at Créteil, c. 1888
Still Life with Peaches and Pears, 1890–1894
Man Smoking a Pipe, c. 1892–1896
Bridge on a Pond, c. 1898

St. Petersburg
The State Hermitage Museum
Girl at the Piano (Overture to "Tannhäuser"), c. 1869
Still Life with Dish, Fruits and Drapery, c. 1879–1880
House on the Marne, 1888–189
Large Pine and Red Earth, 1890–1895
Man Smoking a Pipe, c. 1891–1897
Road Before the Mountains, Mont Sainte-Victoire, c. 1896–1898
Still Life with a Curtain, c. 1899

SWEDEN
Stockholm
Nationalmuseum
Still Life with Plaster Cupid, 1894–1895

SWITZERLAND
Bern
Kunstmuseum
Self-Portrait with Hat, c. 1879–1880
Zurich
Stiftung Sammlung E. G. Bührle
The Boy in the Red Waistcoat, 1888–1890

USA
Boston
Museum of Fine Arts
Madame Cézanne in a Red Armchair, c. 1877
Columbus
Gallery of Fine Arts
Portrait of Victor Chocquet, 1877
Fort Worth
Kimbell Art Museum
Man in a Blue Smock, c. 1897
Kansas City
Nelson-Atkins Museum of Art
Mont Sainte-Victoire (Seen from Lauves), 1902–1906
Merion
Barnes Foundation
Village at the Water's Edge, c. 1876–1878
The Toilette, c. 1880–1890
Madame Cézanne with Green Hat, c. 1892–1894
Still Life with Skull, c. 1896–1898
Chrysanthemums, c. 1896–1898
Portrait of a Woman, c. 1896–1898
Bibémus Quarry, c. 1898
New York
Museum of Modern Art
The Bather, c. 1885
The Metropolitan Museum of Art
Mont Sainte-Victoire and the Viaduct of the River Arc Valley, c. 1882–1885
The Gulf of Marseilles Seen from L'Estaque, c. 1885
Madame Cézanne in a Yellow Armchair, c. 1888–1890
Madame Cézanne in the Conservatory, 1891
Norfolk
Chrysler Art Museum
Bather and Rocks, c. 1867–1869
Philadelphia
Philadelphia Museum of Art
The Bathers, 1898–1905
Washington
National Gallery of Art
Portrait of Louise-Auguste Cézanne, 1866
The House of Père Lacroix in Auvers-sur-Oise, 1873
Riverbank, c. 1895

Chronology

The following is a brief overview of the main events in the artist's life, plus the main historical and cultural events of the day (*in italics*).

1839
Paul Cézanne is born in Aix-en-Provence on 19 January, the son of Louis-Auguste Cézanne and Anne Aubert; he is the eldest of three children.
Louis-Philippe, Duke of Orléans, rules as King of France (1830–1848).

1848
Cézanne's father takes over an insolvent bank and founds a banking firm together with his partner, Cabassol. From now on the family is able to enjoy considerable prosperity.
22–24 February: Revolution of 1848; proclamation of the Republic. Louis Napoléon becomes the president of the nation in December.

1851
December 1851: Coup d'état results in the dissolution of Parliament and a wave of arrests.

1852
Starts school at the Collège Bourbon, where he receives a solid humanist education. Friendship with Émile Zola and Jean-Baptistin Baille.
A new constitution comes into effect in January; it makes Napoléon III hereditary emperor; Second Empire: 1852–1870.

1858
Matriculates from the Lycée. He is interested in music and plays in an orchestra with Zola. He attends drawing classes under Joseph Gibert at the École de Dessin in Aix.
Attempted assassination of Napoléon III by Felice Orsini; Cavour takes advantage of the event to force the emperor to agree to a defensive alliance between France and Piedmont in case of an Austrian attack.

1859
To please his father, he studies law at the University of Aix, though he wants to become an artist.
Second Italian War of Independence. Napoléon III reaches rapid agreement with Austria, the Treaty of Zurich.

1860
Begins to rebel against his father's reservations regarding his artistic ambitions.
Savoy and the County of Nice are annexed by France through the Treaty of Turin with the Kingdom of Sardinia.

1861
Overcomes his father's opposition and is allowed to go to Paris. There he attends the Académie Suisse, where he makes the acquaintance of Armand Guillaumin, who introduces him to Camille Pissarro. Visits the Louvre and the Salon exhibition. The encounter with the Old Masters and the works of the artists whom he meets in Paris precipitates a crisis: disheartened when not admitted to the École des Beaux-Arts, he begins to doubt his talent. Returns to Aix and starts to work in his father's bank, but continues to attend drawing classes.

1862
In November, returns to Paris, where he stays for one and a half years and attends courses at the Académie Suisse. Once again his application to the École des Beaux-Arts is unsuccessful.

1863
Visits the Salon des Refusés with Zola. Manet's *Le déjeuner sur l'herbe* provokes a major scandal when exhibited.

1864
Returns to Aix in July. His works are regularly rejected by the jury of the Salon exhibition.

1866
At the beginning of the year, is in Provence and meets Manet. In August, he returns to Aix, where he begins to paint *en plein air*.

1869
Spends several months in Paris. He makes the acquaintance of Hortense Fiquet, a 19-year-old bookbinder who may also have worked as a model. Lives with her without telling his father.
Outbreak of the Franco-Prussian War. In September, the French army capitulates and the Third Republic is proclaimed. The Siege of Paris.

1871
Paris capitulates in January. The Paris Commune is proclaimed but brutally suppressed. The Peace of Frankfurt am Main leads to the proclamation of the

German Empire. France cedes Alsace and Lorraine to Germany.

1872
His son Paul is born on 4 January, and the family moves to Pontoise. He works together with Pissarro and other painters on landscapes *sur le motif* (in front of the subject) and adopts the lighter color palette of the Impressionists. In the fall he goes with his family to Auvers-sur-Oise, where he remains until 1874.

1874
Lives in Paris. Pissarro invites him to take part in the first Impressionist exhibition, which is held in the studio of the photograph Nadar. He shows *Landscape, Auvers*, *The House of the Hanged Man*, and *A Modern Olympia*. Considered scandalous, his works are ridiculed. His pictures continue to be rejects by the jury of the Salon.

1875
Through Renoir, meets the collector Victor Chocquet, who will support him and collect his pictures.
The constitution of the Third Republic is passed.

1877
Works once more in Pontoise and Auvers; at the third Impressionist exhibition he is represented by 16 works. His pictures are not accepted by either the general public or art critics.
16 May: Attempted coup d'état by Marshal MacMahon. The Republicans win the general election.

1880
Returns to Paris.

1882
Having not been able to show a single work at the Salon exhibitions, he is finally admitted as a result of pressure by the artist Jean Antonie Guillemet. Paints with Pissarro in Pontoise.

1886
Zola publishes his novel *L'Œuvre* (The Masterpiece), whose protagonist, the failed painter Claude Lantier, commits suicide. Sees this as a negative judgment of his painting and ends his friendship with Zola, whom he will never see again. He marries Hortense.

1887
Exhibits his work in Brussels, with the group Les Vingt.

1889
Participates in the World Exhibition in Paris with *The House of the Hanged Man*.
Start of the Dreyfus Affair, in which Jewish army officer Alfred Dreyfus is accused of espionage.

1895
First solo exhibition, in the gallery of the art dealer Ambroise Vollard in Paris.

1899
Second exhibition at Vollard's gallery. Sends three paintings to the Salon des Indépendants.

1900
Participates in the World Exhibition in Paris.

1901
Participates in the Salon des Indépendants and later in exhibitions in Brussels and The Hague.

1905
Once more exhibits his work in the Salon d'Automne and in the Salon des Indépendants. Completes *The Bathers*, on which he has been working for ten years.

1906
On 15 October he is caught unawares by a storm while painting in the countryside; dies of pneumonia in his apartment in Aix on 22 October.

1907
Major retrospective in Paris at the Salon d'Automne, with 56 paintings.

Literature

Roger Fry, *Cézanne: A Study of his Development*, London/New York 1927

John Rewald (ed.), *Paul Cézanne Letters*, Oxford 1941

Kurt Badt, *The Art of Cézanne*, London 1965 (German original 1956)

Jack Lindsay, *Cézanne: His Life and Art*, New York 1969

Laurence Gowing, *Watercolours and Drawings by Cézanne*, London 1973

John Rewald, *Paul Cézanne: The Watercolours*, London 1983

R. Shiff, *Cézanne and the End of Impressionism*, Chicago 1984

John Rewald, *Paul Cézanne: A Biography*, New York 1986

Richard Kendell (ed.), *Cézanne by Himself*, New York 1988

Richard Verdi, *Cézanne*, London 1992

Evmarie Schmitt, *Cézanne in Provence*, Munich/London 2000

Joachim Pissarro, *Cézanne & Pissarro Pioneering Modern Painting: 1865–1885*, New York 2005

Philip Conisbee and Denis Coutagne, *Cézanne in Provence*, New Haven 2006

Alex Danchev, *Cézanne: A Life*, London 2012

Photo Credits

akg-images Berlin: 30–31, 63, 65, 85, 91, 93, 95, 107, 111, 119.

Sergio Anelli, Milan: 11.

Archivio Mondadori Electa, Milan; / Sergio Anelli: 61; / Laurent Lecat: 2,16, 19, 35, 37, 38–39, 47, 49, 50–51, 53, 54, 55, 57, 69, 70–71, 75, 83, 87, 88–89, 97, 101,102, 103, 121, 122–123, 125, 133, 136–137.

The Bridgeman Art Library, London: 15, 20, 27, 59, 73, 99, 109, 113, 114, 115, 127.

Bridgestone Museum of Art, Tokyo: 135.

© Corbis, Milan: 12.

Stiftung Sammlung E. G. Bührle, Zurich: 79, 80–81.

The Hermitage State Museum, St. Petersburg: 24.

Erich Lessing / Agenzia Contrasto, Milan: 8–9, 23, 33, 45, 105, 117, 129, 131.

National Gallery of Art, Washington: 28, 41, 42, 43.

© 2007. Image copyright The Metropolitan Museum of Art / Scala, Florence: 67, 77.